COLOSSIANS

A Study of Authority

Thomas Schaff

Resource *Publications*
An imprint of *Wipf and Stock Publishers*
150 West Broadway • Eugene OR 97401

Resource *Publications*
an imprint of Wipf and Stock Publishers
150 West Broadway
Eugene, Oregon 97401

Colossians: A Study of Authority
By Schaff, Thomas
©2002 Schaff, Thomas
ISBN: 1-57910-960-8
Publication date: May, 2002
Previously published by NPP, 2002.

COLOSSIANS

Table of Contents

Preface i

Introduction iii

Chapter 1 1

Chapter 2 31

Chapter 3 41

Chapter 4 59

Chapter 5 77

Chapter 6 111

Chapter 7 163

Chapter 8 175

COLOSSIANS

PREFACE

Dear Reader,

    This analysis and its associated self-monitored study are not substitutes for your own personal study of the Bible itself. Only when you spend time reading and meditating upon what God has said in His Word, rather than what men have written, will you find the truth that your heart needs. Nevertheless, I believe that God has given me the grace to set down some things that may be a useful guide for your own personal investigation of the Bible.

    What we learn from our study of Colossians depends, not upon our persistence, diligence, insight or observational and analytical skill, but upon God. Colossians is part of His Word and it is up to Him to reveal its contents, according to His will. Therefore, we must approach Colossians humbly, seeking His aid, without any predispositions. We must submit to what we read, trusting it to be true and obeying its commands.

    In this analysis and study, I will not uncover all the wonderful treasures God has put into Colossians. One reason is the Bible is an expression of the infinite mind of God. As creatures, we have limited ability and finite time to study the Bible. Another reason is we do not listen to God's Word as we were originally created to do. As sinful creatures, our ability is corrupted and our desire to seek God's truth suppressed. More than that, I will not teach all that is in Colossians because this study has specific goals that keep it from being an exhaustive study. My plan is to understand the meaning and significance of a few fundamental truths. It will be up to you to use what you learn to help you study those things not discussed in this analysis, as well as apply it to your own personal life. However, I will try to explain those words and phrases which may be difficult to understand, for we do not want to neglect the parts of Colossians that are a puzzle and a challenge, otherwise we will undermine our confidence in whatever conclusions we make.

    It is my prayer that the Lord richly bless you as you behold His beauty in the Bible.

Sincerely in Christ,

Thomas Schaff

COLOSSIANS

Introduction: Understanding Authority

Authority and Will

The word "will" refers to the part of a person that is the seat of his deepest desires. It is a person's will that determines what he wants and does not want, with conviction and passion. More than all the features of a person's body, more than all of his physical and mental abilities, more than all of his acquired skills or lack thereof, more than all of his accomplishments and failures, a person's will defines who he is. It is a person's will that chooses the particular things he wants to think, say and do, marking him as a unique individual, distinct from everyone else.

A person may be subjugated, so that his will is contained and masked, but that situation does not change who he is. He is still the same person, with the same will. His will is still the author of his own, individual set of likes and dislikes, whether he is free and can express his will through what he says and does or whether he is suppressed and cannot.

God has a will. His will reveals who He is. As He expresses His will, He reveals His majesty and the beauty of His Holiness, for all that He wants to say and do is true, pure and right.

People also have wills. But this fact requires some explanation because we must account for sin. The day that Adam was created his will conformed perfectly to God's. Then he sinned, and according to God's command, he died, in his soul immediately and in his body eventually. Yet, Adam still had a will. He still had strong feelings and longings, but they no longer matched God's. In fact, his will could not match God's. That is, it was no longer possible for Adam's will to conform to God's. The reason was that he was spiritually dead. His will was under the control of the members of his sin-infected body rather than his soul, which was dead. That is the heritage of all people and the present situation of all unsaved people. Unsaved people can long for and pursue what their flesh desires but they cannot long for and pursue what God does and commands them to. On the other hand, saved people have been given a new life, Jesus' own life. So, saved people's wills, once again, and in a greater way than Adam's, reflect the image of their Creator and Savior.

With an understanding of a person's will, we are able to answer the question, "What is a person's authority?" First of all, a person's authority means that he has a right to express his will. We do not mean the right of moral purity before God's Law, but the right of privilege. In this sense, a person's authority is the highest expression of his sovereignty. It expresses his right of control that springs out of ownership. In God's case, authority means the right to do His will in and with His universe. If anyone is going to do what he wills, God is the one who will do it. It is God's particular privilege to do what He wants with what He has made (Col. 1:16). God does not need the creation to be sovereign. His authority is part of the essence of who God is. Before He created, there was only God, self-sufficient and wonderful in His sovereign majesty (Col. 1:17). However, He decided to reveal His supreme authority. He spoke and things were created. As sovereign Creator, He has the freedom to do what He wants with what He has made. He has the right to express His will and expect His creation to comply. He says go and people go (Col. 1:25). That is one thing that authority means.

Secondly, a person's authority means that he has the power to express his will. Authority and power are two different words in Greek and express related but not identical ideas. Among men, these two ideas do not always go together. If a man does not have the power to exercise the authority that has been given him, if he cannot carry out his rightful will, what good is his claim to authority? Sometimes we hear of kings and queens in exile. But if they have no power to rule in their land, what kind of sovereignty is that? In God's case, authority always means that He has power to do what He wills. His authority is revealed in His power. No one can stop Him from doing what He wants to do, nor can anyone do what He decides will not be done. The reason is that He has almighty power. He has the power to create (Col. 1:16), to judge His enemies (Col. 2:15), to reconcile sinners to Himself (Col. 1:20) and to keep and strengthen His people in an evil world (Col. 1:11, 3:15). All that is a display of His authority.

Thirdly, a person's authority means that he has control of the opportunity to express his will. What if a person had the right to exercise authority, that is, what if his credentials were proper, and what if he had the power to carry out his will, and yet what if the proper time never came to act? What if his authority was bottled up because circumstances were not convenient or the moment never came to exercise his will? What kind of authority is that? It is possible for a man to have privilege and power but lack the opportunity to do his will, for he does not have complete control over the world in which he lives. God, however, creates His own opportunities (Col.1:26,27, 4:3). God created both the universe and time as part of the arena in which He exercises His authority to do His will, although He had His way from all eternity as well. God does not need His Creation. He can just do things. Nevertheless, His wisdom and ability to arrange things in His universe and work out the sequence of events in time in order to accomplish His will, no matter who or what opposes Him, reveals His authority.

For completeness, we could say that angels, that is, spiritual beings, have wills, too. The holy angels are totally submissive to the will of God, while fallen angels, especially Satan, violently oppose the will of God. But the book of Colossians does not talk about angels. It focusses upon the real authority of God and the assumed authority of man.

The fundamental difference between God's and man's authority is that God alone has dominion over His Creation and all of its inhabitants. That is, God reveals Himself to be completely, autonomously and independently sovereign over all things and all people.

Authority and Character

Besides the right, the power, and the opportunity, a person must have a desire to exercise his authority in order for him carry out his will. As it turns out, everyone who has authority does try to use it. The reason is that people have specific interests and goals that they want to achieve. They want to fulfill their desires. So, a person's attempt to exercise authority tells us a great deal about the person himself. That is, when a person exercises authority, we learn the desires of his heart. Therefore, the book of Colossians, in addition to an examination of God's authority in contrast to man's authority, is also an examination of the character of God who exercise His authority, as well as the character of people, who either submit to or rebel against Him.

God's and people's motives for wanting to do their will, their objectives for which they use their authority, are very different. People's best motives are infected by sin. There always are self-seeking desires and intentions at the foundation of all that people do. And many times, because the needs of other people are secondary to them, people exercise their authority in very abusive and destructive ways. To that, we can contrast God's motives for exercising His authority. His desire is also for personal glory, but the difference is that God is good, very, very good. God deserves the honor He demands. God cannot be glorified enough. The Bible is full of the revelation of God's glory in the exercise of His authority, and it is in Colossians too (Col. 1:18, 2:9,10, 3:17). Additionally, unlike people, God's motives are full of love, not only for His own glory, but also for what He has made. He creates, saves, and keeps His own, all out of the goodness of His heart. Only God uses His authority self-sacrificially for the blessing of others in great need (John 10:11,17,18). In fact, one of the greatest displays of His authority was his incarnation and death on the cross for His people's redemption (Col. 1:20-22, 2:11).

Authority and Truth

Since God is the supreme authority, only what He says prevails and is the standard for evaluating the statements of all others who claim authority in the universe. It is not as though God bullies His way and so forcefully asserts His Word as truth and by His sheer power makes it stick. Rather, this is God's universe (Col. 1:16). He put it together and operates it according to His design and for His purpose. Other rival authorities make statements about what they think is "true" about the universe, but what they say may or may not hold up, no matter how much prestige and influence they have. The reason is if their statements are different than what God has said, then their statements are consequently inaccurate, "untrue," views of the real world, and their actions based upon their own imaginations will not be effective or enduring (Col. 2:23).

Even objective statements about the physical universe reveal God's authority and require peoples' obligatory response of submission to what He declares to be so. Mathematical concepts, principles that describe the structure and behavior of physical objects, as well as the innumerable realities of biology display the wonders of their Creator. The whole physical universe is really a statement of the glory of God and all men are obligated to honor God for it (Psalm 19:1,2). When people ignore, dispute or deny God authority, their thinking of physical truth is full of error and they risk personal harm. They reveal the rebellious opposition they have toward the Creator to whom they must give an account.

Authority, Truth and Compliance

We begin to understand the connection between authority, truth and compliance when we recognize that statements called "true" do not just lie around awaiting discovery and objective examination, like an interesting rock or a pretty flower. Statements that are called true do not just hang in space to be admired as accurate descriptions of reality. Statements that are true always requires a proper reaction to their author. There is always a person's authority behind any statement of truth that demands and seeks to compel obedience. From that point of view, if a man can make his word count, if his word can actually make changes in people's lives, if all who hear conform to what he says, if he is able to fulfill his word in the lives of others, then he speaks with authority. What he says is truth, in the sense that his word sets the standard of behavior for all those who are subject to his authority. Perhaps the following illustration will help us understand the connection between authority, truth and compliance. If you travel on a road and approach a sign that says "Danger! Detour ahead!" you better turn around as the sign directs you. You better obey the statement on the sign or you will suffer the consequences of your disobedience. The reason you must obey is that the sign says what is true about the dangerous condition of the road ahead and what is true about how to avoid disaster. Furthermore, if a policeman catches you disobeying the sign, he could cite you and a judge could fine you.

As we have said, truth is not just a set of neutral propositions which men can discover through proper application of logic and empirical investigation of the physical universe. Truth is the description of God's character as well as an expression of His will (John 14:6, 17:17). So a person's reaction to truth is a measure of his heart's submission to God.

Colossians presents true spiritual statements which are not subject to our evaluation and criticism, but which demand our obedience. The warnings in Colossians are not suggestions. We must heed the counsel to avoid spiritual harm (Col. 2:8,18, 3:16). The promises in Colossians are not wishful stories. We must trust that the blessings are so, now and forever (Col. 1:21, 2:13, 3:24) and display that trust by means of our submission and compliance.

Rival Authorities

The history of the world is the story of the clash of wills. One man's will opposes another's. For example, children's wills clash with their parents', especially as they grow older. Husband's wills clash with wives'. Workers' wills clash with their employers'. The wills of people with religious and political differences clash, many times with great violence. In addition to that, all men's wills oppose God's. For example, unsaved people rebel at God's Law and refuse to submit to His Gospel. That rebellion continues for all people throughout eternity, except for those people who are changed by God's grace. The clash of wills is a big part of the message of the Colossian letter, especially as it describes the conflict between God and rival authorities.

We have to clarify what we mean by the words "rival authorities." If we imply there are people who have sovereign control over part of the universe, ruling autonomously, independently from God, then there are no rival authorities. Even Satan must submit to God (Job. 2:6, Luke 4:8, 10:18, 22:31,32, Rev. 12:7-12, 20:3,10). Nevertheless, people do seek to remove God's rule and assume control of their own lives as well as the lives of others, either foolishly motivated by the illusion that they can be free from God's dominion or blindly driven by their own ego under the influence of Satan. Therefore, we can understand the words "rival authority" in a narrow sense to refer to a person's intention rather than to his pretended or illusionary independence. That is, people try to remove God's constraints upon themselves and seek to dominate the lives of others. In that sense they act as a rival to God's authority, even though they offer no effective competition, in as much as God does what He wants with the hearts and souls of men.

People are encouraged to imagine that they exercise a command over themselves by the fact that God delegates authority on earth in order to accomplish His purposes. For example, God raises up civil governments (Daniel 2:21, Romans 9:17, 13:1), even though most of them are antagonistic toward Him and His Word (Psalm 2:2,3, Acts 2:26-28). God also allows people to design and erect their own religions and peddle their doctrines to their neighbors. People, whom God allows some control in society, imagine that they achieved their position of authority by means of their own wisdom and power. Furthermore, they are sensitive to any threats to their position of authority and react with great jealousy and anger against anyone whom they perceive as a challenge to their control. In their self-deception they even fight against God, who gave them the privilege to rule in the first place (John 19:10,11). So it is these rebellious aggressive people, whether they exercise authority in a secular or religious context, to whom we refer by the phrase "rival authorities."

There were several different spiritual assaults upon the Colossian congregation, but they all really amounted to one thing, namely, rival authorities tried to supplant the headship of Christ and dominate the lives of the members of the Colossian church (Col. 2:8,18,19). So, a prominent message of Colossians is the conflict between the authority of Jesus and the rival authorities of men over people who claim to be Christians. To whose authority would the members of the Colossian church submit? The members of the Colossian church were assaulted by men who tried to assume authority but who were only full of empty words and pride (Col. 2:8,18). The members of the Colossian church were under spiritual attack by men who tried to subdue them by means of rituals and rules (Col. 2:16, 20-22), or tried to intimidate them by judgments and threats (Col. 2:16,18). In addition, the Colossians who professed to trust in Jesus as their Savior and Lord were subjected to the appeal of their own sinful flesh (Col. 3:5). Wonderfully, however, the message of Colossians is that Jesus Christ, who released them from the Law's claim upon them because of their sin (Col. 1:20,21, 2:14), unbound them from the power of spiritual wickedness (Col. 2:15), and to brought them into His Kingdom in the first place (Col. 1:13), also has the authority to keep them faithful amid any assaults (Col. 1:6, 2:6,7, 3:15).

Rival authorities have no answers and offer no help for the needs of men. Men's philosophies promote pride. God's truth produces fruit. Yet as God's truth goes out, human-based authorities press their claims and seek to influence others, especially in the church. It is this two-way pull on people that the book of Colossians discusses. Any yet, as the Bible so emphatically states, the truth is Jesus is the supreme authority in the universe, for the benefit of His people (Eph. 1:20-22).

Jesus' Authority over Saved and Unsaved People

As we have seen, Jesus is the supreme authority in the universe, over all things and all people. He created the universe, sustains it and all of its inhabitants are accountable to Him. However, we must be careful to correctly understand His authority over the lives of people who are saved and over the lives of people who are not saved.

Normally when we say that Jesus is a person's Lord we mean that the person recognizes, acknowledges and even rejoices in Jesus' authority over Him. That is, those people who are saved have a heart that embraces and greatly desires the sovereign control of Jesus over them.

It is easy to see that Jesus is the Lord over all people who are saved.

Jesus' authority can be seen in their fruitful words and actions from hour to hour and day to day. Jesus' authority can be seen in the spiritual blessings they enjoy that reveal His gracious care of their lives over the years. Jesus' authority also can be seen in the confidence and peace of their hearts, for with great joyful expectation and with loving adoration they approach the final destination Jesus has prepared for them, even though they will not see it until Jesus returns at the end of time.

However, it is not so easy to see that Jesus is the Lord over all people who are not saved. We can agree that He is their Lord based upon the fact that He is the supreme authority in the universe, but we may wonder at the fact that unbelievers clearly ignore and sometimes dishonor Jesus. Although unbelievers act and speak differently than believers, Jesus still is the greatest authority in their lives. For one thing, their rebellious life is a reflection of the fact that He "gives them up" to their own desires, as He sees fit (Rom. 1:24,26,28). For another thing, unbelievers reap all the bitter fruits of heartache, fear and hatred as a consequence of their rebellion, as He as planned (Gal. 6:7,8). For one more thing, Jesus controls the eventual outcome of their lives, as they head for eventual destruction of eternal damnation in Hell (Rev. 20:12-15).

Therefore, when we say that Jesus is not a person's Lord, we do not mean Jesus has no authority over him. Instead, we refer to a person's desires. We mean that an unsaved person does not want Jesus to be his Lord. Such a person denies, seeks to suppress and even hates Jesus' control over him. That is, those people who are not saved have a heart that seeks to remove the sovereign control of Jesus over them, even though it is only wishful thinking.

With that in mind, we can say that the Bible is God's word for all men and all men are accountable to what it says (John 12:48), but Colossians is particularly relevant to true born again believers. First of all, it is particularly relevant to them because only they trust the Bible. Only they trust the character of its Author. They know God cannot lie and are convinced that no where else will they find true answers to their questions.

Secondly, Colossians is particularly relevant to true born again believers because they have been given the mind to recognize the value of what they read in the Bible. So, only they really understand or care about the wisdom and counsel found in its pages about the spiritual truths of sin, judgement, grace, the cross, forgiveness and obedience. Only they are honest, willing to face the spiritual situation in their lives as it really is. Only they are discerning and wise, able to avoid the siren call of evil authorities, and cling faithfully to the Bible.

Thirdly, Colossians is particularly relevant to true born again believers because they have been given the power of the resurrected life to obey God from the heart and avoid the appeal and intimidation of evil authorities which try to divert him from God's will. Only they have the power to endure the persecution which attends their obedience and faithful witness. Only they gladly submit to God's purpose in all that happens in their lives.

Through principles and examples, Colossians describes the wonderful way in which Jesus, the supreme authority of the universe, is the wise and loving authority in the lives of His people. The supreme authority of Jesus Christ is wonderful news to a Christian because His Almighty, all-wise Lord has marshaled all His resources for his benefit. For that a Christian is full of thanks (Col. 1:12, 2:7, 3:15-17, 4:2). Jesus is King of the universe, whether men like it or not. How much better it is to have Him as a caring Lord than as an enemy!

Personal Authority

Beyond the issue of whether Jesus is the supreme authority in the universe is the issue of whether Jesus is "the supreme authority in MY life." The book of Colossians, as all of the whole Bible, gets very personal, for it forces people to ask, "Whom do I trust? To whom do I listen? Who is in charge of my life, or more to the point whom do I want to be in charge?" Is the answer to these questions, "myself" or "God"? Colossians forces people to consider "who decides what I must like and pursue or dislike and avoid? Who tells me how and when to spend my own time, energy and resources?" Do they conclude, "I am proud to be the captain of my own life and soul"? Or are they content with God as their Lord and Master?

A person can get idea of how submissive he is to Jesus' authority when he answers the following questions, "Are you humble enough to acknowledge that God alone knows all that there is to know about this universe and its inhabitants (Job. 38-41, I Cor. 2:11), including His own intentions and plans for you (Jer. 10:23,24)? Are you humble enough to recognize that God has set limits to your understanding of the universe, that the Almighty Creator has decided there is a point beyond which you cannot learn things about the universe (Eccl. 8:16,17)? Are you contrite enough to agree that you are sinful and not inclined to learn or recognize anything that is true which conflicts with your own cherished perception of the universe (Rom. 1:18-23, II Peter 3:3-6)? Do you trust God who is in control of all knowledge dispenses it as He sees fit (Matt. 11:27)? Do you seek the grace and mercy of God who reveals Himself and His wisdom only to those whom He saves (I Cor. 2:14-16)? Do you presume to try to amend or improve upon what God says (Prov. 30:5,6, Rom. 11:33-36, Rev. 22:18,19)?"

COLOSSIANS

The Big Picture

The book of Colossians answers some important questions of those people who are submissive to the Lord Jesus Christ. To put it in a more personal way, "God has made you and knows you better than you know yourself. He knows what you are thinking and the questions of your heart. In love, He has answered your questions." We can organize the questions in the following way.

Colossians: The Big Questions of Life

I   Chapter 1:   How Can I Know I Am Saved?
II   Chapter 2:   How Do I Deal with Challenges to My Faith?
III   Chapter 3:   How Do I Deal with My Personal Sin?
IV   Chapter 4:   What Is God's Will for My Life?

With the same idea in mind, we can organize Colossians in a brief way as follows:

Colossians: A Christian on Display

I   Chapters 1 and 2:   What a Christian Is and Is Not
II   Chapters 3 and 4:   What a Christian Does and Does Not Do

Taking into account the theme of authority, we can organize Colossians in this alterative way:

Colossians: God's Authority

I   Chapter 1:   God's Authority Displayed in Jesus Christ

II Chapter 2: God's Authority Meets the Challenge of False Gospels
III Chapter 3: God's Authority Revealed in Believers' Character
IV Chapter 4: God's Authority Revealed in Believers' Service

Finally, we can think of the idea of truth and arrive at the following outline:

Colossians: God's Truth About His Universe

I Chapter 1: God's Truth About Himself
II Chapter 2: God's Truth About His Gospel
III Chapter 3: God's Truth About Christians
IV Chapter 4: God's Truth Goes Out to the World

Chapter 1

Colossians 1:1 - 12

Colossians 1, verses 1 through 12, display and illustrate Jesus' supreme authority over the lives of His people. The character and behavior of Christians reveals the character of their Lord Jesus, in whose image they are being transformed (Rom. 8:29). What they have become also identifies them as people who are under Jesus' authority.

Colossians 1:1, "Paul, an apostle of Jesus Christ by the will of God, and Timotheus our brother."

We immediately meet two men who are exhibits of Jesus' authoritative control over His people. They are "Paul" and "Timotheus," or Timothy. Because there is so much more information in the Bible about Paul than there is about Timothy, we shall spend more time examining Paul's life.

Paul was a Jew by birth and we first meet him in the Bible with the Jewish name "Saul" (Acts 7:58). However, many of the Colossians were Gentiles (Col. 1:27). Since it was his custom to seek some common identity with those people to whom he brought God's Word (I Cor. 9:19-21), he identified himself by "Paul," a Gentile name. Paul's attempt to identify with the Colossians was not artificial or contrived. He was, in fact, a Roman citizen (Acts 16:37, 22:26-28). So, Paul and the Colossians were both part of the Roman, Gentile world.

Paul highlighted that which he shared in common with the Colossians so they would be willing to listen to his message and hopefully reap its benefits (I Cor. 9:22-23). It is as if he was saying, "I am subject to the Roman authorities, just like you. I understand the meaning of submission to authority, both its obligations and its benefits. I also am subject to Jesus' authority, as I trust you are. So, I also have experience in living under His authority. Therefore, I know what I am talking about, listen to me because I have an important message from God for you. If you claim to be saved, take heed to what you read in this letter and obey it rather than the words of someone else with a different message."

The word translated "apostle" means "sent one." It is used in John 13:16 as "he that is sent." Paul was more than just another man with a message. He was a man with God's message, sent into the world by the will of God to bring His Word (II Cor. 5:20).

Apostleship was a unique calling with special authority and was limited to only a few men. That calling included Paul, for he fulfilled the two qualifications of an apostle listed in Acts 1:21 and 22. First of all, Paul was taught personally by Jesus (Gal. 1:11,12). Secondly, Paul was "a witness with us (apostles) of his (Jesus') resurrection," as we read in I Corinthians 9:1. In addition to meeting those two qualifications, his apostleship was verified by God Himself through special signs (II Cor. 12:12, see Acts 13:11, 14:8-10, 19:11,12). Therefore, it was an indisputable fact that Paul was made an apostle by the sovereign, irresistible, authoritative "will of God" (I Cor. 15:7-10, II Cor 11:5).

Paul did not emphasize his apostleship in order to boast, impress anyone or push his weight around, like the false ministers about whom he would later warn the Colossians (Col. 2:16,18). It was not his idea to be "an apostle of Jesus Christ." His apostleship was a divine appointment (Gal. 1:15). Paul was an apostle, sent into the world, by the "will of God."

There were specific historical reasons why Paul asserted his apostleship. His letter was written from a long distance away. Also, few of the Colossians had ever seen him (Col. 2:1), so they did not have the benefit of a personal acquaintance that would lead them to naturally trust him. In contrast to that, other teachers were physically present in Colosse and known to the Colossians. These teachers had a natural advantage in any attempt to gain the attention and allegiance of the Colossians. Despite this handicap, Paul wanted the Colossians to have confidence in what he wrote rather than in the messages of the local, competing authorities (Col. 2:4,8). Paul was saying, "You might only know me by name. And you might wonder if I know enough about your local situation to advise you. But I am what God has made me, a man under Jesus' authority and a man who comes with God's authoritative message. So listen to me rather than anyone else."

Paul was motivated to assert his apostleship because he loved the souls for whom this letter was intended (Col. 1:3, 2:5). There was a lot at stake. He wanted all who were not saved to avoid God's wrath. And, he wanted all who were saved to be strengthen for the spiritual battles they would face each day. Paul knew that it was vital for the Colossians to recognize him as a credible messenger and receive this letter for what it really was, the true, authoritative and valuable Word of God (I Thess. 2:13, Heb. 2:3,4).

This letter came from "Timotheus" as well as Paul. Timothy's support of Paul would tend to make Paul's message more easily accepted. For one thing, Timothy was known personally by the Colossians (notice the use of the word "my" and not "our" in Colossians 2:1). For another thing, Timothy was half Gentile (Acts 16:1-3) and had a physical, common identity with the Colossians. So, it is as if Timothy was one of the Colossians, their familiar friend who vouched for Paul. In addition to that, Timothy's name provided a second witness to Paul's message, in accord with God's formula for establishing an authoritative word (II Cor. 13:1).

If we think about it, Paul's words should have been enough. And they really were enough from God's point of view. He was God's apostle. Paul did not need Timothy's stamp of approval. However, we can think of Timothy's validation as a condescending grace for the Colossians, for Timothy was someone familiar to whom they could turn for corroboration of what they read in this letter, so that they might believe it. God wanted the Colossians to receive and benefit from His Word, which this letter was.

The fact that Timothy had a mixed heritage adds to the message of this letter. Timothy, as a "half-breed" so to speak, represented all mankind. His salvation showed that Jesus is Lord of all nations, tribes and tongues. Therefore, the Colossians could not dismiss the message of this letter as a Jewish doctrine. It is as if Paul was saying, "Jesus is Timothy's Lord. If you are saved, Jesus is your Lord too, even though Jesus was a Jew and you are Gentiles."

Colossians 1:2, "To the saints and faithful brethren in Christ which are at Colosse:"

The words "saints" and "faithful brethren" are not equivalent to "spiritually superior" or "more holy than average." People are made saints and faithful brethren by God's grace. Anyone who is a true believer is placed by God "in Christ" (Rom. 8:1) and stands the same before God (I Cor. 10:17, Gal. 3:28).

The word "saint" (*hagiois*), meaning "set apart" or "separate," could refer to what true believers are in reality (Col 1:12). That is, they are "saints ... in Christ" (Rom. 8:1). They are people who are saved by grace and separate from the world (II Cor. 6:14-17). They have a limited compatibility with people of this world. They do not share the same motives or goals as the people of this world. Also, they are people who are separated to serve God (Rom. 12:1,2).

The words "saint" and "faithful brethren" also could refer to what all the members outwardly identify, whether they truly are people of God or not, for though all members of the church may have called themselves "brethren," some could have been "false brethren" (Gal. 2:4). From that point of view, the letter was meant for every individual in the Colossian church, but with two different purposes. All the members who read the words "saints and faithful brethren" should pause to reflect upon their lives and ask if those words include them. Upon what evidence do they base their certainty that God has separated them and placed them under His sole authority? True believers would recognize that they were submissive to God's authority and be encouraged. For them, the words "saint" and "faithful brethren" describes what they are. For all others, the words "saint" and "faithful brethren" describes what they ought to be. If, after having taken spiritual inventory, they find themselves wanting, then this letter is a message of rebuke and warning, calling them to salvation.

The words "which are at Colosse" really should be rendered "in Colosse." The idea could be expressed as "in the midst of the city of Colosse" or "immersed in the city of Colosse." That is where the members of the Colossian church were when the Gospel found them, and that is where they remained after they were saved. They are still in the world, but not of the world (John 17:15). With this in mind, the message of the phrase could be expressed in the following way. "Don't get influenced by the evil society in which you must live, especially since you are in the minority. You claim to be under the authority of Jesus, so don't act like you are under the same evil, spiritual dominion as the rest of the citizens of the city." Or we could express the message in the following way. "I know that you are preoccupied by necessary obligations of your life in Colosse. But I want to encourage you to remain faithful and seek the wisdom and power of God." That goal is accomplished by the Word of God (Psalm 119:9-16, John 15:3).

"Grace be unto you, and peace, from God our Father and the Lord Jesus Christ."

Grace is the purest display of God's authority and unique sovereignty. Grace starts and ends with God. Before the world even began (Eph. 1:4-6), God expressed grace to those sinners whom He chose to save (II Cor. 8:9, Phil 2:7) for His own purposes, independently of anything in their lives. God took the initiative to wisely plan and sacrificially work to resolve the greatest need of many of the Colossians (Eph 2:5, Psalm 5:10). He is in total control.

We might wonder why the verse says "to the saints ... grace." After all, don't saints already have grace? It is true that saints, that is, people who truly are saints, have already been saved by grace. But the idea here is that grace which saves them also abides in them to sustain them in their walk and causes them to grow, as in the Philippi congregation (Phil. 1:6 and 9). Also, grace refers to the assignment they have from God which occupies them after they are saved, for grace is the word Paul used to label his own job (I Cor. 15:10).

The word "peace" is a label for the results of "grace." When God's character causes Him to be kind to sinners, the result is peace. The word "peace" does not refer to the idyllic calm of a forest meadow, but to the end of war. The peace in view is not the horizontal harmony between men, but the cessation of conflict and the vertical reconciliation between God and man (Isa. 40:2, Rom 5:1).

God is the enemy King (Isaiah 48:22, Rom 5:10, Col 1:21). The greatest threat to sinners is not physical, political war but the judgment and wrath of God. He is a consuming fire (Heb. 12:29). He is the one with whom sinners need to secure peace, and He is the only one with the authority to declare peace, based upon the death of Jesus. It was Jesus' job to fulfill the unilateral terms of peace which God offers to them in the Gospel (Isa 9:6, 40:2, John 14:27, Eph 2:14, Col 1:20).

The words "God **our** Father" do not imply that God is the Father of all men. God is the Creator of all men and gives them physical life. But the Fatherhood of God is God's answer to the spiritual need of men (Psalm 27:10, Isaiah 49:15). It only applies to people through the Gospel (II Cor. 6:18), only to those who are saved (Isaiah 64:8, Rom. 8:15,16). God is "our Father" only if Jesus is "our Lord" (John 8:42). In that light, we could say that the words "God our Father" are an evangelistic greeting, expressing Paul's Gospel desire for them.

Incidentally, we must not let the construction of the phrase "God our Father and the Lord Jesus Christ" lead us to think the wrong thing about Jesus. It may look like the word "God" is attached to the word "Father" but separated from the word "Jesus" by the word "and." However, the Bible uses the same construction to apparently separate God from the Father (Eph. 5:20). So we know the word "and" does not promote the idea of separation. As it turns out, this phrase is meant to bind the Father and the Lord Jesus Christ together. They are two person's of the one Godhead who share the same authority (John 5:23, Col. 1:19, 2:9). They both designed the gracious plan of peace. They both have the same authority to bestow grace and peace. We can understand this phrase to mean, "grace to you, and peace, from God, who is our Father and who is the Lord Jesus Christ."

Colossians 1:3-8

Verses 3 through 8 present some details of the **outward** evidence that a Christian is under the authority of Jesus Christ. From these verses, we learn what people under the authority of Jesus look like, spiritually.

Colossians 1:3, "We give thanks to God and the Father of our Lord Jesus Christ"

When we link the words "we give thanks" to the words "since we heard of your faith in Christ Jesus, and of the love which ye have to all the saints" in verse 4, we see that Paul and Timothy's prayer of thanks was based upon specific and concrete information. Epaphras told them how the Colossians' faith and love was being expressed (Col. 1:7,8). Therefore, their prayers were informed and thoughtful, based upon evidence of grace in the Colossians' lives.

Paul and Timothy's "thanks" illustrated mature christian prayer. Prayer is not vague or sentimental. Instead, it is definite and particular. Prayer expresses a genuine concern for people, revealed by an interest in the details of their lives. Prayer also expresses a deep trust in God, as someone who is capable and caring because He is exact and thorough.

When we isolate the words, "we give thanks to God" together with the words "for the hope which is laid up for you in heaven" in verse 5, from the rest of the passage, it is clear that the focus of Paul and Timothy's gratitude was not upon physical blessings. As nice as physical blessings may be, they can bind people close to this sin-cursed world. Instead, Paul and Timothy's focus was upon the spiritual blessings laid up for God's people in Heaven.

The Colossians showed "faith in Christ Jesus" and "love ... to all the saints" (verse 4), but Paul did not thank them. Instead, he gave thanks "to God." The reason is that every good gift comes from God (Eph. 3:7, James 1:17). It is God who motivates and animates His people to do His will (Phil. 2:13).

The words "the Father of our Lord Jesus Christ" do not reduce Jesus in nature or authority. Because Jesus is a Son does not mean He is somehow less than the Father. In fact, according to John 5:18, when Jesus called God His Father, He declared that He is equal to God. He is honored exactly as the Father (John 5:23). Christians are adopted sons, but Jesus is the one true Son and so is the same as His Father. We cannot understand God, who reveals Himself as the Father, Son and Holy Spirit. But we can say what is true, according to the Bible.

The reason that Paul said he thanked the Father and not the Son is that the Bible tells us to pray "Our Father," in Jesus' name. There are many reasons for this, but the main reason is that true believers are God's children, who adore and depend upon Him. It is true that Jesus is an indispensable person in the salvation plan, for whom all Christians are eternally grateful. But for now, the Bible expects us to address our thanks to the Father.

"praying always for you"

These words do not mean "We are praying every second for you, non-stop." Instead, Paul is saying, "whenever we pray, we pray for you, too." Their prayers were not occasional or sporadic, given whenever something happened to remind them of the Colossians. Rather, their prayers were an enduring, scheduled exercise, revealing a commitment to the spiritual welfare of the Colossians.

The second person pronoun is used in various forms ("you ... your ... ye ...") at least 8 times from verses 3 through 8. From this fact, we see that Paul is an illustration of the message of grace which he brought. In great meekness, he focussed, not upon "I" and "me," but upon "ye" and "your," reflecting God's gracious concern for others. This selfless attitude is a distinguishing mark of those leaders who are under God's authority.

The Colossians were unknown to Paul, personally. Yet Paul prayed for them because he wanted the very best for them. What a work of grace in Paul's heart! Ultimately, Paul's prayers were a signature that he was under the Lord Jesus' authority, for prayer is one of the Lord's commands.

Paul's spiritual concern for someone whom he knew very little is the same as any Christian's, for if we think about it, who really knows the heart of another person? Also, Christians have a prayerful concern for all of God's people worldwide, known and unknown.

Prayer is one outward evidence that someone is under God's authority. Conversely, the lack of prayer is evidence that someone is not under God's authority.

Colossians 1:4, "Since we heard of your faith in Christ Jesus and of

the love which ye have to all the saints,"

We can think of the words "your faith in Christ" as the faith given to them as a gift (Gal. 5:22, Phil. 1:29), which they demonstrated since they were in Christ, or since they were saved. We also can compare the words "your faith in Christ Jesus" with the words "Christ in you, the hope of glory" (Col. 1:27) and conclude that the faith which the Colossians demonstrated is really the expression of Jesus' own character, who abides in them. They received His faith (Gal. 2:16,20 and Eph 4:5), and His life shone through their actions (Gal. 2:20). That is, although the Colossians had a lot to see in the city they lived, they saw spiritual realities with a sight given to them by God. That is why Paul could write that they "seek those things which are above" (Col. 3:1) and expect them to understand.

The love that they had "to all the saints" was a special love. It is love (*agape*) that comes from God. Like faith, it is a gift to those whom He saves.

The word "to" is really "into" (*eis*). We can think about the word "to" in two ways. One idea could be that the Colossians' love caused them to enter "into" the lives of the saints. It is not that they superficially did their "duty" to the saints, but would rather not be bothered. Instead, they cared for the saints as much as God did. A second idea could be that their love penetrated into the lives of the saints. Their love was infectious. Their demonstration of love to the saints resulted in the saints also demonstrating love. Both ideas could be in view because we would expect the love of God that was given to the Colossians to have the same purpose and power as God's own love.

The fruits of love and faith were two witnesses that confirmed many Colossians were under the authority of the Lord Jesus Christ. The idea of verse 4 is that many of the Colossians demonstrated the fruit of "faith in Christ Jesus" and "love to all the saints," which led Paul and Timothy to conclude, based upon that evidence, that these Colossians were saved. Therefore, although Paul emphasized his apostleship, he was not implying that the Colossians were like naughty children who needed a lecture from their parent. Rather, Paul's message is, "I know that many of you are demonstrating the faith and love that is expected of true believers. I can tell you with full authority that God knows that, too."

Colossians 1:5, "For the hope which is laid up for you in heaven"

The word "hope" is a noun which labels an object. The object may be a deferred promise (Rom. 8:24,25), but it is a real object nonetheless. Whether we trust it to be so or not is a matter of our heart, not a matter of the reality of the hope.

Sometimes the word "hope" is a verb, a word that often describes an action. But even in that case, it does not refer to a vague or uncertain expectation, as if it were equivalent to "I wish" or "I hope so, but am not sure." Instead, the action of hope is focussed upon a specific and concrete object, as we read in Hebrews 11:1, "**things hoped for.**"

The Colossians trusted that the promised object was real. That trust sustained their anticipation and joy. God promised something in His Word and the Colossians expected its eventual fulfillment. What is the object for which they hoped? God's people hope for many things. One is eternal life (Titus 1:2). Another is Jesus' return (Titus 2:13). But actually, we should ask, "for whom did they hope?" Above all else, Jesus is the "hope" (Col. 1:27, I Tim. 1:1). He is real, but He is in Heaven and will not come again until the end of time. So in a way He is a deferred promise. That is, even though He is with the believers in His Spirit (John 16:7, Heb. 13:5), He is not personally seen. He is hoped for, but still loved (I Peter 1:8).

Because we can understand the word "hope" to refer to Jesus, we arrive at the idea that Jesus is "laid up" for us "in heaven." This idea makes sense when we recall Jesus is seated on the right hand of God, with full authority (Col. 3:1, Eph. 2:6). So Christians look forward, not to what God can give them, but to God Himself, with whom they want to be and will be, forever.

The mark of true Christians is that their desire or expectation is not for political influence, social justice, material prosperity, or physical health. They have heaven's hope instead of the world's hope. As they now rejoice in and live obediently under the authority of Jesus, they eagerly look forward to the same thing when they go to be with Him in heaven.

"whereof ye heard before in the word of truth of the gospel"

The word "gospel" identifies "the word of truth." In fact, in Ephesians 1:13, the word "gospel" functions as an appositive, in the sense that it is equivalent to the words "the word of truth." Inasmuch as the whole Bible is the word of truth, we can conclude that the whole Bible is the "gospel." The Gospel is a very large word, including all that the "word of truth" contains, not only the promises described in the Old Testament but also their fulfillment described in the New Testament (Acts 20:24-27, Gal. 3:8, Heb. 4:2).

There is a common misunderstanding that the word "gospel" only refers to the basic facts about Jesus' life and death, as if I Corinthians 15:3,4 were a summary of the Gospel. That is a very wrong way to think about the Gospel. According to the phrase "the word of truth of the gospel," the Gospel is the same as the word of truth, without any modifying or limiting phrases. That is, the Gospel is in all of God's Word of truth, the entire Bible, including both passages of judgement (Rom. 2:16) and salvation (Rom. 1:16). In fact, without an understanding of judgment and the wrath of God, no one can understand salvation. The Gospel is the complete revelation of what God planned before time, how He carries out that plan through the ages, and how He will complete it at the end of the world and into eternity.

The Colossians "heard" about the hope in "the word of truth of the gospel" (Col. 1:23). And that same "word" sustained their hope, as they were assaulted by the appeals of competing messages (Col. 2:4) and as they fought against the desires of their flesh (Col. 3:16).

Colossians 1:6, "which is come unto you, as it is in all the world;"

The antecedent of the word "which" is the word "gospel." The Gospel "came unto" them from Epaphras (Col. 1:7) among others. But how do we understand the phrase, "as it is in all the world"? Colossians 1:23 states, "the gospel, which ye have heard, and which was preached to every creature which is under heaven." However, at that time, the Gospel of redemption in Jesus Christ had not come to the Americas or to many parts of the Far East.

One way to think of the words "in all the world" is to recognize that the Bible sometimes uses the word "world" to refer to a limited part of the whole world, as for example in Luke 2:1. The idea then would be that the Gospel is "in all the known world," known to and visited by the Christians at that time.

Another way to think of these words is in the sense of Roman 1:19-20, "Because that which may be known of God is manifest in them; for God hath shewed it unto them. For the invisible things of him from the creation of the world are clearly seen, being understood by the things that are made, even his eternal power and Godhead; so that they are without excuse." From the information found in the creation, God expects all men to repent (Rom. 2:4) and seek after Him (Acts 17:25-

27). But, doesn't Romans 10:17 states that salvation comes through the "word"? Yes, it does. However, in Psalm 19:1-4 we read, "The heavens declare the glory of God; and the firmament sheweth his handiwork. Day unto day uttereth speech, and night unto night sheweth knowledge. There is no speech nor language, where their voice is not heard. Their line is gone out through all the earth, and their words to the end of the world. In them hath he set a tabernacle for the sun." Though no one is saved through observing the creation, there is enough of a message to drive people to seek God. And God directs the lives of His elect so that they will have an encounter with His Word. In that sense, we could say that this phrase in Colossians 1:6 is a prediction of eventual worldwide evangelism.

One important point is that the Gospel that came to the Colossians, as in this letter, is not a local cult or regional religion, with limited application or authority. It is the universal plan of the one true God, revealed in the "word of truth, the gospel, which is come unto you." There is no alternative "truth" in this universe, different from that which is found in the Bible, despite the false claims of men.

"and bringeth forth fruit, as it doth also in you, since the day ye heard of it and knew the grace of God in truth."

The words "as it doth also in you" imply that Gospel brought forth fruit in "the world," just as it also did in the lives of the believers in Colosse. The Gospel has worldwide application, the proof of which is the fruit it produces everywhere it is heard, in all nations. Christians in one nation think and behave similarly to Christians in other nations, even if they look differently and speak a different language.

Incidentally, the word "heard" means really heard, not just with their ears but also with their hearts. They heard so well that they became saved, the evidence of which is the fruit they brought forth. Similarly, the word "knew" must mean more than head knowledge. It must mean the actual experience of salvation that resulted in "fruit" (Gal. 5:22-25). The Gospel which came to the Colossian congregation brought forth fruit in all of its saved members. That is how it always is. The fruit identifies the true Gospel and marks the true believer. In terms of the parable of the sower, we can say that fruit identifies the Gospel as good seed, full of vitality. Also, the fruit marks the people as good ground, with "an honest and good heart, having heard the word, keep it, and bring forth fruit with patience" (Luke 8:1-15)

The fruit in the Colossians' lives also was evidence that they were under God's authority rather than someone else's. The principle is that a person's authority determines and is revealed by his ethics, whether it is good (Phil 2:13) or bad (John 8:34,44). The big question of a person's life is not "Do I have the right knowledge?" Instead, it is "Who is my authority?" Different authorities, with different principles, truths and rules, cause people to think and behave differently. We know something about the authority behind people when we observe them. Their fruit reveals the character of the authority that controls them and that they follow (Matt. 7:15-23, John 8:41-44).

It is true that for a short time span a man who is under God's authority may falter. After all, if a person has lived in the world as an unsaved person for a while, he takes time to grow and demonstrate his submission to his Lord Jesus. Some evidences of salvation are immediately apparent, others reveal themselves slowly. It is also true that for a short time a man who is under an evil authority outwardly may live obediently in one area of his life. But in either case, the true nature of a man and his authority eventually will be exposed. The authority under which he lives will show because he cannot keep it hidden very long. The Colossians demonstrated fruit, "since the day ye heard" the Gospel, evidence that they were saved and under God's authority.

Verse 6 provides one answer to the big question of Chapter one, "How can I know I am saved? How do I know the Gospel I trust is the true one that will make me right with God, and that I truly trust in it?" The answer is that a true believer trusting in God's unique true Gospel "bringeth forth fruit."

Colossians 1:7, "As ye also learned of Epaphras our dear fellowservant, who is for you a faithful minister of Christ;"

Actually the words "of Epaphras" mean "away from Epaphras." The idea is that the word went away from Epaphras toward the Colossians. The idea is that Epaphras passed out the hope of the Gospel, just like someone passes out tracts. So, they learned about the true hope of the Gospel from Epaphras.

The words, "Epaphras ... is for you," mean "... is over or above you." He was in a place or in a position above them to dispense the truth to them. One way we could think of this is that Epaphras had some kind of position of rulership over them. Another way we could think of this is graphically. It is as if he were like a tube that starts in heaven and ends in Colosse. Into the top end God put His Word and out of the bottom end they received it. The idea is that he was "a faithful minister of Christ." He was a steward of God's word, and it passed from God through Epaphras on to the Colossians without any modifications. He was a Colossian (Col. 4:12) who was a "faithful minister," from whom they "learned" the truth. He was an example of someone working faithfully under Jesus' authority.

Incidentally, Epaphras' name means "lovely." That is appropriate because the Bible says people who bring the Gospel have "lovely" feet (Rom. 10:15).

Colossians 1:8, "Who also declared unto us your love in the Spirit."

Epaphras also brought back an encouraging report to Paul and Timothy. It was that information for which they gave "thanks to God" (verse 3). However, the word "declared" does not mean "to speak." Instead, it means to "signify," in the sense "to be a picture of." For example, the word is used in Hebrews 9:8 which explains that the "Holy Ghost" used the Old Testament tabernacle and its rituals to signify, or picture spiritual truth, namely that those physical things were not the way to God. With this in mind, we could say that Epaphras not only verbally told Paul and Timothy about the spiritual affairs in Colosse, but also was a picture of the Colossians' "love in the Spirit." Perhaps they expressed their love for Epaphras by caring for his physical needs in some way, which Paul and Timothy noticed.

The phrase "your love in the Spirit" refers to one of the fruits which the Gospel brought to them (verse 6). The phrase refers especially to a love for God, which is a gift of God given only to believers (Gal. 5:22, I John 5:3). Love for God is the proper motivation for personal obedience to God as well as the proper basis for love between people.

Colossians 1: 9-12,

Verses 9 through 12 complement the message of verses 3 through 8. As Colossians 1:3-8 present some details of the **outward** evidence that people are under the authority of Jesus, Colossians 1:9-12 present some details of the **inward** evidence that people are under Jesus' authority. These verses complete the message of Colossians 1:1-12, which is that God has done something **to** His people to mark them as people under His authority, seen in their words and deeds..

Colossians 1:9, "For this cause we also, since the day we heard it,

do not cease to pray for you."

The antecedent to the word "this" is the report of their faith and love mentioned in verse 4, as well as the fruit mentioned in verse 6. The evidence of God's grace in their lives prompted Paul and Timothy to pray.

Paul and Timothy's incessant prayers were a testimony to the affection they had for the Colossians and a testimony to the proximity and seriousness of the spiritual challenges they all faced.

Prayer is the most effective way for Paul and Timothy to minister to them. One reason is that they were so far away from the congregation and could not counsel them, except through an occasional letter. Another reason is that only God has the authority and power to help them. The previous verses testified that many Colossians demonstrated that they were under God's authority. Paul responded to that news with prayer that God would lead them to mature in knowledge and practice. In that way, they would remain bright advertisements for God's Gospel as well as understand how to answer the challenges of false teaching and practice.

The response of prayer highlights the fact that the Christian experience is not complete the day people become saved. Unless a person dies and goes to Heaven the moment after he become saved, he has an unceasing need to pray for God's guidance and care during his spiritual pilgrimage on earth. Prayer is needed to strengthen a person's trust in God since sin within and false teaching without can lead to doubt and confusion, especially in the face of the world's contemptuous and hateful reaction to the Gospel. A Christian's reaction of prayer amid sin, temptation, confusion, doubt and fear reveals his abiding trust in his Lord, no matter what.

"and to desire that ye might be filled with the knowledge of his will in all wisdom and spiritual understanding."

The whole Bible is "the knowledge of his will." It is knowledge beyond the reach of human investigation (I Cor 2:9-16) and is knowledge distributed to people according to His decision and schedule (Matt. 11:25-27). That is why we must ask God for "all wisdom and spiritual understanding" (James 1:5). He alone has the authority and power to supply it.

Paul and Timothy prayed that "all" or the **whole** Bible fill their lives. They knew that selective and partial study of the Bible results in sloppy and fuzzy thinking concerning what the Bible says about God, about men, about sin and about salvation. Poor thinking, in turn, makes people vulnerable to the persuasive influence of false teachers. Therefore, the two men wanted the whole Bible to be the authority that shaped the Colossians' thoughts and behavior. They knew that a person's ability to think accurately and clearly about spiritual things is evidence that he is submissive to all that God says in His Word. And that was their objective for the Colossians.

Colossians 1:10, "That ye might walk worthy of the Lord unto all pleasing, being fruitful in every good work, and increasing in the knowledge of God."

Paul and Timothy did "not cease to pray" that the Colossians would be "filled with the knowledge of his will in all wisdom and spiritual understanding" in order "that" they "might walk worthy of the Lord." That is, the men prayed that the Colossians would be spiritually smart in order that they be obedient. They wanted the Colossians to be filled with all knowledge in order to avoid error in thought and behavior, and so not dishonor God's name.

The word "worthy" refers to the worth of God and so reminds us of the honor and praise people owe the Lord, for who He is and what he has done (Rev. 5:9,12). To "walk worthily" means to live in a way that encourages people to give Him the honor and praise He is due.

Paul explains, in verse 10, what it means to "walk worthy of the Lord." It means to walk **"unto all pleasing."** Pleasing the Lord means to walk by faith (Heb. 11:6). That is, trusting the Lord is a walk that honors God because it is a comment upon His competency and sovereignty. Trusting the Lord is saying, "He is worth trusting because He is in total control, for good to them who love Him." Pleasing the Lord also means to serve others (Heb. 13:16). That is, trusting the Lord is a comment upon His family. Trusting the Lord is saying, "the people who matter to God, matter to me too. I value what God does. His priorities are right."

So, "walk worthy of the Lord" also means to walk **"fruitful in every good work."** Bearing fruit in every good work is a walk that honors God because being fruitful is a display of God's own work in His people. He alone causes them to be fruitful (John 15:5,16, Phil. 2:13, I Peter 2:9). Being fruitful in every good work is saying, "this is what God would do if He were here, and He is in me. That is what kind of God He is." It also is saying, "God is worth obeying because His way is best."

To "walk worthy of the Lord" also means to walk **"increasing in the knowledge of God."** Increasing in knowledge of God is a walk that honors God because He is the only fountain of knowledge. The knowledge and wisdom a person displays comes from Him (James 1:5). The word "increasing" reminds us of the fact that the more a person studies the Bible the more he wants to and the less a person studies the Bible the less He wants to. The amount of knowledge in a Christian's life is always increasing. When God's people grow in "the knowledge of God," they advertise the value of His Word. They are saying, "it is worth studying and remembering God's word. His word is that precious." Also, when God's people grow in "the knowledge of God," they advertise the power of His Word to help them walk more and more faithfully as time goes by.

Colossians 1:11, "Strengthened with all might, according to his glorious power, unto all patience and longsuffering with joyfulness."

Paul and Timothy did "not cease to pray for" the Colossians, that they may be "strengthened," because the Colossians needed strength to "walk worthily." The Christian walk always is spiritually difficult, with dangers to discourage, with personal sins to impede and with false teachers to beguile. One more witness to the fact that someone is under the authority of God is the power they demonstrate to "walk worthily" amid all these hindrances.

The three words, "strengthened," "might" and "power" are close in meaning. The words "strengthened" and "might" are similar, both based upon the word, *dumanis*. It is a word that is used for Gospel power to save (Rom. 1:16). It highlights God's ability. The word "power" is based upon the word *kratos*. It is often rendered "dominion," as in a doxology (Rev. 1:6). It highlights God's control. The idea of verse 11 is "we pray that your walk reveals God's sovereign, irresistible ability working in you (Phil 2:13)."

Christians must deal with difficulties and obstacles in their pilgrimage on earth, day after day, month after month, year after year, without an end in sight. According to this verse a Christian can do more than endure with grim teeth-clenched determination. A Christian has the power to turn from despair, bitterness or resignation and display "patience and longsuffering with joyfulness." Their stamina does not come from a proper diet. Their endurance is not a result of exercise.

Their toughness is not a product of human discipline or philosophy. A Christian lives according to God's power.

We should also add that the power of God is not given to Christians in one big jolt the day they are saved. Christians have power because they abide attached to Jesus the power source, without whom they could do nothing (Psalm 119:28, John 15:4-5).

The word "patience" could be more clearly understood as "stand under." The idea is that Christians are given the power to stand under or submit to God's plan, no matter what their own assessment of hard circumstances may lead them to conclude, or no matter how persuasive other people may be. Christians have the power to say, "His way is best, no matter what." Their stubbornness is an expression of faith (Daniel 3:17,18, Matt. 15:25-28).

Also, they can be "longsuffering." They can continue to run despite the exhausting circumstances and temptations to quit the race. Christians have the power to refrain from changing their objectives and methods to conform to the ways of the world, even though conforming would give them some temporary relief from the struggle against it. Their persistence is an expression of faith (Matt 10:22).

The word "joyfulness" highlights the fact that Christians have a clear view, beyond their present difficult situation, to eternity, in imitation of Jesus (Heb. 12:2). It isn't that Christians do things God's way because they have to, but that they are obedient because they want to, are happy to. Their optimism and cheerfulness are expressions of faith (Phil. 4:4,13).

Colossians 1:12, "Giving thanks unto the Father"

The words "Giving thanks unto the Father" complete the idea that was begun in verse 9, with the words "we also ... do not cease to pray for you." The idea is that Paul and Timothy gave thanks to the Father for all that is listed in verses 9 through 11 because they were confident their prayer would be heard and answered (Psalm 65:2). How did they know? First of all, they had confidence in the "Father" to whom they prayed. They recognized the Father as someone who has the authority and power to do all things well, in His great way and in His great time. Secondly, they trusted that the Father was willing to help (Luke 11:11-13). They knew that God has only two answers to every Christian's prayers. One is "Yes." The other is "I have something better in mind." They knew that God wanted the best for them. Thirdly, they prayed according to God's will. That is, they asked for what was already in

God's mind and heart to do, namely, all that is listed in Colossians 1:9-11.

"which hath made us meet to be partakers of the inheritance of the saints in light."

The words, "which hath made ..... meet" are a translation of one word (*ikanosanti*), that is based upon a word meaning, "to arrive." The idea is that "we" were someplace else (Eph 2:12, Col 1:21) but finally "we" arrived, like the Israelites who were in the wilderness but then entered in the promised land in order to inherit it. Sometimes the word is translated as "sufficient" (II Cor 2:6), or "worthy" (Matt 3:11). The idea is that we are fit, or properly prepared, to partake of the inheritance. God has something to give to His children and has the power to work in their hearts to make them fit to receive it. Colossians 1:13, and following, will explain what He did for and to His people in order to allow them to be "partakers of the inheritance."

The word translated "inheritance" sometimes is used as "lot" (Matt. 27:35 "lot"). It is a "lot" in the sense of a token which determines who gets an assignment, like a short straw among many longer ones used to choose one person among many. In the Bible the "lot" refers to a person chosen by God (Acts 1:24-26). So, we could think of the Colossians' inheritance as their right to be part of the Kingdom because God has chosen them to be citizens. The inheritance includes all the blessings that are part of salvation. Essentially, the inheritance is salvation.

The document that describes an inheritance is called a will. God's will is His eternal plan of salvation, most details of which are revealed in the Word of God, the Bible. It is instructive to make a few comparisons between God's plan of salvation and the human rules of inheritance, with which we are more familiar. For example, just as the author of a human will decides who inherits his wealth, so God alone decides who will receive the inheritance and knows their names. That is, God alone determined before the foundation of the world who would be saved and inherit eternal life. Also, just as the author of a human will must die before the wealth listed in his will can be distributed among his beneficiaries, so Jesus' death was required before God's children could receive what was promised to them. Also, just as a human will normally cannot be altered after the death of the testator, so the promised inheritance can never be taken away from those people to whom it is given.

As we see, the word "inheritance" is an expression of God's authority. God alone designed the Gospel, named the beneficiaries and did what was necessary to fulfill its terms.

The words "in light" or as it is, "in the light," refer to God's Word (Psalm 119:105,130). The inheritance is "in light" in the sense that it is found in the clear revelation of God's Word (Psalm 119:105,130). The fact that God's Gospel promises are part of His word show that the inheritance is bestowed according to His will (Eph. 1:11). That is, He is the one who set the rules and wrote them out for all to see. Also, the fact that God's Gospel promises are part of His word obligates God to fulfill the promise which He has made (Heb. 6:18). God does not change the rules. The people named in the will are never removed at some later time. The blessings promised are never modified. Paul's confidence is based upon the trustworthiness of God's promised word, for He has done all that is needed in Jesus in order to justly make the saints "meet to be partakers in the inheritance."

According to verse 12, "we" are made "meet" or fit to partake of the inheritance by means of "the light" or the Word. That is, the Word, in which we read about the promised inheritance, creates the faith to believe the promise (Rom 10:17) and removes the sin that keeps people from enjoying it (John 15:3). Also, saved people remain in "the light" (Eph. 5:8, I John 1:7). The Word guides them how to think, speak and act as inheritors of salvation. It is the only light they have in this world.

In addition to that, Jesus calls Himself "the light" (John 8:12). With that in mind, verse 12 means "we" inherit because we are in Jesus, being saved and not condemned (Rom. 8:1,17).

Additional notes related to Chapter 1

Colossians 1:1-12

Additional notes for Colossians 1:1 concerning the words, **"and Timotheus our brother"**

Timothy's name was not added because he was equal in authority to Paul. We say that to emphasize that the message of this letter, a letter which is part of God's Word, is not a result of human conference and consensus, nor was it a ratified by committee vote. Paul did not first get Timothy's approval before he wrote this letter. In fact, the first person singular pronoun, "I," is used about twice as much as the plural "we" (e.g. Col. 2:4). The letter to the Colossians was supported by Timothy. But, the apostle Paul wrote it by the authoritative decree of the King of the universe.

Additional notes for Colossians 1:2 concerning the words, **"at Colosse"**

There is not a lot of historical information in the Bible about the church in Colossi, but a few things can be pieced together. Evidently, Paul never visited the Colossians church (Col. 1:4, 2:1), although he intended to (Philemon 22). However, it seems that God used him to build the church in an indirect way. It is possible that Christian travelers from Colosse who heard him preach during his more than two year stay at Ephesus, another city of "Asia," brought the Gospel back home with them (Acts 19:1-10). We say that because Paul personally knew many people from the congregation of Colosse. For example, Paul knew Epaphras, who cared much for the church and may have brought the Gospel to Colosse in the first place (Col. 1:6,7, 4:12). Paul was a friend of both Onesimus (Col. 4:9), a man who was converted under Paul's ministry (Philemon 10), and Onesimus' former master Philemon, who was also a convert of Paul, in whose house the Colossian church may have met (Philemon 1,2,16,19). Also, Paul knew Archippus, who had some kind of ministry in either Colosse or neighboring Laodicea. Not only that, it seems that Mark, Luke and Aristarcus, traveling companions of Paul, spent time in Colosse (Philemon 24). Through conversation with these men, and through news from Tychicus who carried the letter to Colosse, Paul had contact with members of the church in Colosse, grew to care for them and believed that they had a concern for him too (Col. 4:7,8).

Additional notes for Colossians 1:2 concerning the words, **"Grace be unto you, and peace, from God our Father and the Lord Jesus Christ."**

Here again we encounter the principle of 2 or 3 witnesses. The couplet "grace" and "peace" as well as the couplet "Father" and "Jesus Christ" testify that the Gospel is a message with unquestioned authority. The first couplet testifies to the credible content of the Gospel message. The second couplet testifies to the trustworthy author of the Gospel.

Additional notes for Colossians 1:2 concerning the words, **"Grace be unto you"**

The testimony of the Bible, which our own experience confirms, is that we are weak, needy and rebelliously sinful. What will God do to us? Will He help us out of the mess we have made and the trap in which we are? He doesn't have to. A just response of a Holy God is to destroy sinners. The only proper sinners' cry is for mercy. The only hope is that God is gracious.

In Luke 18:13 we read that publican prayed, "God be merciful to me, a sinner." And in Luke 18:38 as well as 39 we read that a blind man cried to Jesus, "Have mercy on me." Notice that the publican did not say, "be merciful because I am a sinner." Nor did the blind man refer to his handicap. In both cases the men made a simple declaration and admission of their need. The point is that God does not have an obligation to save based upon the fact people are so sinful and needy. We might be inclined to find fault with someone who withholds help when it is in their power to do something, especially when faced by someone in great need. But God does not have to help. In fact, peoples' sin merits wrath not mercy.

However, God is the only one who can help. Grace comes exclusively from God. Sinners can find grace no where else. Unless God is gracious, there would be no kindness to sinners at all. God alone has the authority to bring wrath or to save. So we read of the two men who recognized the one and only possibility of help and asked for it. From the conversation in Matthew 8:1-4, the issue is put, "if thou wilt, thou canst make me clean" (verse 2). That is, the question is "Does God have the will to use His authority to save?" There is nothing automatic about grace. It all depends upon God's sovereign will. Wonderfully, His answer is, "I will" (verse 3). The words "Grace be unto you ... from God our Father and the Lord Jesus Christ" mean that the great, holy, perfect and powerful God has shown grace toward sinners.

In Numbers 6:25 we read, "The LORD make his face shine upon thee, and be gracious unto thee." Notice that grace is linked to God's face. Why His face? The reason is that a person's face identifies who that person is. The idea is that when God is gracious to sinners He wants them to recognize Him, that is, to really know Him (John 17:3, similar to Matt 5:8, I Cor 13:12, I John 3:2, Rev. 22:4). Again, grace is a word that describes the heart of God, who He is. Notice, for example what we read in Jonah 2:4, "are gracious." That is, Jonah does not say, "you do gracious things," but "you are gracious." God has the gracious character that causes Him to use His authority to be kind to people who are not kind to Him. Amazing! When Colossians 1:2 says that grace comes "from God," it means grace comes from His heart.

Additional notes for Colossians 1:4 concerning the words, **"the love which ye have"**

Let us briefly examine a few of the many beautiful and sparkling facets of the jewel of God's love, which Christians, to some degree, exhibit. First of all, God's love is self-motivated and self-sustaining. That is, it is not dependent upon the appearance, behavior or character of the person whom He loves. Secondly, God's love is realistic. That is, God is not motivated by an expectation of love requited. God is not surprised by the evil that people return to Him for the good that He bestows upon them. He recognizes that people are sinners and that they live in a world that promotes rebellion against Him. Thirdly, God's love is purposeful. He always desires the spiritual best for people, whether those people understand their souls' need or not. To that end, God shows His love by spending Himself to benefit other people, regardless of their own lack of concern for their soul, for God is selfless and sacrificial, not concerned with the cost to Himself. In other words, God's love is sacrificial. Fourthly, God's love is wise. His love is under the control of His own Word. He knows His own will that He prepared from before the foundation of the world and he knows how to fulfill it in His perfect time. He is faithful to His commitments. He knows whom He intends to save, as well as how and when He plans to save them. His love motivates Him to complete the job of securing His peoples' salvation.

Now we can understand why Paul gave "thanks to God" when he heard of the Colossian's love. Paul recognized the quality of love they displayed and concluded that it was from God, who then deserved thanks. In addition to that, Paul was grateful to God for the benefit that God's love was to them personally. Let us explain in the following way. I John 4:8 states, "God is love." Colossians 1:27 states, "Christ in you." Putting those two verses together, we can say the Colossians who were saved lived by means of and in the love of God Himself. God and His love dominated the personality and behavior of the Colossians. In other words, Paul was not impressed by their outward piety, devotion and compliance to the Bible, which in themselves are not necessarily evidences of submission to the one Authority in the universe (I Cor. 8:1, 13:1-3). Rather, love was the supreme evidence for which Paul was thankful. The love that motivated God to design and fulfill the Gospel, was the love that motivated their thoughts, words and deeds.

Perhaps we can understand God's love better if we compare it to human love. One kind of human love is described by the Greek word *eros*. Although, the word *eros* is not used in the Bible, the Bible does describe that kind of love (II Sam. 13:1-2, 14-15). We can call that kind of love, erotic love, or even lust. It is really a love for self. This kind of love is based upon the perceived attractive qualities of the person who is loved. This kind of love does not endure, but vanishes when the person who is loved loses his appeal. Someone with this kind of love is driven to conquer, possess, control and use the person whom he loves, in order to satisfy his own selfish desires, without regard for the benefit of the person he loves. This kind of love leads to disappointment, jealousy and hatred.

Another kind of human love is described by the Greek word *philos*, which is used many times in the Bible (Matt. 10:37). We can call this kind of love fraternal love. It also is love for self, but it is self that is seen in other people. That is, it is love based upon the fact that the person who loves sees in the person they love qualities they both have in common. A person with this kind of love prefers the exclusive company of other people with whom he shares similar ideas, similar cultural background or similar ethnic heritage. It is often expressed as the love of family. This kind of love leads to exclusiveness, pride, prejudice and condemnation.

As we see, God's love is unique and so different from man's love. Anyone who is controlled by it, thinks and behaves in a way that is distinct from anyone who is controlled by their own human emotions.

Additional notes for Colossians 1:5 concerning the words, **"the word of truth"**

I would like to tie the word "truth" to the idea of authority which we have highlighted as the theme of Colossians. There are no independent truths in the universe, that is, independent from God. Truth is not a neutral propositional statement, or a curiosity. We do not read true statements for amusement, with an objective, detached attitude. We cannot compare truth to an object along the side of a road, like a pretty flower or an interesting rock that we pick and examine and put down again, which has no impact upon our lives. Since all truth is what God says (John 17:17), it carries authority, with the expectation of compliance from the people who hear it. A statement of truth carries the obligation of submission and obedience by all who are confronted by it, because truth describes God's expectations and demands. There is always a moral and spiritual dimension to the truth in the universe. Even truth such as scientific data requires a proper spiritual response. For example, the apparently objective facts of astronomy demand a response of humbleness and worship before the Authority who created the universe (Psalm 8:1-9, 19:1,2).

With that in mind we can see that Gospel truth is a dynamic expression of an authoritative God who is both a Creator and Redeemer. The truth of the Gospel not only informs man, it is also a revelation that forms man as well. The Gospel not only shows a man the truth, it also is the power to shape a man's heart to want to and be able to obey the authoritative God whose truth it is (Psalm 119:47,48,97,140-143, John 15:3, I Peter 1:21-25).

Additional notes for Colossians 1:6 concerning the words, **"the grace of God."**

Although we discussed the word "grace" in our examination of verse 2, there are a few things that we should add to our understanding of it and reinforce what we already know. First of all, "grace" is a word that highlights God's sovereign choice in bestowing His benefits. God is the King over all things and the final authority over **all** men. But He uses His authority for good only for some people, those whom He saves by "grace." For example, by grace God makes some people "meet" or ready to receive the "inheritance" (Col. 1:12), but only those whom He has "delivered" (verse 13) or who have "redemption through his blood" (verse 14).

Secondly, "grace" is a word that labels a kindness from God that is unconditional. No circumstances or powers outside of God cause Him to bring words of grace. For example, people are not so pitiful in their sin and misery that God is compelled to be gracious. Nor are people so delightful in their devotion that God is disposed to be gracious. God's righteous law obligates Him to bring wrath, but nothing outside of Himself obligates or motivates Him to show His grace.

Thirdly, "grace" is a word that labels a condescension from the greater to the lesser. That is, it a word that describes a character trait that leads God to help undeserving needy people, who can do nothing for themselves. The blessings expressed in Colossians are more than anyone deserves and has a right to expect. If it was not for the authority behind the statements of blessings no one would believe that God would be so kind to sinners. So, "grace" is a word that labels God's character which disposes Him to be kind. It is not just that God acts in a gracious way, and He does toward His people, but that God **is** gracious. That is, grace is a word that describes His heart. He alone is gracious because He wants to be.

Additional notes for Colossians 1:10 concerning the words, **"worthy of the Lord" and "the knowledge of God."**

Walking "worthy of the Lord" is related to "the knowledge of God." One leads to and is dependent upon the other. Let me explain in the following way. A person's careful attention to his "knowledge of His will" results in careful attention to his "walk." That is, a vague and neglected knowledge of God's will result in a life that seeks to get as close to the world as possible and still remain a Christian. Conversely, a life that seeks to please self or the world promotes a lack of interest in the knowledge of God's will. But a good "knowledge of His will" results in a walk that pleases God, for such knowledge will motivate and guide that walk.

Additional notes for Colossians 1:10 concerning the words, **"the Lord."**

The words, "the Lord," might lead us to the question, "Over whom is Jesus Lord?" Normally when we say that Jesus is a person's Lord we mean that the person recognizes, acknowledges and even rejoices in Jesus' authority over Him. That is, the word "Lord" is usually associated with those people who are saved and so have a heart that embraces the sovereign control of Jesus over them. But from a larger perspective, we must recognize that Jesus is the supreme authority in the universe, Lord over all things and all people. After all, He created the universe, sustains it and all of its inhabitants are accountable to Him. However, we must be careful to correctly understand how His authority is revealed in the lives of people who are saved and in the lives of people who are not saved.

It is easy to see that Jesus is the Lord over all people who are saved. Jesus' authority can be seen in their fruitful words and actions from hour to hour and day to day. Jesus' authority can be seen in the spiritual blessings that reveal His gracious control of the direction of their lives over the years. Jesus' authority can also be seen in the outcome of their lives. With peace in their hearts, with great joyful expectation and with loving adoration, they approach the final destination or end Jesus has prepared for them.

It is not so easy to see that Jesus is the Lord over all people who are not saved. We can agree that He is their Lord based upon the fact that He is the supreme authority in the universe, but may wonder at the fact that unbelievers clearly ignore or blaspheme Jesus. It is true that unbelievers act and speak differently that believers, even though Jesus is the greatest authority in the universe, including their lives too. And yet, Jesus has not lost control over them, for He allows unbelievers' wicked hearts to guide their actions and words, hour by hour and day to day. Even though the path unbelievers take through life is full of selfishness and rebellion, with its attendant bitter fruit of heartache, fear and hatred, the outcome of their lives is eventual destruction of eternal damnation in hell, in accordance with the will of the Lord.

Additional notes for Colossians 1:9 and 10 concerning the words, **"do not cease to pray (verse 9) ..... that ye might."**

We should clear up one common misunderstanding of prayer. Although Paul and Timothy prayed "that ye might," we must not get the impression that the prayers of believers, including the prayers of faithful men such as these two, can cause a change in circumstances, initiate God's actions or alter His plans. We bring up the problem with these kind of prayers because it is related to the issue of authority. After all, who is in charge, the one who prays or the One to whom the prayers are offered?

In the first place, we must acknowledge that people who pray are finite creatures who do not know all the facts of a situation or of a problem, even though they might think that they do. This is especially true in salvation, for God alone knows who will be saved (Rom. 8:28-30). Therefore, prayers of a believer ought to be in accord with God's plans. In other words, believers who pray must always keep in mind that they are praying to their Lord, who truly is their Lord as well as the Sovereign of the universe. He is the One who knows what is best and does it on behalf of those who are under His authority.

In the second place, we must recognize that God is all wise and makes perfect plans which need no amendments. He does not need to be informed about things through prayer nor do people need to appeal to Him so that He would change things for the better. The fact is that no one changes God's plans, for they express His will and His will is always done just as He has planned that it would be done. In as much as the Bible is the description of God's will, as believers grow in their understanding and obedience to it, their prayers will align with God's will. The thing that prayer changes is the heart and mind of a believer who prays.

We should add that although Christians have a healthy respect for who is in control in the universe, they still pray to Him, not because they insist in obtaining their desires, but because God is their heavenly Father to whom they delight to talk and in whose presence they are always welcome. Christians are not intimidated, discouraged or stifled in prayer even though God is the Sovereign One who knows all, and does all according to His perfect will. Rather, they confidently talk to Him who wants the best for them and works to bless them in His great way and in His great time.

Chapter 2

Colossians 1:13-14

In Colossians 1:1-12 we learn about the wonderful effects of God's authority in the lives of those whom He has saved by grace. Colossians 1:13-14 explain what God did to make the effects described in verses 1 through 12 possible. In terms of the theme of authority, we can say that these verses answer the question, "How did Christians come under the authority of Jesus?"

Colossians 1:13, "Who hath delivered us"

Why is it that the Colossians had a reputation for "faith in Christ Jesus" and "love to all the saints" (Col. 1:4)? How is it that they were so different from the rest of the citizens of Colosse, so different from who they were before? Verses 13 begins the explanation with the fact that they were "delivered." This deliverance is the basis for the wonderful effects of Jesus' authority in their lives.

The words "hath delivered" are a translation of a verb in a grammatical form that describes a one time past action with present effects. Also, the words "hath delivered" are a translation of a verb in the middle or reflexive voice. A reflexive verb describes an action performed by the subject of a sentence that is directed back upon that subject. The phrase "the man hit himself" describes a reflexive action. Therefore, the idea in verse 13 is that God, by means of one act, has delivered Himself.

With all of this in mind, we can understand the words, "hath delivered" or rescued, in two ways. One way is that God Himself, alone, delivered or rescued His people from sin. He had no assistants. Another way is that, in the deliverance of "us," He also had to deliver or rescue Himself. This second idea is a statement of the fact that, although Jesus Christ was innocent in Himself, He bore the guilt of His people and was condemned to endure the punishment they deserved (II Cor. 5:21, I Peter 2:24). However, Jesus was not utterly and forever consumed by the wrath that descended upon Him as payment for the sins that He bore, otherwise the payment for our sins would not be complete. Jesus was delivered from that awful wrath to which He was subject (Psalm 16:10, 116:4,8,13, John 17:4, 19:30, Rom. 8:3, Gal.3:13). That was what His resurrection revealed.

"from the power of darkness"

The word "from" is better rendered "out of." It highlights an extraction or relocation. The word "power" means authority, as in Matthew 7:29 or 9:6. The picture is that God entered into where darkness had authority, found some people and then took them out (Psalm 107:14).

Our understanding of the whole phrase depends upon our understanding of the word "darkness." On one hand, we could connect the word "darkness" with the evil of sin. The Bible does not directly equate "darkness" with sin or evil deeds, but it does describe "darkness" as a place where people cannot see to do what is right and so sin (John 3:19, Rom. 1:21, 11:10, Eph. 4:18). The idea is that "darkness" refers to the environment of sinful deeds. It is where sinful deeds belong because that is where they are found (Eph. 5:11). The idea is that we are delivered out of a place of darkness (and therefore into a place of light).

If we rewrite the phrase "power of darkness" as, "darkness' power," then the focus is upon "darkness" as an agent in control. That reminds us of Satan who has authority to dominate unsaved men so that they continue to live blindly in sin (Acts 26:18, Eph 6:12, Heb. 2:15). With this view of "darkness" in mind, we understand deliverance as an issue between two authorities, God's and he who is master of darkness. The idea is that there is a wicked authority which opposes God's redemptive plan, in the sense that the evil authority tries to preserve its control over its subjects and resist God's plan to capture those over whom it rules. That is the picture in Matthew 12:29, where we read of deliverance as spoiling the house of the "strong man," or Satan.

Another view of "darkness" is based upon its association with the evil of God's judgment, which He brings in response to man's sin (Isa. 45:7). Darkness, in this sense, reminds us of the complete darkness of Hell and eternal death (Matt. 22:13, Jude 13). Again, it is the environment of sin. But in this case, it is not where people practice sin, but rather where they are assigned to pay for their sin. With this in mind, the word "darkness" refers to the Law of God and the word "power" refers to its authority to condemn men to death for their disobedience (Gal. 3:10), as well as to sentence them to eternal darkness. We understand deliverance, then, to be salvation from the condemnation of God's Law. According to Colossians 1:14, that means Christ shed His blood in order to satisfy the demands of the Law and bring us out of its condemnation. That is the picture in Psalm

107:6-14.

Actually, sin, Satan's dominion and the Law's authority are all in view here, as they are in the rest of Colossians. Adam entered into the dominion of darkness when he listened to and obeyed Satan rather than God. Adam abrogated his position as ruler over God's creation in the Garden of Eden and submitted to Satan's words. God honored Satan's usurpation as a legal right, even though Satan obtained it through deceit. From then on, all of Adam's descendants were bound by Satan's authority. Also, when Adam obeyed Satan, he became liable for God's promised wrath against sin and the destruction that will come upon Satan and all who are under his dominion.

"and hath translated us into the kingdom of his dear Son."

How we understand the words "translated us into the Kingdom of his dear Son" depends upon how we understand the word "darkness." If we think of the power of darkness as the environment or the country where sin and Satan rule, then the idea is that God has the authority of a conquering King who has the right to enter a vanquished country and take the spoils of battle. In this case, the spoils are people whom he captures and puts into His own kingdom (Isa. 49:25, Matt. 12:29). It is not that because God is so strong He bullies His way in and does whatever He pleases. Rather, it is that God properly addressed the claims of Satan upon his slaves and so designed a plan to properly rescue them. God sent Jesus to earth as a second Adam, who perfectly obeyed the demands of the Law. He was a worthy sacrifice for sin and paid for the sins of His people. Therefore He could legally release His people from the dominion sin and Satan had over them, to whom they previously listened and obeyed.

On the other hand, if we think of the power of darkness as the authority of the Law to judge sinners, then the words "translated us into the Kingdom of his dear Son" mean that God has the right to release His people from the just condemnation of the Law. Men who live in darkness are not innocent victims of a violent and illegal kidnaping. Rather, men who live in darkness are in need of mercy (Eph. 5:8) because they are rebellious and wicked people who willingly serve Satan and hate God (Rom. 1:21, 3:10,11). They are in need of "forgiveness," as verse 14 states. Only when their legal problem is resolved, can they be moved to God's kingdom.

Notice that the Kingdom of Jesus is a present reality. At the time a person is saved, he is "translated into the kingdom of his dear Son."

Jesus is a King now, and His Kingdom is real now. We must never think that Jesus' Kingdom is some future reality. Jesus' Kingdom may not be earthly (John 18:36) or physical (I Cor. 15:50), but Jesus is a real king (Psalm 47:7,8, Jer. 10:7,10, Heb. 1:8) over His subjects (Luke 17:21, I Thess. 2:12) who presently display His authority in their lives on earth (Col. 3:1).

Also notice that a person is either in the dominion of darkness and out of the Kingdom of God or he is out of the dominion of darkness and in the Kingdom of God. He cannot be a citizen of both. As he lives his life, he will eventually show to whose authority he is subject and loyal. A person cannot continue to live a self-centered life of sin and also be under Jesus' authority. A man who seeks to serve God shows that he is a citizen of Jesus' Kingdom.

Not only that, the transfer of a person's citizenship from the dominion of darkness to the Kingdom of Jesus is both one way and permanent. It is a work of God that cannot be altered or reversed. It is forever (John 10:27-30).

Colossians 1:14, "In whom we have redemption through his blood"

A redemption is a very special kind of purchase. One important thing to keep in mind is that the objects which are redeemed, or purchased, are those that originally were owned by the person who redeems them. The emphasis is upon the restoration of objects to their original owner.

The Bible discusses the rules of redemption in many places, such as in Leviticus 25, especially verses 23-27. The rules are shadowy and involved pictures of the redemption found in the Gospel. For our purposes, in trying to understand Colossians, we will focus upon the basic idea of redemption, namely, a restoration of an object to its original owner upon the payment of a price. Briefly, the rules stated that, when an object was transferred from the possession of its original owner to a new owner, it remained there until payment of the price of redemption was made. The new owner did not possess the object in the same way that he owned other things. The new owner had limited rights to the object. The new owner was obligated to honor the privilege of the original owner to purchase the object when the original owner was able and willing to do so. It is as if the original owner had pawned the object, rather than really sold it. That is, it is as if when the original owner gave the object to the new owner, the object was held in bond awaiting redemption.

Now let us try to understand the idea of redemption in Colossians. It is easy to identify the objects to be redeemed. They are people, the "we" of this verse. It also is easy to identify the original owner. He is Jesus. Jesus owns all people because He is their Creator (Eph. 3:9, c.f. Ezek. 18:4). But Jesus especially owns the elect, people who were given to Him before the foundation of the world (John 17:2,24). It is not so easy to identify the new owner, for it depends upon our view of the words "power of darkness." We could think the words "power of darkness" refer to Satan's control over unsaved people. Or we could think the words "power of darkness" refer to Law's authority to condemn sinners and send them to Hell.

If the words "power of darkness" refer to Satan's control, then the idea of redemption is as follows. Adam and all his descendants became slaves of Satan when Adam submitted to Satan in the Garden of Eden. God eventually sent Jesus to pay for the release of those people among Adam's descendants whom He had chosen from before the foundation of the world. After Jesus made the necessary and sufficient payment with His life, He had the authority to loose His people from the control of Satan and bring them into His kingdom (Matt. 12:28-29, Acts 26:18).

The idea that Satan is not the original owner of unsaved people but instead is identified as the new owner might be a little puzzling. After all, it seems that all people, born as sinners, begin life under Satan's dominion. That would seem to identify Satan as the original owner. However, people cannot have originally belonged to Satan, for Satan cannot receive credit for their existence. It is true that as soon as a person is conceived he is under the dominion of darkness. There doesn't seem to be any span of time between people's creation in their mothers' wombs and their infection with sin. Yet, from God's point of view, who had His people in His mind before the foundation of the world, they belong to and were given to Jesus first (John 17:2, Eph. 1:4). Their conception and birth began a series of events that eventually would lead them out from "the power of darkness" and "into the kingdom of his dear Son."

If we think the words "power of darkness" refer to the Law's condemnation, then the idea of redemption is as follows. Because of the sin of Adam, all people became subject to the punishment demanded by the law and deserve eternal death in Hell. But Jesus came to redeem them from the law by means of His blood, that is, His death. Then He arose from the dead to prove that the price of redemption had been fully paid. Also, He arose so that He could claim them as His possession (Acts 20:28, I Cor. 3:23, Rev. 5:9).

Whether we think of redemption from Satan or from the Law of God, both views repeat our explanation of the words "translated us into the kingdom of his dear Son." Therefore, at the very least, the idea of redemption in verse 14 supports and reinforces the idea of translation in verse 13.

The words "in whom," are equal to "in Jesus Christ" (Rom. 3:24). They mean that the price of the redemption of the believers is in Jesus Christ. That is, if you want to locate the currency used to satisfy the price of redemption, you must go to Jesus. It is "in Him." He doesn't have a purse which contains the currency. Rather, He Himself is the currency used for the redemption. And that gets us to the words "through his blood."

Why does the Bible bring up the word "blood?" For many people it is an uncomfortable subject. Blood is unsightly. It makes a stain in our clothes that stands out and, once set, is almost impossible to remove. Blood also is alarming. It is evidence of a wound. And to lose a lot of blood is a mortally serious matter. But God created blood to be noticeable for a more important reason than any physical concern. Red blood should remind us of our conspicuous sin (Isaiah 1:18). Spilt blood should remind us of death (Lev. 17:11).

To that we can add the picture of the alter in the tabernacle or temple upon which the Old Testament sacrifices were placed and upon which blood was sprinkled. It must have been a physically offensive place. The blood would smell bad after a while. The alter probably looked terrible with the sticky, brown oxidized blood all over it. There was nothing attractive or cheerful about the blood on the alter, but it provided the proper picture of Jesus' sacrifice. Blood reminds us that Jesus' redemption was a horrible experience for Him (Luke 22:44). Jesus shed blood because "he was wounded for **our** transgressions" or "he was cut off out of the land of the living" (Isa. 53. 5,8). We don't gladly think that, "He was a man of sorrows and acquainted with grief" as He bore the wrath of God for "us." Therefore, "we hid as it were our faces from him." (Isa. 53:3). Jesus' sacrifice was as gross, as stark, as serious, as frightening as the sight of blood.

"even the forgiveness of sins:"

The word "forgiveness" is a translation of a word that means "to send away" or "to let go." In Luke 4:18 it is used as "deliverance," or in another form as "liberty." The Old Testament picture of this is found in Leviticus 16 (verses 7-10, 21-22). The law commanded the priest to put his hands on a goat, which ceremonially transferred the sins of the people to the animal. After that, the priest sent it away into the wilderness, as a figure of removing sin from the people, which was the basis for forgiveness.

In this verse, the words, "the forgiveness of sins" are linked to the words "redemption through his blood." That is, it is only because of the redemption that forgiveness is legally possible. Forgiveness does not mean that God says, "O well, I'll just be a nice guy and forgive you." God must provide a legal basis for pardoning or separating His people from their sins. That He did that in Jesus is the basis for His people's confidence and relief that there will be no horrible surprises in eternity. That is, God's forgiveness is complete and enduring.

Even though sin still easily besets God's people (Heb. 12:1) and they struggle with sin all their lives (Rom. 7:17,22-23), from God's judicial point of view, their sins are gone and forgotten (Heb. 10:17). They continue to sin and struggle to gain victory over their sins. Of that God is aware, and for that He provides counsel (Col. 3). However, their sins are no longer a barrier to fellowship with a Holy God because their sins have been completely forgiven (Col. 2:13). And when they eventually go to heaven, there will be a total separation from the presence of sin.

As a general comment upon verses 13 and 14, we see that the Bible does not paint the picture of salvation as a romantic drama in which Christ plays the part of a brave knight with shining armor riding upon a white stallion, who assaults the evil enemy's castle, rescues the fair damsel from her distress and carries her off to his kingdom to live happily ever after. The problem with people is not "out there" somewhere. It is in their own hearts (Jer. 17:9). People have a spiritual problem that needs a resolution. If we wished to retain the drama of a rescue, then the damsel is as ugly as sin and unwilling to be rescued, even fighting against the Savior, for sinners are willing servants of sin and Satan. To continue with the drama, the knight is stained by blood because He dies a horrible death, for He is a redeemer. Jesus redeems sinners from death's claim upon them (Hosea 13:14, Heb. 9:12,14,22-28).

Additional notes related to Chapter 2

Colossians 1:13-14

Additional notes for Colossians 1:13 concerning the words, **"and hath translated us into the kingdom of his dear Son."**

Paul was an illustration of the message he brought. Paul had been an arrogant and aggressive opponent of the Gospel, as he described himself in Titus 3:3, "For we ourselves also were sometimes foolish, disobedient, deceived, serving divers lusts and pleasures, living in malice and envy, hateful, and hating one another." But then he could say in I Corinthians 15:9-11, "For I am the least of the apostles, that am not meet to be called an apostle, because I persecuted the church of God. But by the grace of God I am what I am: and his grace which was bestowed upon me was not in vain; but I laboured more abundantly than they all: yet not I, but the grace of God which was with me. Therefore whether it were I or they, so we preach, and so ye believed." He who had been an unwitting servant of sin and Satan (John 8:34,44), defended the Gospel (Phil. 1:7,17). Paul's new obedient life was a testimony to others that he was under Jesus' authority and could be trusted.

The dramatic and conspicuous contrast in Paul's life also revealed and highlighted the difference between the character of the master whom he used to serve and the character of One whose authority to whom he afterward became subject and who controlled his life. Paul's new obedient life was a testimony to the kind of person Jesus is and the nature of the authority that He exercises. The fruits that Paul displayed in his life revealed Jesus' objectives, methods and power and therefore reflected the beauty of His character.

Finally, Paul's new obedient life was a testimony to himself. It gave him assurance that he was saved. Paul was certain that Jesus was his Savior because it was clear that Jesus was his Lord. Based upon the evidence of his obedience, Paul was confident that although he had been the citizen of an enemy country (Col. 1:21), he had been transformed into Jesus' kingdom and would avoid the destruction that will come against the dominion of darkness on Judgement day. His ready submission was a mark of being under Jesus' authority, of being saved. It is true that obedience is not equal to salvation. People are saved by grace alone, apart from anything they do. Also, people who are not saved outwardly can conform to what the Bible says for a while.

However, over time, a person's allegiance, whether to self and Satan or to Jesus Christ, will show. In other words, obedience is a necessary companion to salvation because Jesus is either a person's Lord or He is not.

The exchange of authority in Paul's life illustrates the fact that people are always under some authority. People are never autonomous and independent (Rom 6:16-18,22). Whose authority people are under will be revealed in their lives because their authority commands obedience and their authority has the power to enforce compliance.

Additional notes for Colossians 1:14 concerning the words, **"even the forgiveness of sins."**

Interestingly, Leviticus 16 discusses two goats (v7). One goat was slain, whose blood was shed as a sin offering. And the other which was let go into the wilderness, as we mentioned in the main part of this study. That double picture matches the double message of Colossians 1:14. Colossians 1:14 first states that God's people have redemption through Jesus' blood, which coordinates with the first goat that was slain. Colossians 1:14 then follows with the forgiveness of sins, which coordinates with the scapegoat. The idea is that the sequence is the same in both the picture found in Leviticus 16 and the fulfillment of that picture described in Colossians 1. First there must be the payment for sin, only then can people's sins be sent away.

Chapter 3

Colossians 1:15 - 20

Verses 1 through 12 illustrate **what** Jesus' authority does in the lives of His people. Verses 13 and 14 explain **how** Jesus places them under His authority. Verses 15 through 20 answer the question, "**who** has done all of this?" In these verses we see the Son, who is God and man. He is the Creator and the Redeemer with supreme authority. Since He is in charge in the universe, all people are expected to submit to Him. True believers submit now and unbelievers will submit at the end of time (Revelation 1:5-7).

Colossians 1:15, "Who is the image of the invisible God,"

The antecedent to the word "who" is the word "Son" in verse 13. So the phrase "who is the image of the invisible God" can be rewritten, "The Son is the image of the invisible God."

We must be careful what we say about the phrase "the image of the invisible God." It focusses upon God Himself, and who can fully understand God? If we think we do, we are kidding ourselves and believe a lie. At this point of our analysis of Colossians, we are standing upon holy ground and must proceed very humbly.

Let us begin with a brief investigation of the word "image." An image is a picture we can see that gives an approximate but accurate idea of what we cannot see. For example, in Matthew 22:20, the image of Caesar that could be seen on a coin was a picture of the man who could not be seen because he was hundreds of miles away in Rome.

Now, the Bible states that man is created in God's image (Gen. 1:27). That image is unique to human beings and is the essence of who they are, in contrast to the animals. Parts of people's nature and character that we see give an approximate but accurate idea of the invisible God.

Animals die and cease to exist (Psalm 104:29). The whole physical universe will end (Psalm 102:25,26). But people, like God, continue forever (Psalm 102:27,28). The fact that their souls continue to exist beyond the grave cannot be seen today. But that aspect of their "image" will be seen at the time of the general resurrection.

Animals, along with the rest of the universe, are not sensible to moral good and evil, nor are they accountable for their behavior before the Law of God. It is true that most animals are given an inclination to protect and care for their families. Also, many animals can be trained to behave in a humanly acceptable ways. Furthermore, animals can be loyal, even to the loss of their own lives. But only people are created under the law, and like God, are measured by the Law. Unsaved people's sensitivity to good and evil is greatly diminished. They have no inclination or capacity to obey the Law. But people are created to recognize the difference between the beauty of holiness and the ugliness of sin, as well as conform to God's will. The fact that people are accountable to the law is not clearly seen today. But that aspect of their "image" will be seen on Judgment Day.

Animals are designed to fulfill their amazingly complex role in the ecology of the earth. But only people, like God, have a spiritual purpose for their lives (Col. 3:17,23), which continue into eternity (Rev. 5:12,13). That aspect of their "image" is more easily seen today, in their words and actions that glorify and serve God..

Even though the word "image" is associated with humankind, we must be cautious. We cannot jump to the conclusion that Colossians 1:15 teaches the Son is only a human picture of God and not very God Himself. The word "image," in the phrase, "Son ... is the image of the invisible God" is not a description of the nature of the Son, as if the Son is only an image of God and so he is less than God. Instead, it is a description of what happened to the Son. What happened to Him? The Son, who is God, added or attached to Himself an "image," a true human nature, a man part whom we call Jesus the Christ. That is why in II Corinthians 4:4 we read, "Christ, who is the image of God." As man is created in the image of God, so Jesus is the part of the Son that is made in the image of God. The Son is God and man is not. But the Son added or attached to Himself a man part, an image part. How? When His man part was conceived and born in Bethlehem as Jesus the Christ, with all the attributes that make him truly human, including the fact that He was subject to the Law (Gal. 4:4) and devoted to fulfill it (Luke 2:49, John 4:34, Heb. 10:7). From that point of view, then, the word "image" refers to Jesus, the human attachment to the Son. Therefore, in Jesus, the Son has an image, we can see, of God whom we cannot see.

It is true that the Son is God Himself, the invisible God. We cannot see the Son as God, for God is Spirit (John 4:24). That is good because God is holy and people are sinners, and no sinners can see God and live (Ex. 33:20). However, Jesus is image we can see, the visible human attachment to the Son, who is part of an invisible God (John 1:18, I Tim. 1:17). That does not mean Jesus' body was a replica or representative of the invisible God. Rather, in Jesus' character and behavior was the image of God, as we read in John 1:14, "And the Word was made flesh, and dwelt among us, (and we beheld his glory, the glory as of the only begotten of the Father,) full of grace and truth." Jesus is the only truth (John 14:6), in contrast to all others who claim to bring truth.

In terms of the big picture of Colossians, which deals with the authority of Jesus above all other authorities, we must recognize that even though He was human, His authority was not reduced in any way. In fact, His authority was enhanced, as we shall see. It is that His humanity made it possible for Him to do His job as a Redeemer. Jesus is not simply another human. Rather than just one more person among the many other teachers whom the Colossians heard and wondered who to follow, Jesus was a display of God's authority and power.

"the firstborn of every creature:"

These words do not mean that Jesus was born before Cain or before any of the animals were created. He is not the first of the created creatures and therefore less than God. The focus of the word "firstborn" is upon the first child of a family who has the rightful claim to the inheritance (Gen. 49:3, Deut. 21:17). The idea is that the Son is the heir of **all** things (Heb. 1:2). The Bible uses the word "firstborn" to remind us that the universe belongs to Him and uses the words "of every creature" to remind us that His ownership includes all of its inhabitants. Psalm 89:27-29 supports our claim that the word "firstborn" highlights the Son's supreme authority over every creature, His eternal rulership as the "eldest brother," so to speak.

If "every creature" in view is every created human, then the Son is over them as the second Adam, fulfilling the responsibility to rule over the world which the first Adam abrogated (Gen. 1:26, Eph. 1:21). If "every creature" in view is every saved human, then the Son is over them as the head of His church (Col. 1:18). In either case, the Son has eternal authority as the invisible God and authority over all creatures as the firstborn man.

Colossians 1:16, "for by him were all things created"

The word "for" connects this verse to the preceding one. The idea is, "Let me explain how the Son is the firstborn and so heir over all creation." God the Son created it through Jesus Christ (Eph. 3:9).

Without Jesus as the agent of creation, nothing would have been created (John 1:3). It would not exist unless He willed it into being. He was not a helpful participant, but the sole actor in the drama of creation (Isaiah 48:12,13, Heb. 1:2). As the Creator, He owns everything (Psalm 24:1) and has uniquely supreme authority over all the universe.

The Colossians had to realize that they did not have an option to whom they could submit, whether to a teacher who came to them with strange doctrines or to Jesus whom Paul proclaimed. Paul brought a message about and from the Almighty Creator which they had to heed. How ever they reacted to Paul's message, they eventually would face Jesus of whom he spoke and wrote, either as Lord or Judge (Heb. 4:13).

"in heaven, and that are in the earth, visible and invisible"

If the words "(all things) in heaven, and that are in (on) the earth, visible and invisible" refer to the physical extent of the universe, then they include all the objects in space as well as on earth. They include all the objects which man can see with his naked eye together with all the objects to small or too remote for him to see with the aid of his instruments .

If the words refer to all things whatsoever, that is, all things besides Himself, then both the physical and spiritual parts of the universe are in view. In that case the words "earth" and "visible" highlight the physical creation made up of atoms and various forms of energy, while the words "heaven" and "invisible" highlight the spiritual, non-material realm.

The point is that the scope of Jesus' authority is total, for if He is not Lord of all things, then He is not really Lord of anything. The fact is that Jesus has the authority of the Son of God, whose jurisdiction is unlimited, including all of the members of the church in Colosse.

"thrones, or dominions, or principalities, or powers all things were created by him"

There is no purpose served in emphasizing a distinction among the words "thrones," "dominions," "principalities" or "powers." The reason is that there is no authority in this list which is not subject to Jesus' control. None of the words refer to an authority that is an especially effective rival to Jesus' authority.

The message that we draw from this list is the same as what we draw from the phrase "Lord of lords," found in Revelation 1:5. The words in Revelation are not just a statement of high praise, as if to say, "most Lordly." They are a statement of fact, as if to say, "of all the lords in the world, Jesus is Lord of them all." Therefore the list in Colossians 1:16 can be thought of as an inventory which is meant to be exhaustive. That is, the Son is over any kind of lord that we can think of and mention (Eph. 1:19-22). He has the only legal right as Creator to that position. The idea can be expressed as, "You name it, and Jesus is over it." Or, in the words of this verse, **"all** things were created by him."

Since there is only one supreme authority, there really are no rivals, whether, "thrones or dominions, or principalities, or powers." Anyone who challenges Jesus' authority is bringing a false message and living a nonsensical illusion. Worse than that, the denial of and challenge to God's authority is the seed of many human evils. For example, people's attention to the occult is based their belief in an imagined, irrational and evil authority that they are driven to appease. In another example, human cruelty is based upon the attempt of people to assert their own authority, often expressed by the forced imposition of one person's will over another. In fact, as we shall see later in our analysis of chapter 2, coercion is often a mark of a false teacher.

The words "by him" or as it really is, "through him," mean that the Son is the agent through whom the universe came into being. The universe did not exist until He rolled up His sleeves and started to work on it. Therefore, the Son is distinct from creation, as a maker is distinct from the thing he makes. No one can bring the Son down to a level with His creation, even though he added to Himself a human nature.

The words "by him" also mean that creation has the stamp of His personality. Creation has God's fingerprints all over it. For example, creation has a rational structure and operation that reflects His rational wisdom. Creation has a beauty that reflects His loveliness. And creation has an intricacy and detail that reflects His loving care of all things He has made, no matter how small.

"and for him."

These words actually are, "and into him," in the sense of "toward Him" or "in His direction and penetrating into Him." We can try to understand these words as, "creation is presented toward the Son." Inasmuch as He also is the Creator, we could say that He presented it to Himself, as an offering or gift. He gave Himself creation to do with as He willed. And He willed to redeem it (Rom. 8:21, Col. 1:14).

Colossians 1:17, "And he is before all things, and by him all things consist."

The word "before" means the Son existed when there was no universe. The Son had a glorious existence with the Father and the Holy Spirit before anything was made (John 17:5). He could say, "Before anything was, I Am" (e.g. John 8:58). The Son does not need the universe. In fact, the words "by him all things consist" mean that the universe needs the Son. Without His sustaining power it would collapse or vanish.

The word "consist" means "together stand." In Luke 9:32 it is found as "stood with." Sometimes the word "consist" is explained to mean that in Jesus the different parts of the physical universe are held together, as if He were glue. That idea is supported by the Bible (Heb. 1:3). With that in mind, we could understand the word "consist" to mean the universe stands together by the personal will of Jesus. Without His continual intervention, it would collapse, especially because it is subject to the corruption induced by the curse. Consequently, the universe has no independent existence and therefore nothing in it has any independent authority, including the false teachers who seek to influence the Colossians.

We also can think the word "consist" means that the universe is standing with or next to Jesus Christ in support of His will and plans. The Son does not need the universe to exist or find personal fulfillment, honor or joy, nevertheless He uses it for His purposes, the greatest of which are His own glory and the redemption of His people (II Cor. 4:15). The universe is cursed and in many ways can be an impediment to missionaries who bring God's Word. However, God is really in control of the physical universe. It ultimately serves Him, who is its supreme authority, as a tool in His hands. Jesus arranges times and events so that His elect will eventually be translated into His kingdom.

Colossians 1:1:18, "And he is the head of the body, the church:"

Verses 16 and 17 develop the idea that Jesus is the "firstborn," remembering that the word "firstborn" highlights Jesus' ownership of all things. These two verses emphasize His ownership from the point of view that He is the Creator of all things. Verses 18 through 20 continue to develop the idea of Jesus as the "firstborn." In these verses the emphasis is upon Jesus' ownership from the point of view that He is the Redeemer of His people. Verse 18 also is connected to verse 17 in the following way. Reasoning from the greater to the lesser, if in Jesus "**all** things consist," then certainly that includes the smaller group called "the body, the church."

If we compare the discussion in verses 16 and 17 to verses 18 through 20 we notice that Paul discusses Jesus as Creator before He looks at Jesus as Savior. It is not that the work of creation is preeminent above salvation. In fact, salvation is the greatest work of God and displays His glory is a far clearer and greater way than His work of creation. But the sequence in these verses highlights the dependence of salvation upon creation. One reason we say that is that for Jesus to be the Savior, He must be the Creator. If he is not a Creator, than He cannot be a Savior. Besides the obvious fact that if He did not create anything, there would not be anything to save, His creative work is a necessary part of His salvation work (Psalm 51:10, II Cor. 5:17). For example, in those who are spiritually dead, He must create life.

Another reason we say that salvation is dependent upon creation is mechanical. The Son had a plan and He designed and created the universe in order to fulfill that specific plan. That plan is the universe's reason for existence. His plan was to display the salvation of His people to the glory of God (Eph. 1:5,6, 9-12). The universe is a platform or arena He created and prepared where He could work out the drama of salvation, or do the job of a Savior.

The word "head," in the phrase "he is the head," is a clear reference to authority, as it is used in I Corinthians 11:3,10. It is not a figurehead authority, in title only, but a real authority, in power.

The words "the body" and "the church" do not refer to a specific local church. Their focus is not limited to the single congregation in Colosse. Instead, they refer to the body or the church throughout the world. We do not mean one worldwide organization. We mean one worldwide organism composed of saved people from every nation, where ever they happen to be found in the world, even though they may not be connected to each other in any official way, or even be aware of each other.

Jesus is the authority to whom all members of the church's body are subject (Eph 5:23,24). He is the only authority of the church (Phil 2:9-11) and earthly leaders rule according to His Word.

The words, "the body" refer to Christ's one body, of which "he is the head." That is, Christians do not form a body separate and distinct from Jesus. They are one with Him (John 17:11). In an act of great grace, Jesus declares Himself incomplete without the church (Eph 1:22,23), even though He really is complete without it (Col. 2:9).

Not only is the body or the church a collection of people beyond political borders, it also is beyond the barrier of time. That is, the concept of "the church" not an exclusively New Testament idea. Saved people from all times are part of "the body" or "the church." For example, the word "church" is the label given to Israelites in the wilderness (Acts 7:38). The point is that Jesus' authority extends over and dominates the lives of all His people, in all places and times. The Colossians must not trust a teacher who comes to them ans says, "You guys are far removed by geography and time from Jesus. I have a message for you that is more contemporary and fitting for you than that which Paul brought you. Listen to me. My message is more authoritative." Instead, Paul said that Jesus is the only "head of the body, the church." Other false prophets were trying to impress the members with some kind of message (Col. 2:8,18,19). But the Colossians had to recognize that Jesus has no real competition. They had to listen to His word only.

"the firstborn from the dead;"

We previously learned that the Son, in Jesus, as the "firstborn," is the heir of every creature because He is the Creator of all things. Now we meet the word "firstborn" again, except this phrase adds that the Son is "firstborn" or heir because He came "from the dead." That is, the words "firstborn," together with the words "from the dead," mean that Jesus came from the dead to be an heir. The idea is that Jesus was resurrected, not only to complete and verify the atonement, but also to claim an inheritance.

In support of this, we can turn to Acts 13:34. We can understand this verse in the following way. The words, "as concerning that he raised him up from the dead ..." mean, "the purpose of God in raising Jesus from the dead is ..." The words, "he said on this wise, I will give you the sure mercies of David" mean "God said some time ago that the purpose in raising Jesus from the dead was to give him the sure mercies of David." The logic of the whole verse can be expressed as, "one purpose of the resurrection is that Jesus must inherit the mercies of David" or "Jesus was raised so that he could be given the mercies of David." What are the "sure mercies of David"? Isaiah 55:3, from which Acts 13:34 quotes, equates the inheritance of the "sure mercies of David" with the "everlasting covenant," which is another name for the Gospel. So, Jesus was raised to inherit or own the Gospel.

What does it mean that Jesus was raised to inherit the Gospel? The Gospel promise is that, before the foundation of the world, Jesus was given people to save (John 17:2,6,9,11,12,24). In terms of another picture, Jesus owns a field of wheat as well as the harvest that it contains. Therefore, Jesus was raised to inherit the harvest, the people who were given to Him to save. His people include all the saved Gentiles (Isaiah 54:3, where the words "thy seed" refers to Jesus, as in Galatians 3:16) and all saved Jews (Zech. 2:12). In terms of Colossians 1:18, we can say that Jesus was raised from the dead so He could inherit all saved people throughout the history of the world, including those in Colosse.

The significance of the resurrection "from the dead" is that it clearly shows the authority of Jesus. The resurrection reveals that Jesus is God (Rom. 1:4). The resurrection shows that He has complete control over death (John 10:18). The resurrection shows that He is the great King and Judge of the universe (Rev. 1:5,18). The resurrection shows that Jesus has completed the payment for sin and has the authority to be the Savior and Lord over believers (I Cor. 15:17,20, II Cor. 4:14). The resurrection shows that He can bestow life to others (John 11:25,26). All these details of redemption were carefully designed so "that in all things he might have the preeminence."

Now we see how the phrase "the firstborn from the dead" explains why Jesus is "the head of the body, the church." By virtue of the fact that He completed the job of Savior, that is, because He endured the wrath of God and rose from the dead, both the organized local churches exist and all true believers exist (Eph. 5:23,24). He is the head of the organized churches in the world, doing with them what He wills. He counsels, builds up and blesses those that are faithful. He condemns those that are not. He is the head of the saved members who are a part of the organized churches, being the Lord of their lives. And He is Judge of those who are not saved (John 12:48).

The message of verse 18 is tied to verses 16 and 17 by the fact that, as we pointed out before, it is necessary that Jesus be the Creator in order to be the Redeemer. Only the Creator has the right to do what He wants with a ruined universe, saving whom He wills (Isaiah 45:9-12, Rom. 9:20-23). Only the Creator has the wisdom and ability needed to redeem His people. Only the Creator could apply the blessings of redemption to their lives, for it is an act of creation to bring life from the dead and change a person's heart (Ezekiel 37, Psalm 51:10, John 11:25, II Cor. 5:17).

Colossians 1:19, "For it pleased the Father that in him should all fulness dwell;"

"For," can be thought of as, "for all the reasons given above ..." Verse 19 gives the ultimate goal or objective for creating and redeeming the world and its inhabitants through Jesus.

The closest antecedent to the pronoun "him" is the noun "Son" in verse 13. The words, "the Father," are not in the original verse. So, the verse is better rendered, "For the Son Himself was pleased ..."

The word "fulness" can be thought of as "fulfill or keep a promise," or "make a promise real," as in Colossians 1:25, "to fulfill the word of God." The promise of salvation in the Word of God is more than words. The resurrection is proof that it became real in Jesus. The idea is that the Son was pleased that "in him" there was the place where the promise became real. In Jesus Christ, the promise of a redeemer was kept, when the Son added to Himself a human part and finished the job that was promised.

The word "fulness" also can be thought of as "filling a container to the top, without any space left." That is the sense in which it is used in Matthew 13:48 ("was full") or Colossians 2:10 ("complete"). The idea is that the Son was pleased that "in him" is the complete amount of all His people (Rom. 8:1), both Jews (Rom. 11:12) and Gentiles (Rom. 11:25).

The word "dwell" refers to a place to live, to a home. It is used in Hebrews 11:9 as, "dwelling in tabernacles." The idea is that the Son was pleased that "in him" humanity found a place to dwell. That is, humanity "came home," so to speak, when it was added to the Son. There is a place "in him" for all redeemed humans to dwell forever (Rom. 8:1).

Verse 1:20, "And, having made peace"

The words "having made peace" bring us back to the fundamental problem of people and their real need. People need peace, but not the peace based upon self-insight, self-control and meditation, not the horizontal peace between each other, not any kind of mental, physical, political, financial or social peace.

The peace in mind is the cessation of war, the war between God and all people (Isaiah 40:2). God is the real enemy people must fear (Luke 12:4,5). God is angry with all people because they are rebellious wicked sinners (Psalm 5:5, Isaiah 48:22, 57:21, James 4:4). Only by taking care of that issue (Isaiah 9:6, Ezek. 34:25, 37:26, Rom. 5:1,8) can sinners be freed from the dominion of darkness. Only God has the authority to declare peace from the relentless pursuit of the law and the fright of Hell, peace based upon the high cost of the death of Jesus Christ.

"through the blood of his cross,"

Peace with God is made "through the blood." We briefly looked at the word "blood" in verse 14. Let us add a few more ideas to give a more complete understanding of why "blood" is mentioned. As we said before, according to Leviticus 17:11, "the life of the flesh is in the blood." What does that mean? If we rewrite it as, "**THE** life of the flesh is in the blood," we see a clear reference to Jesus, THE one special life. Jesus says "I am the life" (John 14:6), and we are reminded of the fact that peace cost the life of Jesus. Jesus gave His life for the purpose that only His life would do which, as Leviticus goes on to say, is "to make an atonement for your souls: for it is the blood that maketh an atonement for the soul." Therefore, Jesus' blood refers to the fact that Jesus paid for His people's sin by sacrificing His life.

In addition to that, according to John 14:6, Jesus is the exclusive source of life. Jesus' blood is the only blood that really counts (Heb. 9:22, 10:4) because He is the only worthy sacrifice. There are not different plans for finding peace with God, one for Jews another for Romans, one for Paul and Timothy another for the Colossians. Jesus' one sacrifice applies to all who are saved. That means no one must take it upon himself to secure salvation by his own effort. No one can add his own blood to make payment for sin. Nor can anyone find someone else's blood for payment. Only Jesus' blood will do. This emphasis anticipates and lays the groundwork for the answer to the false message assaulting the Colossian congregation (Col. 2:8,16-17).

There are many mistaken ideas about the blood of Jesus. It is important that we think clearly and accurately about it, in order to avoid misunderstanding the atonement. For example, some people draw the mistaken conclusion that the phrase "blood of his cross" highlights Jesus' physical agony and trauma. That focus is not only misplaced, it also reveals a confusion about what Jesus did to pay for sin. Even more dangerously, that focus leads to and encourages a physical rather than a spiritual hope, and a physical hope is not the hope of the Gospel found in the Bible.

Jesus' physical blood and the wooden cross are part of Jesus' real historical experience. He shed His blood and hung on a cross in real time and space. But Colossians 1:20 is not pointing to Jesus' physical loss and pain.

For one thing, Jesus' physical death on the cross did not pay for sin. Wrath is the proper reaction of a Holy God against sin (Rom. 1:18). Jesus' atonement is His experience of bearing the wrath of God, a spiritual payment to which physical death does not contribute. Jesus' physical death on the physical cross, to which Jesus was nailed, and upon which He said, "It is finished" and gave up the ghost (Mark 15:37), was not the payment that secured peace with God.

Secondly, physical crucifixion was not the Jewish way of execution. The cross was a Roman instrument. That is, the Law of God did not prescribe death by crucifixion. The Law insisted upon death by stoning (Deut. 21:22). Death by stoning was a sign that the person was evil. According to the Law of God, someone was hung on the "tree" (crucified) only after he was stoned to death (Deut. 21:22). Crucifixion was an advertisement that he died a cursed death (Deut. 21:23).

Was Jesus stoned prior to His crucifixion, according to the law? Yes, in a figure, He was. In Luke 22:41 we read, "And he was withdrawn from them about a stone's cast," which indicated if the disciples would have thrown a stone at Him, it would have reached Him. He was within stoning distance. He had to be. He was not physically stoned to death because there were other things that still had to happen to complete the atonement. But the disciples were close enough to stone Him, in order to picture the fact that Jesus died because of His people's sins. In fact, Luke 44:41 describes the moment that Jesus was within a stone's throw was the moment He was enduring the wrath of God, as we read in Luke 22:42 and 44, "this cup ... in an agony ... blood." The picture of Jesus being stoned is part of His actual enduring the wrath of God in order to put away the evil of His people. But it is the agony of Jesus under the curse of God and not His physical trauma that was important for the atonement for sin. His physical crucifixion was the advertisement that He gave His life as a curse for the sins of His people. Clearly, Jesus has every right to claim them as His own and lead them as their final authority.

"by him to reconcile all things unto himself; by him, I say, whether they be things in earth, or things in heaven."

The "all things" which are reconciled are things "in (actually 'upon') earth, or things in heaven." The "things" reconciled must refer to the physically created things on the earth, in the sky and beyond. The word "heaven" could not mean spiritual beings because there is no salvation provision for them. The idea of verse 20 is that the universe shares in the tragedy of sinful men (Lev. 26:19-22, Psalm 107:33,34, Jer. 4:23-28, Hosea 4:1-3) and it also shares in the hope for which the redeemed wait (Rom. 8:19-22, II Peter 3:13).

The point of verses 15 through 20 is that the amazing work of creation and redemption reveals the Son's nature. What He has made, redeems and continues to sustain shows something of what kind of person he is (Rom. 1:20). That is, the Son did not become a Creator because He made the universe. He was always a Creator, even before Genesis 1, in the sense that He had the wisdom and ability to create as He willed. His work of creation simply revealed Him to be the Creator that He always was. In the words of Psalm 19:1, the universe **declares** His glory. It does **not make** Him glorious. We see the amazing creation and give Him honor for who He is, who He always was and will be. And He used His creative authority and power to redeem His people, separate them from the penalty and power of their sins and bring them into His kingdom.

Perhaps to clarify or magnify this point we can contrast the situation of men. If a man says he is a shoemaker but he never made a shoe, is he a shoemaker? No. He is a shoemaker in title only. It is a self-proclaimed title, but not a reality. In fact, if he tried to make his first shoe, his lack of understanding and training would show in a poorly made shoe. What he made, or attempted to make, would reveal that he was not a shoemaker. Also, the man would not be able to repair a shoe that was broken. Similarly, God **is** a Creator and therefore a Redeemer. He only had to decide to begin to create and then do it, perfectly (Gen. 1:31). Therefore, He has all the authority in this universe that He claims to have, including the authority to "deliver," "translate," "redeem" and "forgive" (Mark 2:10-12).

We can use both the idea of Jesus as Creator and Jesus as Redeemer to help us apply the fact of Jesus' supreme authority to a person's life. Maybe we can express the practical reality of Jesus' authority in the following way, "If Jesus is Creator, is He your Lord? Do you look to Him alone for all your provision? If Jesus is Redeemer, is He your Savior? Do you look to Him alone for your comfort? In addition to that, is Jesus both your Lord and Redeemer? He cannot be one without being the other, too."

Additional notes related to Chapter 3

Colossians 1:15-20

Additional notes for Colossians 1:15 concerning the words, **"the firstborn of every creature."**

The Son's nature, as both God and man, is often a matter of theological or academic discussion. It is a popular amusement to "talk about" Jesus, especially in an intellectual arena like college. A place that is dedicated to study and discussion considers Jesus to be another subject for debate. Furthermore, it is a popular ruse to make Jesus an object of analysis rather than submit to Him as a Person of authority.

But the words "every creature" make a person's relationship to the Son very personal, especially if we understand them to refer to all humanity. No one can escape the obligation to acknowledge Jesus as the Lord of the universe.

If the Son is God, then all people must submit to Him as ruler of the universe, every moment of their lives (Psalm 2:12). If the Son also has attached to Himself an image, a creature-human part, then all people must flee to Him as the Savior, with haste (Luke 19:10).

Therefore, good advise for a true believer is to avoid an involved argument about the nature of Jesus, whether He is God or not. Such a conversation is a waste of time. It diverts the attention off of the real issue, namely people's sins and their accountability to Jesus as the Judge of their souls.

Additional notes for Colossians 1:16 concerning the words, **"for by him were all things created"**

The Bible states that the world was made by the Word of God (John 1:3, Heb. 11:3). This supports the idea that Jesus is the Creator, for He is the Word of God. Jesus, is the Son of God, the person with that kind of authority.

Interestingly, the universe was created simply by means of the spoken word (Gen 1:3). This reveals to us Jesus' awesome power that backs up His authority. What He says goes, both for salvation (Matt. 9:6) and for judgment (John 12:48).

The connection between Jesus' authority and His display of creation is based upon the power of His word. When Jesus speaks, Jesus creates (John 2:8, 11:43). There is a similar connection between

Jesus' authority and His display of redemption. When Jesus speaks, Jesus saves (I Peter 1:23). His is a life-giving word (John 11:25), a cleansing word (John 15:3) and a healing word (Matt. 8:8,13, 9:5).

Additional notes for Colossians 1:19 concerning the words, **"that in all things he might have the preeminence."**

    Jesus Christ is the supreme sovereign of the universe, the all wise and all mighty King (Phil. 2:10,11, Rev. 4:11, 5:12,13). What are the nations of the world before the one eternal King (Psalm 47:2,7, Isa. 40:9-31, Jer. 10:7-16)? What are the kings of the earth before Him (Psalm 89:27)? What are the man-made gods before Him (Psalm 95:3)? What is the pride of men before Him (Dan. 4:34-37)? The nations of men shall be brought low before His throne in judgment (Rev. 19:11-16).

    The whole Bible is a revelation of the power and majesty of this great King, and His authority also is displayed in every chapter of the book of Colossians (Col. 1:18, 2:10, 3:1, 4:1). One message of Colossians is that Jesus' authority shapes the destiny and life of His people (Col. 1:13. Another message is that Jesus overwhelms all who oppose His sovereign will (Col. 2:15).

Additional notes for Colossians 1:19 concerning the words, **"through the blood of his cross,"**

    Sometimes people will ask questions, "Well, if God really is the supreme authority that the Bible declares Him to be, then why doesn't He just decide to forget all the sins of men and declare them forgiven, thereby bringing peace between Him and them without all the agony and sorrow of the cross? After all, He doesn't answer to anyone, so couldn't He do what He wants?" The response to this challenge is that God answers to Himself. He is righteous. In the integrity of His own heart He will be true to His own word, which declares that the wages of sin is death. Therefore, the souls that have sinned must die, even if it has to be His own dear Son in substitution for the elect. Jesus' death shows that God means what He says. Judgment **must** come against sin because he said it would. And He must decree that judgment comes as a consequence of disobedience otherwise the universe would not operate according to any order and He would not be in control; He would not be God.

    As another challenge to the Gospel, sometimes people who

question God's authority in their lives will ask, usually faithlessly and in malice, "If God is so infinite and almighty, why would He concern Himself with a infinitesimal speck on the surface of a small planet? After all people are so small and weak in comparison to the rest of the universe. It's arrogant to think that God would come to this planet and do so much for humans. It doesn't make sense that the Son of God would endure the agony of the Cross and shed His blood for inhabitants of such a minor planet in the universe." It is true that man is insignificant from a physical point of view, although humans are amazing physiological creations, and their brains are the most complex structure in the universe. However, we only will find answers to these questions when we ask them in faith (Psalm 8:4) and look at things from a non-material, spiritual perspective.

The physical comparison is irrelevant. After all, what is the size of a person's soul? It really has no physical dimensions. A conclusion of value based upon physical measurement is meaningless The value of a human is not measured by his physical "size," it is measured by value of his soul. The value of people is based upon the fact that they are created in God's image. The measure of that value is seen by the extent God went to save them. In a manner of speaking, the value of a human is seen in the "size" of the salvation, of which its "breadth, and length, and depth, and height" is beyond measure (Eph. 3:18). The value of a human soul is seen in the "size" of God's love for those whom He redeemed. People are as important as God has made them to be and He expresses that value in His willingness to send His Son to die for them.

Chapter 4

Colossians 1:21- 2:3

Colossians 1:1-12 displays the evidence that Christians are under the authority of the Lord Jesus Christ. Colossians 1:13-14 describes Jesus' great work that was required to bring them under His authority. In Colossians 1:15-20 the focus is upon their Lord Himself, the Person with supreme authority. Now we come to Colossians 1:21-2:3, which describes the value of His authority, both for their character (Col. 1:21-23a) and for their service (Col. 1:23b-2:3). That is, after we answered the questions "What?" "How?" and "Who?", we now answer the question, "So what?"

Colossians 1:21, "And you,"

The words "and you" reminded the Colossians that sin is not an academic idea or a problem which only applies to some very bad people out there someplace. The words bring the issue of sin home to the hearts of the members of that congregation, as if to say "think about how much trouble you were in and what God had to do to reconcile you." Sin had been their dominating problem, and the memory was painful. But recalling their former foolishness was instructive and clarified their view of themselves and of God.

"that were sometime alienated"

The word translated "alienated," meaning alienated from God, is related to the word that means "stranger," and is based upon a word that means "other" or "change." It is as if God looked at the Colossians and saw them as "other" people, that is, not people who belonged to His kingdom. Spiritually, they did not look like or fit in with God's people. They, like all unsaved people, were aliens because they were citizens of another authority (Eph 2:12). They acquired the alien citizenship after the Fall in Eden, when the allegiance of Adam and all of his descendants changed from God to Satan. Since then, they were dominated by sin and Satan (Isaiah 26:13, Acts 26:18). As aliens, they had no rights or privileges that belonged to the citizens of God's Kingdom.

The word, "sometimes," does not imply that they occasionally were alienated from God, estranged only when they sinned but not at other times. Such a notion would lead to a gospel dependent upon the works of men. Besides, people sin all the time, not just some time. Furthermore, one sin is sufficient to permanently alienate people from God, despite any other "good works" they may do. Instead, the idea of this phrase is "you were alienated from God some time before," that is, before they were saved.

This embarrassing and uncomfortable memory is meant to highlight the exclusive work of God in reconciling people to Himself. God is the only one who has the authority and ability to reconcile people. The point can be expressed as, "Your rescue certainly was not accomplished by your own ability or your own resources. You were aliens, opposed to God, when He found you."

"and enemies in your mind by wicked works,"

Before the Colossian Christians were saved, they were "enemies" (Rom. 5:10). They were are not citizens of a neutral kingdom that was located next to the kingdom of God, which coexisted in a friendly way with God and His people. Rather, they belonged to and were loyal to an enemy kingdom that actively opposes Christ and His kingdom.

The fact that they were "enemies" was displayed "by (actually 'in,' or 'being immersed in') wicked works" (Eph. 2:2,3, Titus 3:3). It is a certain principle that a person eventually will reveal his authority through his behavior (Matt. 7:22, John 8:44, Phil. 1:28). The reason is that people are slaves to their authority and must march to its tune. Their works are the evidence of who is in command in their lives (John 8:34, Rom. 6:16).

Their problem was "in your mind." This refers to the deepest part of them (Matt. 22:37). When they were alienated, they were not just people who outwardly disobeyed God. Rather, they had a mind to sin, they wanted to sin in their hearts (Gen. 6:5, Jer. 17:9). In their minds they imagined themselves independent of Christ, so they deliberately opposed Him, whose laws impeded and threatened them. They also hated His people, who reminded them of His demands upon them and their liability for their disobedience. That was an attitude with which Paul could personally identify (Acts 7:58-8:3). Unbelievers not only defend themselves from the assault of the Gospel (II Tim. 3:8), but also attack the claims as well as the conduct of those who identify with Christ (I Peter 2:12, 3:16). More than that, as we shall see in Colossians 2, unbelievers sometimes are subversive, seeking to draw away people from the truth.

When the Colossians were alienated, their need was for new minds (Heb. 8:10, 10:16). In fact, they needed the mind of Christ Himself, which is given only to those who are saved (I Cor. 2:16, Phil. 2:2,5).

"yet now hath he reconciled"

As the word "alienated," the words "hath he reconciled" also are based upon a word that means "other" or "change." In this case, change in view is the one that God makes in the lives of people whom He brings under His authority.

In a way, this phrase is the surprise of history. Why would God bother with people who were enemies and had no desire to be at peace with Him, who were afraid of and hostile toward Him? For people who were not nice and who were not nice to Him, God took the initiative and diligently worked until peace was made. It is a display of love to sinners that makes them speechless.

Colossians 1:22, in the body of his flesh through death,"

Jesus "made peace" and was "reconciled" to His people when He was "in the body of his flesh." What happened in the body of His flesh? The biggest event in His body was His "death." In fact, the reason that the Son added to Himself a body was to prepare for His assignment to die as a man (Heb. 10:5-10). Jesus' "death" was real because He died in real time in a real body of His flesh (Rom. 8:3) for the purpose of reconciling undeserving, rebellious, hateful sinners to Himself (Rom. 5:8-10). But as we discussed before, his "death" refers to His spiritual death under God's wrath, the only death that could make a change.

Incidentally, the words "in the body of his flesh" do not imply that, when the Son added to Himself a body when He was on earth, He reduced His authority (Matt. 7:29, 9:6). It was simply that he needed a body to complete the assigned atonement (Heb. 2:14,15). Only Jesus had the authority to do that job (Isaiah 59:6, 63:5), so He attached to Himself a human nature and did it. There was no other body (not another man's not an animal's), that would do. The result of His finished work "in the body" was reconciliation (Heb. 10:19-22).

"to present you holy and unblameable and unreproveable in his sight:"

We could think that these words describe the goal of the reconciliation. Or we could think that these words list some of the effects or the changes in the Colossian believers' lives. One goal or change is that they were "holy." In other words, they were separated from the world and reserved for God's use.

Another goal or change is that they were "unblameable." The word from which "unblameable" comes is better translated "without spot," as in Hebrews 9:14, or "without blemish," as in I Peter 1:19. The idea is that, from God's point of view, the Colossians were pure, that is, in their hearts (II Tim. 2:22, Titus 1:15). God saw them in Jesus, without sin.

One more goal or change is that they were "unreproveable." The word "unreproveable" comes from a word that is closer to the idea of "unblameable," for it is composed of a prefix that means "no" attached to a word that is translated "accused," as in Acts 23:28,29 or "shall lay to the charge of," as in Romans 8:33. The idea is that there was no record of their former life as an enemy which anyone could use to blame them (Rom. 8:1,33, Heb. 10:17).

The message of verses 21 and 22 is, "Look at the change. There was a lot of reconciling to do. It was nothing you could do. Your rescue was not accomplished by your own ability. It was all of God." Reconciliation is a BIG DEAL. Reconciliation is based upon the amazing completed work of God in the past and also is dependent upon the abiding grace of God to make it secure and eternal. All of this compels our trust and praise. Reconciliation is one of the many ways in which God displays His "preeminence" (Col. 1:18).

Colossians 23, "If ye continue in the faith grounded and settled, and be not moved away from the hope of the gospel, which ye have heard,"

Verse 23 explains the enduring quality of God's work. His people will remain faithful to the end despite the sinful desires of their flesh and the corrosive spiritual environment in which they live (Rom. 8:38,39).

The conditional statement beginning with the word "if" does not imply that it is uncertain whether believers will make it to the end. Neither does it imply that believers must work very hard in order to remain faithful, as if by "grim determination" or "hanging in there no matter what" they will endure to the end. Rather the idea is that "You will continue in the faith and you will not turn from the gospel you have heard, if you truly are under the authority of Him who alone has the power and authority to keep you." That is, the condition is not their effort but God's sovereign gracious decision to save them. If Jesus saves them and places them under His authority, then they will be pure and holy when He returns (Phil. 1:6).

Anyone who is truly saved will not "be moved away from the hope of the gospel, which (they) heard," despite any appeal or coercion from false teachers. That is, the Gospel does not offer an opportunity for believers to work hard and so persevere, rather it is an announcement of God's power to change people, a change which will always show and a change which will last forever. Colossians 2 will discuss the means that God uses to make sure that His people do endure, especially when they are attacked by false messengers.

The word translated "grounded" means "to lay a foundation." The only foundation that can be laid is Jesus Himself (I Cor 3:11), and is a foundation that God lays alone, without the participation of men (Heb. 11:10). The foundation is "the hope of the gospel" which God sovereignly promised and described in the Bible (Eph 2:20).

The word "hearing" is not referring to the natural ability of humans to respond to the sound waves that enter their ears. Rather it refers to really hearing, with the heart and soul, to hearing which produces a spiritual work in the heart (Luke 8:15). Again, the emphasis is upon the work of God and not men (Isaiah 35:5, Mark 7:31-37).

These words highlight the sovereign authority of God. Not only is salvation dependent totally upon God's work in a person's life, but also it is not universal. That is, salvation is limited to those people who "continue in the faith" that God has given them and sustains in them.

"and which was preached to every creature which is under heaven;"

The word "creature" refers to people (Rom. 10:18). The word "creature" emphasizes that people are created creatures and dependent upon God. They especially are dependent upon God to hear and respond to what is preached.

One important idea that comes out of this phrase is that there is one and the same Gospel for "every creature." There are not different gospel messages for different people. People who bring the Gospel must be sensitive to the local culture of the people to whom they preach. For example, a missionary's effort to understand the culture of the people to whom he ministers shows the people he really cares about them. However, he must not alter the Gospel to accommodate it to their spiritual beliefs and moral habits. The "hope of the gospel" found in the Bible was written by God who knows the cultures of all men. It is true that God separated people by languages at the Tower of Babel, but He wrote only one book to call them to His one kingdom. Therefore the Gospel that is "preached to every creature" is independent of any local tradition or culture. It fits the needs of all the different creatures "under heaven." The reason is that there is only one kind of a human, a sinner in trouble with God, and there is only one kind of solution to their need, salvation through Jesus.

"whereof I Paul am made a minister;

Beginning with the last words of verse 23, the focus of the passage changes a little. Now the passage considers the effect of God's authority upon a Christian's life of service, particularly the service of bringing God's message to the world. Paul begins with himself as an example, for he was sent by God to be a minister of the gospel, "to every creature which is under heaven" (Acts 9:15).

Colossians 1:24, Who now rejoice in my sufferings for you and fill up that which is behind of the afflictions of Christ in my flesh."

Colossians 1:24 teaches that believers rejoice in God's assigned service for them on earth, even though the assignment includes suffering. This verse gives very surprising and helpful counsel in dealing with affliction and suffering. Let us look at a few of the details and then put them together to get the idea of the verse.

When we read the words "(I, Paul) Who now rejoice in my sufferings," we might wonder, "What's the matter with Paul? Is he a masochist? The answer is "No!" Then, we can then ask, "Does this make sense? Is it possible to rejoice **in** suffering?" The answer is "Yes!" And this verse tells us how.

First of all, let us look at the words "and fill that which is behind of the afflictions of Christ in my flesh." The point of these words is not that there is something lacking in the afflictions of Christ, as if there were more for Christ to suffer. Christ was afflicted once, sufficiently for all that was needed to pay for the sins of all His people (Heb. 10:10-14).

The problem is with the word "behind." It seems to imply that there is something missing in Christ's sufferings. We know that cannot be. However, we cannot modify the word in order to understand it. It means a real lack as in I Corinthians 16:7 ("that which was lacking"), II Corinthians 11:9 ("that which was lacking") or I Thessalonians 3:10 ("that which is lacking"). The word means to have nothing. It is a word upon which our English word "austerity" is based. The key to understanding the word "behind" is in the words "in my flesh." That is where the lack is. It cannot be that Christ lacked anything (Col.1:19).

The words "of Christ" are not in the accusative case. That is, Christ is not the direct object which receives the action of affliction. The afflictions are not directed toward Christ personally. The words are in the genitive case, a grammatical construction which means that the afflictions belong to Christ as a possession, to do with as He wills. The image is as if Christ had a bag of afflictions into which He reached and then gave to Paul the kind and amount reserved for him to endure in his flesh. The affliction mentioned in this verse is the suffering that Christ had to give Paul in order to further whatever plan He had in mind (Acts 9:16). It is as if Christ had prepared some afflictions that were just right for Paul and then He put Paul's name of on them. Christ then gave them to Paul as a gift to accomplish some purpose.

Now we can properly understand the phrase "that which is behind ... in my flesh." Paul lacked Christ's full allotment of sufferings to which he had been appointed. There was a predetermined amount and kind of suffering, decided by God's will. Paul had yet to complete or fulfill the quota of suffering in his flesh while he was yet on this earth. This verse is not a complaint but a statement of fact. Paul knew that he still had to fulfill the sufferings that God had planned for him. Paul still had to complete his course.

God had a plan, the Gospel plan of the ages. Part of that plan meant that Paul was a marked man. God had marked him for a certain amount and kind of suffering. Paul knew that he had not suffered it all yet. Therefore, he rejoiced because each episode of affliction meant that he was closer to fulfilling God's plan. Paul knew that God's plan of suffering was purposeful for each of His people. It is a plan rooted in the mind of a God who is all-wise and who knows what is best for His glory as well as what is best for His people. God always has the best interests of His people at heart. God's plan is motivated by His love for His people. It may include affliction (Acts 14:22, II Tim. 3:12), but it is meant to draw them closer to Christ, to forsake their own foolish ways and to trust and depend upon Him more. It is meant to display the power of the Gospel in their obedient reaction to the troubles that come their way. It is meant to encourage other believers who suffer. It is meant to attract unbelievers to the Gospel who, in their wonderment of the peace they see believers have in the midst of their own affliction, seek the same peace.

Paul did not, nor did he counsel others to, rejoice in affliction for its own sake. Suffering is not fun. Instead, Paul's joy was in fulfilling God's plan for his life. Paul could not, nor did he want to, evade the allotted suffering which God had determined was best to fulfill His plan for all of His people.

Paul knew that things are never out of control, because God has supreme authority. He knew that affliction never catches God by surprise so that God has to quickly give His people strength on the spot. God has it all purposefully scheduled for their good (Rom. 8:27,28). His people do not suffer any less or any more than God has planned. God knows each of His people and knows what is good for each of them. Therefore, Paul knew that his afflictions were limited to a predetermined amount. Paul was not abandoned to an undetermined amount of affliction nor had he been temporarily forgotten and therefore endured an amount that was more than he should. He was not a victim of unfortunate circumstances that could have turned out differently. Instead, Paul knew that he was called to be a witness in his suffering which God used as a display of His work of grace (II Cor. 12:9).

"for his body's sake, which is the church:"

Affliction is planned for "his body's sake." That is, God's plan of suffering for each of His people is purposeful for each member of the "body" or "church" and for the "body" as a whole. He has their benefit in mind.

For one thing, suffering separates true believers from pretenders (Phil 1:28, II Thess 1:4-6). True believers draw closer to their Lord. True believers see by faith the wise and good hand of God in the difficulties of life. Unbelievers are repulsed from God. Sometimes unsaved people are full of anger and bitterness because of a personal wound or loss, which may even lead them to seek revenge or aggressively pursue their rights. Sometimes unsaved people are full of despair because they cannot understand God's ways, which leads to confusion, fear and hopelessness.

Secondly, suffering instructs believers in what is real and important (II Cor. 2:4). They see afresh that the world is a source of frustration and disappointment while the Lord is ever faithful. They know that beyond the physical affliction, there is a spiritual reality upon which they must focus (II Cor. 4:10-18, Heb. 12:2).

Thirdly, suffering is an opportunity for true believers to shine as trophies of God's grace and power (I Peter 2:9,20,21). Though they may stumble from time to time, true believers display patience, trust and even joy amid their suffering.

Fourthly, suffering can be used of God to draw unbelievers to His kingdom. Suffering may cause them to begin to see the vanity of trusting in themselves or in the world. Suffering may cause them to be attracted to the wisdom and peace of true believers, who endure the same grief as they (I Peter 3:1,2).

Colossians 1:25, "Whereof I am made a minister, according to the dispensation of God which is given to me for you, to fulfil the word of God."

This verse states that God has authority over the selection of His staff and their individual assignments. From the words "am made" and "given to me" we learn that God is sovereign in how He delegates jobs to His workers. People do not fill out applications for work in the Gospel. They are "made" servants and are "given" work by God's authority. That was God's promise (Isaiah 43:21, Jer. 3:15) and Paul's personal experience (Gal. 1:15, Eph. 3:7, I Peter 2:9).

The antecedent of the word "whereof" (or "of which") is the word "church" in verse 24. The message is that Paul was assigned as a minister to a specific group of people, namely, the church. This refers both to the organized churches found in different locations throughout the geographical area in which he ministered and to the true believers found in and out of the organized churches. To that assigned group, Paul was committed. He was dedicated to the church and cared for the spiritual welfare of its individual members.

We may think of the word "dispensation" as a compound word put together from the words "house" and "law." The idea is that Paul was a minister "according to" the law of God's house. It is as if Paul was responsible for administering the affairs of God's house on His behalf, and like a trusted domestic servant, he followed the instructions in God's law. The law shaped Paul's job. What he said and did as well as how he said and did it was done "according to" or determined by the law of God.

The words, "for you" highlight the fact that God determined for whose benefit Paul's ministry was intended. When the Colossians received and read this letter it was a divine encounter, planned by God. God directed His servant, Paul, to those people whom He has in mind. That is, Paul was sent with a message "for you" so that the word of God would be fulfilled. God did not mention the Colossians by name in Old Testament. However, God did refer to "my people" (Isaiah 51:16), which included those elect in the congregation of Colosse for whom the Gospel was intended and to whom He sent His servants to fulfill His promise to gather them into His Kingdom. So we see that Colossians 1:25 states God has the authority to determine to whom the Gospel applies. In that way, God shows His authority to control the lives of His servants so that they do their job "to fulfil the word of God."

Colossians 1:26, "[Even] the mystery which hath been hid from ages and from generations, but now is made manifest to his saints."

This verse, together with verses 27 and 28, has more to say about God's control over "the word of God," which is the message He distributes by His ministers throughout the history of the world. These verses refer to "the word of God," as "the mystery." The word "mystery" is another label for the Gospel (I Tim. 3:16). It does not mean that the Gospel is a puzzle that needs careful thought, time and insight to solve. Instead, it means the Gospel is only understood when God reveals it to someone (I Cor. 2:7,10). The Gospel is a "mystery" to unbelievers and clear to people who are saved (I Cor. 2:14,15, II Cor. 4:3).

The Gospel was "hid from ages and from generations." That does not mean that in the past believers did not understand the Gospel. After all, Abraham knew (John 8:56, Gal. 3:8). So did Isaiah (John 12:41). Rather, the idea is that prior to the fulfillment of the Gospel in Jesus and its announcement to the world after Pentecost, few people of the world besides the nation of Israel heard or understood the Gospel. There were a few cases, as when the Gospel went to the city of Niniveh. But that was an exception, anticipating the Gospel's world-wide distribution through the work of evangelists like Paul. Even in the nation of Israel, the Gospel was not revealed with the clarity that it was declared by Paul and ministers "now to his saints." That is, "now" is God's time to reveal it clearly (II Cor. 6:2). From this we see God's authority over the timing of His revelation to His people (Rom. 16:25,26).

Colossians 1:27, "To whom God would make known what [is] the riches of the glory of this mystery among the Gentiles; which is Christ in you, the hope of glory."

This verse continues to describe God's control over His "mystery." According to verse 27, God intended to make known to the saints how rich His Gospel was. The riches refer to people whom God saves (Mal. 3:16,17), including some "among the Gentiles." Those riches glorified God, both in the sense that saved people praise Him and in the sense that the fact that sinners are saved is a glory to Him, for the salvation plan demonstrates His love and wisdom.

We should point out that the words "among the Gentiles" together with the word "you" imply that some members of the church at Colosse were Gentiles. But not all were. Colossians 3:16 implies that false teachers insisted that the Colossians return to obedience of the Jewish ceremonies, an appeal that would not have influenced the Gentile members.

We also should add that the inclusion of Gentiles in redemption and in the kingdom of God is another meaning of the term "mystery," as we read in Ephesians 3:3-6. The fulfillment of God's Word God "now" is in the work of His Gospel in the lives of the Gentiles (Acts 10:34,35, 15:14-17, Eph 2:11-22). This verse shows that God has authority or control over the scope of the impact of the Gospel, namely that it includes people from all nations.

The word "in" means "inside of" or "within." We cannot completely understand the words "Christ in you," at least not in any physical or graphic way. After all the Bible also states that God's people are "in Christ Jesus" (Rom. 8:1). So which is it, Christ in you or you in Christ? Rather than try to get a mental picture of the preposition "in," we should be content with some of the things that the Bible clearly states. One is that people who are saved live because Jesus has given them life, His life, and continues to sustain His life within them (John 11:25,26, Gal. 2:20). Another is that people who are saved obey because God works in them (Phil. 2:13). Even then, we do not really understand how Christ is "in" a believer. However, one message is that the control of Christ in the lives of His people is total and intimate.

Colossians 1:28, "Whom we preach, warning every man, and teaching every man in all wisdom; that we may present every man perfect in Christ Jesus."

This verse states God has authority over the content of the Gospel which He gives to His ministers to distribute.

Notice the words "whom we preach." The word "whom" refers to Christ, the hope of glory. God's people preach Christ (I Cor 2:2-4). The emphasis of preaching must be upon Jesus (I Cor. 1:31). The foundation of the Gospel is not a system of propositions that must be adopted and obeyed in order to gain acceptance with God. The foundation of the Gospel is a Person, someone who did something for His people in real time and space and did something in their souls to give them eternal life.

When God's people preach Christ, they must include both "warning" and "teaching." That is the only method by which God's purpose to "present every man perfect in Christ Jesus" can be achieved.

People who preach Christ do not have a choice about the kind of Christ they preach or serve. The word "warning" highlights the fact that Jesus Christ is the Judge (John 5:26,27, 12:48, Acts 17:31, Rom. 2:16, Rev. 19:15). Jesus has the right to judge, for as the Creator of the universe He has jurisdiction and authority over all of its inhabitants. Jesus is qualified to judge, as the perfect sinless one. Jesus is obligated to judge, for, as the one who was judged Himself, He demonstrated that sin must be punished without exception. Therefore, "warning" is a necessary part of the job of preaching (Ezek. 3:17-21, Jonah 3). Also, warning is motivated out of a personal concern for those people to whom a person preaches (II Cor. 5:11).

In addition, people who preach Christ do not choose the information they research or the words they use. They must teach "in all wisdom." That is, they must teach "all" of it because the whole Bible and only the Bible is the wisdom of God. Jesus is the wisdom (I Cor. 1:30, Col. 2:3) that is found in all of the Bible (Luke 24:27). The requirement of God's people who preach is that they be faithful to all of God's Word (I Cor. 4:2).

The objective to "present every man" is a display of God's holy love. According to Ephesians 5:27, it is what a husband wants for the wife he loves. He sacrifices his own desires because he wants the very best for her. Similarly, preachers sacrifice their own cherished opinions and ideas in order to bring all of God's Word for the benefit of God's people.

God's servants are obligated to warn and teach one message to "every man" because the content of the Gospel is the same no matter to whom they preach, as we discussed in verse 23. Also they are obligated to preach to "every man" regardless of that person's eternal destiny. "Every man" is a candidate for the Gospel, for God does with the "mystery" as He will. For some it is a blessing and for others it is a curse (II Cor. 2:15,16).

Colossians 1:29, "Whereunto I also labour, striving according to his working, which worketh in me mightily."

Colossians 1:29 through 2:2 show that God has control of and shapes the attitudes of the people who serve Him as they bring His Gospel.

In Colossians 1:29, we see Paul as an example of someone who diligently worked, despite weariness and trouble, because of his personal interest and commitment to the job. Paul made that great effort because he was under the control of God. Hindrances and adversaries did not paralyze him or reduce his enthusiasm for the job, because those barriers are not too much for God, who worked in him with irresistible power. God's servants diligently labor in their arduous service to their Lord because they trust Him who conscripted and assigned them. God's servants faithfully labor because they see the value of His message for themselves and for the people to whom they are sent. They labor, not uncertain of its impact, but confident that it contributes to the fulfillment of some larger and wonderful plan, such as bringing praise to God and producing fruit in the lives of the people for whose sake they work (Col. 1:6).

Colossians 2:1, "For I would that ye knew what great conflict I have for you, and [for] them at Laodicea, and [for] as many as have not seen my face in the flesh."

The words "great conflict" label the agony of a man who is in a violent struggle accompanied by great pain. It is a conflict due to a collision of opposing forces. The word translated "conflict" is used only a few times in the Bible. It is similar to the word translated "striving" in the previous verse and is a form of the word translated "fight" in I Timothy 6:12, or "have fought" in II Timothy 4:7. Also, it labels the tension of competition and is translated, "race" in Hebrews 12:1. In this case, a believers' opponents in the fight and in the race are the rival messengers who have another view of Jesus and His salvation.

Paul wanted the Colossians to know that he willingly spent himself for their benefit and in defense of their spiritual life. His motivation was not to gain the Colossians' sympathy or admiration. Rather he labored because most of the members of the congregation "have not seen my face in the flesh." This was a problem because, although he was an outsider to the Colossian congregation, the false messengers were close at hand and therefore were more familiar to the Colossians than Paul. Also, Paul's competition was in a position to speak more often to the congregation of their "philosophy and vain deceit (Col. 2:8).

There was little history of personal human contact between Paul and the believers of Colosse or Laodicea that would normally be the foundation of and sustain a close, trusting relationship. Therefore, Paul wanted the Colossians to know about his "great conflict" for them because he wanted them to know, though he was more remote, he was far more jealous for the welfare of their souls than anyone else, as revealed by his labor on their behalf. For example, he questioned all who had visited the Colossians to learn of their spiritual welfare (Col. 1:8,9). He prayed much and wrote letters based upon what he had learned (Col. 4:16). He encouraged others to pray for and minster to them (Col. 4:8,12). He willingly endured the conflict that came to him because of his outspoken concern for them (Col. 1:24).

That Paul would consume and exhaust his energy and resources on their behalf also was evidence that he was a true ambassador with God's authority, for his agony had the same motive and purpose as Jesus Christ. That is, God labored sacrificially for the sake of His people (Eph. 5:25), and so did he. In contrast to that, the people who brought a false message to the Colossians, as well as false messengers today, were on a power trip that promoted their own welfare. They never had their listeners' best interests at heart. False prophets make bright and generous promises but have dark, self-serving purposes.

Colossians 2:2, "That their hearts might be comforted, being knit together in love, and unto all riches of the full assurance of understanding, to the acknowledgement of the mystery of God, and of the Father, and of Christ."

The word "That" implies Colossians 2:2 and 3 state the objectives of Paul's service. Paul never thought first of all, "What do I get out of this effort for them?" He did not think, "What is the least I can do to help meet their needs and then get on with my life." He always was liberal with his time and labor because he always had their best interest in mind. He wanted them to be "comforted." He wanted them to be "knit together in love." He wanted them to have "all riches" and have "full assurance," based upon an understanding "of the mystery of God." Paul wanted to give, rather than take as the other messengers did.

One objective was that "their hearts," the total essence of them, be "comforted." The word "comfort" means to speak along side of and is used as another name for the Holy Spirit (John 14:16,17,26), who speaks along side of His people on their behalf. There is no comfort in hoping to convince God on our own, by means of our own clever words or expert logic, that we should be admitted into Heaven. The only comfort is for someone who is able and worthy to plead our case (Rom. 8:16, 34, I John 2:1, Heb. 7:25). The Spirit's pleading is successful. The argument is a good one, namely that Jesus paid for our sins. Even though God's people are people who ought to weep because of their own rebellion, God provides comfort for weepers (Jer 31:13, Matt 5:4). The "comfort" is in the certainty of the Gospel of salvation and in the power of God revealed in that Gospel (II Cor. 1:3-9).

Also, there is little comfort if a believer's pilgrimage is a solitary journey, if he must go it alone. The Gospel's comfort is reinforced in a believer's heart when he is "knit together in love," not only with Jesus Christ, but also with another christian brother or sister. From Ephesians 4:15,16, we see that the idea is Christians belong together and help each other when they speak the same truth because they have the same mind (Phil. 2:3,4). The words, "every joint suppieth," remind us that God has designed His people to be dependent upon Him and supportive of each other, for God works in an individual Christian's life through the ministry of other Christians, as each "joint" supplies the truth needed for the whole body.

In addition to that, there is no comfort for a believer's heart if what he believes comes out of his or someone else's imagination. There is no comfort if something for which he hopes is not real but only a fairy tale. Trusting something to be so does not make it so. There is comfort only because of the certainty of the Gospel based upon the authority of God to keep his Word. The Gospel is true. Paul knew it was true. That is why he was so ardent and insistent. The Gospel's comfort is based upon that "understanding" of the "mystery of God" (Col.1:26).

It is not that Christians are comforted because they are thinking correctly. Rather, they are comforted because what they know is real and true, namely that God is sufficient for all their needs. They don't have to wonder if the basis for their comfort is in jeopardy, if God has missed something. They are assured because God is sovereign, that their trust is in the one Person who has control over all things because He has the all wisdom and resources to provide for all their needs. That is the point of the next verse.

Colossians 2:3, "In whom are hid all the treasures of wisdom and knowledge."

The words "in whom" imply "in Christ and not anyone else" or "in Christ alone." The words "are hid" mean that God hides the Gospel in Christ. Therefore only those who find Christ find the "treasures." The treasures are all the blessings of the Gospel of salvation in Jesus Christ (II Cor. 4:5-7). Since they are hid in Jesus, they are hid to them who are not saved (Matt. 11:25-17, II Cor. 4:4).

The Bible states that "treasures" are stored or set aside for future need (Matt. 6:19,20). The future need is to escape the wrath of God. The idea is, as we say, "set aside something for a rainy day," in which the rainy day is the flood of Judgment Day. Jesus, who is wisdom itself (I Cor. 1:30), is the treasure who we have in Heaven, for He hides us from the wrath of God forever.

The Bible also states that "treasures" are valuable or what is desired and important (Matt. 6:21, Heb. 11:26). There is nothing more valuable or important than to secure the blessing of Heaven. Jesus Christ alone has all that is necessary to secure that salvation and has all that is sufficient to live a faithful Christian life. In other words, in anticipation of the problems that will be discussed in Chapter 2, the counsel is that there is no need to seek wisdom and knowledge in anyone else, for Jesus has it "all.".

Additional notes related to Chapter 4

Colossians 1:21-2:3

Additional notes for Colossians 2:1 concerning the word, **"Laodicea."**

It is helpful to note that while the congregation at Laodicea may have been fairly faithful at the time that Paul wrote this letter, not too many years later the apostle John would write, "I know thy works, that thou art neither cold nor hot: I would thou wert cold or hot. So then because thou art lukewarm, and neither cold nor hot, I will spue thee out of my mouth" (Rev. 3:15,16). It is possible that the signs of unfaithfulness already were beginning to show. With that in mind, we could surmise that the false teaching assaulting the Colossian congregation was coming from Laodicea and the warnings as well as the personal concern of this letter was directed to both congregations. Perhaps the letter with a message for both congregations (Col. 4:16) was sent to the Colossian congregation because it was not as far down the slippery path of unfaithfulness and so it would be a more likely candidate to receive the message for its own benefit and deliver it to others.

Chapter 5

Colossians 2:4 - 23

Chapter 2, from verse 4 through the end, warns Christians who "preach ... in all wisdom" (Col. 1:28) about people who oppose and try to subvert what they say. God sends His people into the world with Jesus' authoritative message. But that message is feared, hated and challenged by people who are not saved. God explains in this chapter how His people can recognize the character and methods of rival authorities, as well as avoid being influenced by their conflicting and subversive message.

Colossians 2:4, "And this I say, lest any man should beguile you with enticing words."

The word "this" refers to the previous verses, especially verse 3, in which Paul taught that in Jesus is all wisdom and knowledge. All that Jesus said and did was enough for all the needs of His people's souls. But not everyone agreed with that message. Therefore, Paul was motivated to write what he did "lest any man should beguile you with enticing words." Paul was saying, "I want you Colossians to believe me lest you be inclined to believe someone else." It was his words against the words of other teachers.

The word "beguile" (*paralogiztai*) means "next to logic." The word "beguile" implies that rival authorities use words "next to" or close to God's Word but do not actually bring the message of the Bible. That is, the vocabulary and logic of rival authorities seem biblically sound and sensible, their warnings and promises are reasonable and appealing, but the foundation of their message is not the Christ of the Bible. They are false angels of light (II Cor. 11:13,14), deceiving even themselves (II Tim. 3:13).

In a passage that explains the character and methods of false teachers, this verse gives the first warning. The warning is that we must never be impressed by what men say, no matter how well they express it, even if they use Bible words and phrases. What men say is not the measure of truth. Rather, their words are measured by a truth with a higher authority than they, namely the Bible. In fact, according to this verse, false teachers pile up words next to the truth in order to confuse their listeners and divert people's thinking away from the truth.

In addition to that, we must keep in mind that false teachers can bring truth for a long time until they gain the confidence and trust of their listeners, at which time they can slip in lies that will also be believed. So, the counsel is that we must always be vigilant. Any teacher, false or true, is but a man. Though someone may say a thousand things that are true, there is no guarantee that the thousand and first thing is true. It may be wrong, or even calculated to lead people astray. We should never receive anything unprepared by our own personal study of the Bible or unquestioned. Anyone, even a man who has proven himself faithful in the past, must continuously be compared to the Bible.

The false teachers hope their persistence, eloquence and clever logic will gain them credibility in the minds of people and capture the hearts of their audience thereby. Could someone be captured by words? Yes, it is possible, but only if a person listens to the false message and does not have the power to withstand the words (Genesis 3:1, Rom. 16:18, II Peter 2:18,19). The beguiling words of false teachers will not be a problem for God's people if they have the "treasures of wisdom and knowledge." Not only does verse 4 express Paul's desire for them (Col. 2:2), it is also the command of God (Col. 3:16). Paul is saying, "know who and what you believe and stick to it." Paul can expect God's people to listen and obey. True believers will turn away from deceivers, for God keeps His own (John 10:3-5).

Colossians 2:5, "For though I be absent in the flesh, yet am I with you in the spirit, joying and beholding your order, and the stedfastness of your faith in Christ."

The words "absent in the flesh," "with you in the spirit" and "beholding" are a curious combination. The word "beholding" is sometimes used for physical sight, as in Matthew 12:22. Sometimes it refers to mental perception or understanding as in Ephesians 5:15. Therefore, the verse states that Paul was physically absent from Colosse, yet in a sense he was with the members of that church and saw evidence of their faith.

How could Paul see the evidence if he was not there? One straightforward answer is that Epaphras told him about the congregation (Col. 1:8). And so, we can understand the word "beholding" to mean Paul saw in his mind. That is, he made a conclusion about their spiritual situation based upon what he heard (I Cor. 5:3, Col. 1:4). Another answer is that, in a unique way, Paul did see their faith. It is not that Paul had a special ability and could actually see them as God did (Matt. 6:4-6), for John 2:24,25 applies to Jesus and not to Paul. Instead, Paul's situation was similar to the time when God gave the prophet Elisha insight about Gehazai's attitude and behavior that Elisha could not have humanly known without special revelation (II Kings 5:25,26). The idea is that Paul's message of approval was a real encouragement to the Colossians because it was backed by the authority of God. His message was, "You're on the right track. I know that because God told me personally. I have joy that each of you have a properly assigned job and persistently work in your own place as part of a team, cooperating to do God's will."

The evidence of their faith, as this verse puts it, is that God gave the Colossians "order" and "steadfastness." They were like a group of soldiers marshaling obediently under the urging of their authoritative leader. Their orderly, faithful behavior reflected upon the authority and work of their commander, that He is not a God of confusion, but a God of order and faithfulness (I Cor. 14:33, Lam. 3:23). In the flow of the logic in the discussion of this chapter, we could say that Paul noticed they were not tossed about with every wind of doctrine but their thinking was ordered by God's Word and they remained faithful to the Lord Jesus, listening only to Him (Eph. 4:14). They had "faith in Christ" and not faith in a man, whether that man was a true of false teacher.

Colossians 2:6, "As ye have therefore received Christ Jesus the Lord, so walk ye in him."

Two important words in this verse are "as" and "so." They help define the Christian walk. Actually, the word "so" is not in the Greek, but is a permissible insertion that properly relates the first part of the verse with the second part. Recognizing that the word "receive" refers to salvation (Rom. 5:11, 15:7), we can express the idea of the whole verse in the following way, "As, or in the same way that, a believer is saved, so he walks."

God does not have two separate plans for a Christian's life, one for his salvation and another for his walk in grace. Instead, God uses the same method to nurture and strengthen Christians in the faith (II Tim. 3:14-17) that He does to save them in the first place (I Peter 1:23). It is as if a Christian's life was described in a book whose first chapter is entitled, <u>Amazing grace working through God's Word</u>. And when we turn to the other chapters, we find that they all have the same title. The idea is that as believers grow in their Christian lives, it is not that they learn more and more new and different doctrines, but that they learn more and more deeper things about the same basic doctrines of grace. God's work of mercy for undeserving sinners is so great that believers are fully occupied in their study of the Bible to understand the depth, height, or breadth of God's one plan of redemption.

The word "walk" *(peripeteite)* can be rendered "walk in a perimeter or circle," like an animal that is tethered to a stake in the ground. It is as if Christians walk around in a circle tied to the stake who is Jesus Himself. He determines their path. This understanding of the word "walk" supports our explanation of Christian maturity, which is that Christians continue to grow as they began, namely by grace through faith, for the word "walk" emphasizes the fact that Christians walk over the same territory, limited by the rope of God's authority.

If we recall that Christians are people who have been transferred from one authority to another (Col. 1:13), we can say that Jesus first unties them from the post of sin and Satan, then ties them to His post, forever. Both the original tethering to Jesus and the ongoing walk around Him reveal the total sovereign work of God. First of all, people cannot untie themselves from the old post anymore than a donkey can use his hoofs to untie himself, nor can they untie anyone else. Secondly, it is a matter of the heart. People tied to the new post or stake do not yearn and mourn for freedom. Once people are tied to Jesus' stake, they never want to be untied again. They abound with "thanksgiving" (Col. 2:7) to be tied to Jesus.

In terms of the problems expressed in this letter, we can say that rather than wander astray due to the attraction of another messenger who offers some new knowledge and wisdom, Christians remain close to Jesus. Their attention and interest remain fixed upon Jesus alone. Jesus is the stake in the ground and believers are tied to Him by a rope of trust and love. They will never wander so far that they will be fettered by false prophets. Not only that, believers rejoice that God tied them to that stake by grace. They are content to walk within the wise limits imposed by God and they find in Jesus sufficient "treasures of wisdom and knowledge" (Col. 2:3). Christians need and desire no one else.

It is true that, as we just learned, Colossians 2:6 is a statement of confinement, in the sense that believers should be busy understanding and obeying the true Gospel of the Lord Jesus rather than search for something more (II Tim. 2:15, 3:14). However, the verse also is a statement of comfort in the sense that believers know that they will never wander too far from the Lord who loves them and who is their only refuge and strength (Col. 1:23).

The point of the verse can be expressed in the following way, "Therefore, ye received Christ rather than any men with enticing words," or "ye received Christ and that was enough; you did not listen to any men with some new words in addition to Christ's words."

Colossians 2:7, "Rooted and built up in him, and stablished in the faith, as ye have been taught, abounding therein with thanksgiving."

This verse explains how people who have "received Christ Jesus the Lord" ought to "walk."

First, the Colossians were taught to walk "rooted and built up in him." How can someone walk if he is rooted? How can he simultaneously be active and stationary? The word "rooted" means to "abide," as it is used in John 15:6. It is a walk rooted in Jesus. The word, "rooted" is a participle, a grammatical form of a verb that refers to what something is, instead of what it does. That is, we could say it is a rooted-kind of walk. Also, the word, "rooted" is in the passive tense, a grammatical construction that refers to an action done, not by the subject of the sentence, but upon the subject of the sentence. That is, the person does not root himself. Instead, he is rooted by an agent outside of himself. So, someone who has "received Christ Jesus the Lord" is someone who walks obediently because God has connected him to Jesus, the source of the power to obey.

The words, "built up" come from a word made of three parts, each which mean, "on top of," "house" and "gift." We could express the parts altogether as, "the gift which remains on top of the house." Also, the word is in the passive tense, which mean the subject is inactive, and is acted upon by an outside agent. We could say, in an awkward way, that the believing Colossians were added upon the house of God as a gift. That is, Jesus decorated or adorned the house of God as He caused them to walk as they should (Isaiah 43:21, I Peter 2:9).

Secondly, Christians are taught to walk, "stablished in the faith, as ye have been taught." The word "stablished" is also used as "confirm" (Heb. 2:3, 6:16) and refers to something made sure by the unalterable force of God's will. The "faith" in view is THE faith. One way to think of it is as the Word of God that defines the faith. Also it is the Word of God through which God creates the faith. The Colossians were "taught" the faith by the Bible and there was no reason to seek some new knowledge or experience. So, the Bible directs their walk.

Paul prayed that the Colossians "might be filled with the knowledge of his will in all wisdom and spiritual understanding; that ye might walk worthy of the Lord" (Col. 1:9,10). That prayer was answered by means of the word of God which was their contact with God's knowledge, wisdom and understanding. A biblical education was the basis for their vital walk. It also kept them from the seduction of others who challenged God's authority.

Thirdly, we learn that Christians walk, "abounding therein with thanksgiving." The word, "thanksgiving," highlights the expected fruit of anyone who is under the authority of God (Col. 1:12, 2:7, 3:15,17, 4:2). It is not just a walk of "thanksgiving," but a walk "abounding with thanksgiving." A person who walks "in him" is impressed by all that God has done for and to him in the past, as well as joyful for all that he is promised in the future. Christians do not long for anything more or covet anything that God has not given them. They are content, because they trust and are satisfied with God Himself. So, "thanksgiving" is a result or product of being "rooted and built up in him and stablished in the faith" as they were taught.

Verses 6 and 7 give the foundation for the proper response to the attacks from rival authorities. The counsel is that there is no need to experiment with any new ideas. The process by which believers were saved, which is trusting in God's Word alone, is the same procedure by which they continue to live faithfully amid false gospels. As God's authority dominates their lives, revealed in their walk of faith, they will be filled with gratitude, joy and satisfaction, rather than restlessly pursue another gospel peddled by someone else.

Colossians 2:8, "Beware lest any man spoil you through philosophy and vain deceit, after the tradition of men, after the rudiments of the world, and not after Christ."

The word "spoil" is used in II Corinthians 11:8 as "robbed." Jesus robbed the dominion of "darkness" when he took His people to His kingdom (Matt. 2:29, Col. 1:13). That was something good. But in Colossians 2:8, the word "spoil" refers to the reversal of that situation, namely the capture of people by unsaved teachers in order to bring them into the dominion of darkness and thereby spoil their "walk."

When we properly understand the salvation of God, we realize that if someone is truly saved, they can never be spoiled (John 10:27-29). Therefore, while this verse is addressed to the congregation as a whole, only the unsaved members are vulnerable to the "philosophy and vain deceit" of the men who seek to spoil anyone in the congregation they can. The whole congregation is warned for at least two purposes. One is to encourage individuals to build up each other in the faith in anticipation of and in preparation to defend against the evil aggression directed toward their fellow members. Another is to motivate every member to examine himself in the light of the doctrinal assaults of false teachers and verify to himself that they are saved.

Wicked men seek to spoil through "philosophy." Philosophy is the love of wisdom. That in itself can be good or bad. It depends upon what wisdom is in view. There is only one true Wisdom (I Cor. 1:30). But in this verse wisdom refers to man's wisdom, the logic and reasoning which is impressive but is based upon man's imagination and leads people away from the true Gospel.

Wicked men also seek to spoil through "vain deceit." That is, the words that false teachers use are empty of true wisdom, and their words are lies intended to lure people away from the truth (II Pet 2:18,19). Their words are empty in the sense that they promise wisdom, power, hope and peace but they have none themselves. Their words are lies in the sense that their words promote the popular, brave and exhilarating idea that people are basically good and captains of their own lives. Their words also are lies in the sense that they appeal to and encourage their listeners' sin, which is the ultimate deceiver (Eph. 4:22 Heb. 3:13).

This verse gives an insight into the "philosophy and vain deceit" false teachers use. It states that their wisdom and lying words are based upon "the tradition of men" and "the rudiments of the world."

The word "tradition" can be good (II Thess. 3:6). It is used in I Corinthians 11:2 as "ordinances," referring to the word of God. The problem is with tradition "of men" (Mark 7:8, I Peter 1:18). Men's traditions are faulty as they are. Yet tradition is an important weapon in the arsenal of false teachers. Tradition is the glue that keeps man-made religions together. People naturally are comforted by habit and familiar ideas. People fear change. These tendencies are exploited by false teachers to maintain their dominion over other people.

The words "rudiments of the world" refers to the objects and phenomenon in the universe that can be seen or sensed physically ("elements" in II Peter 3:10,12), especially those used for religious rituals ("elements" in Galatians 4:9,10, Col. 2:20-22). The elements of the universe are not divine and have no spiritual power within them. But God sometimes uses the rudiments of the world to set up pictures of His promised work of grace, such as the brass serpent which Moses held up on a pole, physical circumcision, water baptism and the communion supper. But men focus upon the pictures of the promises of the Gospel and turn them into objects of devotion (II Kings 18:4). It is to that unholy use of physical elements that Christians have died in Christ and are no longer bound (Gal. 4:9,10, 6:15, Col. 2:20). But it is those rudiments that false teachers use to try to spoil the members of the congregation at Colosse.

In a passage that explains the character and methods of false teachers, this verse gives the second warning. The warning is beware of someone who has a physical focus to their message and ministry. Anyone who emphasizes or insists that certain physical objects or activities are important for a right relationship with God is contradicting the counsel that we are saved by grace through faith and not by works (Eph. 2:8,9), as well as the counsel that after we are saved we walk by faith and not by sight (II Cor. 5:7).

Colossians 2:9,10, "For in him dwelleth all the fulness of the Godhead bodily. And ye are complete in him, which is the head of all principality and power."

These two verses should be looked at together. First of all, we shall present the overall view so that we keep our understanding of the verses clear and so we see how they fit into the logical flow of the whole chapter. Then we shall look at a some of the details.

The point of verse 9 is that in Christ dwells God. This is emphasized by the added word "fulness." That is, in Christ is the complete Godhead. All the wisdom, power and authority that is God's dwells in Christ, even though Christ has a body like all other humans. Therefore, the words of Christ that Paul brought have far more authority than the enticing words of other teachers, who come with their pretended authority. Verse 10 follows with the statement that true Christians are complete in Christ. Jesus Christ provides all the wisdom and power they need. In context of this book the idea is, "if Almighty God is your supply, you have no reason to listen to or follow anyone else. That is, what Jesus Christ has said and done for you is enough for all your needs and true desires (the ones He creates in you), so don't believe anyone else who says to look for more." When we get to them, we will see in verses 11 through 15 how Jesus supplied and continues to supply all of His people's needs.

Verses 9 and 10 are an answer to the old lie that we find back in Genesis 3:5. By using the words, "for God doth know" Satan was implying that God knowingly forbad Adam and Eve to eat something that would be a benefit to them. Satan had just said that eating of the forbidden tree was not fatal, implying that God was lying simply because He did not want them to have its fruit. In other words, Satan's message is that God was depriving them of something unfairly, that God was cheating them. That notion is part of the progress of sin in a person's mind. People who insist upon something that is against God's will justify their indulgence by blaming God for denying them something that they think they have every right to have. Such is the enormity of sinners' rationalizations. The bottom line is that sin is marked by a restlessness for more than what God has provided in His Gospel, an attitude whose foundation is a lack of faith in God's plan and ability.

Now let us look at some of the details of verses 9 and 10. The word "for" directs our attention to what was said before, and alerts us that now we will learn why verse 8 is true. To put it another way, inasmuch as verses 9 and 10 are true, the Colossians are warned to avoid the spiritual appeals that could "spoil" them.

The words "in him ('Christ,' see verse 8) dwelleth all the fulness of the Godhead" is a clear statement that Jesus Christ is God. It is not that the qualities of God are in Christ, in the sense that Christ is God-like. It is not that Christ is replica of God. Rather, Christ is fully God.

The word translated "dwelleth" is composed of a root that is the normal word for dwell plus a prefix that means down, the emphasis being that God lives down in Christ and truly is bound to Christ. God is at home in Christ and continues to be found "in him." We will not spend a lot of time defending the full deity of Christ, but for reference we shall list a few of the verses which show that to be true. Compare Isaiah 42:8 with John 1:14. Compare Isaiah 45:22,23 with Philippians 2:10. Compare Isaiah 45:21 with Luke 2:11. Read John 10:30, 20:28, Titus 1:4 together with Titus 2:10 and 3:6, and Hebrews 1:8. Also notice that His resurrection showed that He is God with all of His authority and power (John 10:17,18, Rom. 1:4, Col. 1:18)

It is upon the word "bodily" which people often stumble. How can a spiritual God and a material body be compatible? Hebrews 2:14 states without apology that "as the children are partakers of flesh and blood, he also himself likewise took part of the same." However limited our understanding may be, the Bible declares that the Word that was God also became flesh (John 1:1-14).

That the Son of God became a human in Jesus Christ gives us hope. First of all, He took upon Himself a human nature so He truly represented us when He paid the penalty demanded for sin, which only a human could pay (Rom. 5:15, 8:3, Heb. 2:14-17, 10:1-10, I Pet. 2:24). Secondly, He will never abandon His humanity (Heb. 7:25). In Christ, humanity has a permanent place in Heaven and so we believers, who are human, can be assured that we also belong in heaven forever (I Thess. 4:17). Thirdly, Jesus who is our brother also is our Creator. He knows us better than we know ourselves and knows what is needed to help us. Yet, as a human, He understands from first-hand experience the problems we face as we struggle to live faithfully for Him on earth (Heb. 2:17,18, 4:15), including the pressure from false messengers who seek to turn us aside from the truth.

Since, according to Romans 8:1 anyone who is "in him (Christ)" is saved, verse 10 is stating that when Christians are saved they are "complete." We can think of the word "complete" in two ways. First of all, in Colossians 1:9 it is translated as "ye might be filled with," as in filling a container to the top. This means that "in him" Christians' are full of God's forgiveness as promised in the scriptures (Psalm 130:4). Once "in him" they experience the full amount of God's care for their souls and have the promise of God's full care for their bodies in the future. Secondly, in Colossians 1:25 it is translated as "to fulfill," as in keeping a promise made previously. This means that "in him" Christians find the full amount of God's wisdom and strength to deal with their sins and temptations, as promised in the scriptures (Isaiah 33:6). Also, "in him" Christians are able to turn completely away from the appeal of false messengers and walk obediently to the Gospel, as promised in the scriptures (Psalm 141:4).

Jesus' authoritative plan and provision for the lives of His people is sufficient. He is able to complete all of their needs. If he can't provide, who can? People who bring a false religion try to create an appetite for a need and then claim they can fill that need. False teacher's tactics are as smooth as a salesman. However, only God knows what His people's true needs are, and only He can fulfill those needs. Therefore, in contrast to false teachers, true teachers simply bring the Christ found in God's Word (I Cor. 2:2, 4:2).

Paul's message to the Colossians was, "You must not look for or expect any thing else than what God has promised in His Gospel. If you claim to be God's people, you must trust that He is able to provide for all your needs as He has promised in His Word." God's people must value His deliverance from the wrath to come and be content with His promise of Heaven. Since Jesus Christ provides the total solution for all of His people's needs, that must be enough for them. They must not yearn for some other or additional experience, philosophy, or material support for their faith or seek to fulfill some artificial, imagined need (II Tim. 1:9, Titus 3:5, Heb. 4:10). No additional mediators are needed to make them complete (I Tim 2:5, Heb. 4:14, 7:25). The best antidote to the appeal of a false gospel is contentment with the true Gospel.

According to verse 10, Jesus Christ is the "head," especially of believers (Eph. 1:22, Col. 2:19). The head controls the body. Also, the head is responsible for recognizing what the body needs and figuring out how to supply those needs. Similarly, Jesus is the head of His family. So he is its final authority as well as responsible to care for every member of that family. As man, Jesus understands the needs of each of His people. As God, He has full wisdom, authority and power to execute His responsibilities to His people. Therefore, Christians run to Jesus if they have a need, rather than to man (Psalm 146:3,4).

Colossians 2:11,12, "In whom also ye are circumcised with the circumcision made without hands, in putting off the body of the sins of the flesh by the circumcision of Christ. Buried with him in baptism, wherein also ye are risen with [him] through the faith of the operation of God, who hath raised him from the dead."

Verses 11 and 12 explain the meaning of the phrase "ye are complete in him." Jesus used all of His power and authority to pay for His people's sins. Based upon His work, the Colossian believers have "complete" forgiveness of all of their trespasses and have "complete" separation from both the power of sin and the influence of false teaching. Verses 11 and 12 describe that completeness in the form of two pictures, one picture is called "circumcision" and the other picture is called "baptism." The two pictures are really one. They are equivalent illustrations of that "complete" forgiveness and separation.

Paul chose the words "circumcision" and "baptism" because he wanted his readers to consider two ceremonies found in the Bible. The ceremonies are pictures God created to help His people understand His atonement and its consequent benefit to their lives. The point of the pictures is that when Jesus made His people just before the Law through His sacrifice, He also earned the legal right to perform a spiritual operation that separated them from the power of their sins.

The words "circumcision" and "baptism" in Colossians 2:11,12 do not refer to the physical rituals but the actual spiritual work of God in a person's life. Nevertheless, the words come from physical ceremonies that were given in the Old Testament for the spiritual edification of God's people. Therefore, we should briefly examine those physical ceremonies in order to properly think about the message they have for the Colossians.

The explanation is complicated by a double meaning of the words "circumcision" and "baptism." In the book of Colossians, they refer to both the spiritual operation of God within Christians that makes a dramatic difference in their lives and His work of atonement that makes that operation possible. Since the book of Colossians is a message to the Colossians about their need to "walk in him," the first meaning is prominent. However, the second meaning, namely the foundation of their "walk," is also in view.

First, let us look at the picture of physical circumcision. Physical circumcision refers to cutting off a piece of skin or flesh. It illustrates the fact that God cuts off or separates a Christian from his sinful flesh. As verse 11 puts it, "ye are circumcised ..... in putting off the body of the sins of the flesh." That does not mean that when a person becomes saved he is separated from his physical body. Rather, it means that his sinful body, with its sinful passions, no longer dominates him. It is as if he were separated from His body that is still infected with sin.

The words "circumcision made without hands" highlight the fact that Christians are separated from their sins without the aid of human hands, without any contribution by men. God alone separates His people from the dominion of their sinful flesh.

The words "circumcision of Christ" could be understood in two ways. In one way, we can think they refer to the fact that the operation of circumcision belongs to Him. It is His to distribute and administer according to His will. Christ designed the operation of circumcision and His "hands" do the work of circumcision in all of His people's lives.

In another way, we can think that the words "circumcision of Christ" refer to the circumcision that Christ personally experienced. From this point of view, circumcision highlights Jesus' personal work of atonement which allowed Him to separate His people from their sins. Two physical features of the ceremony point to Jesus' atonement. One is that the skin cut off in the ceremony of physical circumcision is a male's foreskin. Because it is part of the reproductive organ, the ceremony points to the man's "seed." That is, the ceremony is called the "circumcision of Christ" because it points to Jesus, who was the "seed" cut off. Secondly, the ceremony of physical circumcision cannot take place without the shedding of blood. Therefore, the ceremony is called the "circumcision of Christ" because it points to Jesus, who shed His blood. With all of this in mind, we can think that physical ceremony of circumcision as a picture of Christ, laden with the sins of His people, being cut off in death (Isaiah 53:8). In His death he was cut off from God and from His people. However, the full story is that He also was separated from His people's sins when He left those sins in Hell after He rose from the dead.

With all of this in mind we see that the message of verse 11 is that the "body of the sins of the flesh" are put off "by the circumcision of Christ." That is, the value of Christ's atoning circumcision is that it results in the circumcision or separation of Christians from their sins, or rather, even though they still are beset by sins as long as they are on the earth, they no longer are under the dominion of their sins.

We should add that throughout the Bible, whenever the physical rite of circumcision is mentioned, it is not really the physical rite that is in view. Instead, it is the spiritual work of salvation to which the physical ceremony points (Deut 10:16, 30:6, Jer. 4:4, 6:10, Rom. 2:29, Phil 3:3). It is just that God institutes the physical rite in order to aid our understanding of His spiritual work. In salvation, Christians are separated from the penalty and dominating power of their sin, even though sin continues as an annoyance, over which they must gain victory through their Lord (Rom. 7:18,24,25).

Next, let us look at the picture of water baptism. Physical baptism in the Old Testament refers to the washing of the priests. The priests represented all believers, who must be clean to stand before God and serve Him. Because of the salvation work of Jesus Christ, a believer is clean before God. The idea that baptism, washing and salvation are interchangeable ideas is supported by many verses in the Bible (Psalm 51:7-9, Jer 4:14, Ezek. 36:25-29, Mark 7:4, Luke 11:38, Titus 3:5, I Peter 3:21).

When we say that a Christian is washed clean of his sins, that does not mean that a believer no longer sins while he lives in this world. Rather, when he is saved, God does not see his sin anymore because the penalty required in payment for his sins has been remitted by the sacrifice of Jesus. It is as if his sins have been washed away.

However, there is a part of a Christian where it is not just "as if" his sins were washed away but actually are. Though a Christian's body is infected by sin, his heart is pure, without sin (I John 3:8). That fact is revealed by his desire to please God and obey Him, even though for now, in his body, he stumbles in his Christian walk (I John 1:9).

As with circumcision, the word baptism has a double meaning. It refers to the changes in Christians' lives when they are saved. And it refers to the atoning work of Jesus which makes those changes possible. That is, baptism pictures Jesus as the high priest who Himself had to be baptized in order to represent His people before God. Jesus calls His personal suffering under the wrath of God His baptism, as we read in Mark 10:38,39.

That brings us to the phrase in verse 12, "buried with him in baptism." That strange expression is explained in Romans 6:4 to mean "therefore we are buried with him by baptism into death." In other words, a person's baptism reminds us of his burial, which in turn reminds us of his death. Baptism is a picture of death. That makes sense because we only bury people after they are dead. So we must ask, "What death is in view? Verse 12 states that it is "with him." That is, the death we experience is simultaneous with Christ's death. We can explain this in the following way. In Mark 10:35-40, Jesus equates His "baptism" with His obligation to "drink the cup" of God's wrath. He also states that the disciples, representative of all His people who will be saved, will partake in that baptism. The disciples did not personally drink the cup of God's wrath, but Jesus Christ did it for them. He was their proxy. So they were baptized "with him." Having died with Him, they were then "buried with him."

Whether we think of the ceremony of water baptism from the point of view as a washing or as a death, the message is the same. Baptism is a picture of the fact that when a person is saved, he is separated from his sins, just as physical washing separates him from dirt or death separates him from his body. Again, salvation is not a physical separation, but as we are taught through the picture of circumcision, salvation means his sinful body with its sinful passions no longer dominates him. In addition to that, he is no longer condemned for the sin that is in his body.

The words, "wherein also ye are risen with him" are connected to the picture of baptism as a death. Christians do not remain dead "in him." The moment they are saved, they receive new life, eternal life, His life. It is a life that dominates rather than is dominated by sinful carnal desires.

The words "the operation of God," can be associated with "circumcision" and "baptism" as pictures of the changes within true believers. The idea is that the blessings of new thoughts and new behavior are a result of what God does, for He alone can raise someone "from the dead" and give them new life.

Before we leave these pictures, let us fit them into the general discussion of Colossians 2:4-23. Verses 11 and 12 reveal that Jesus has done everything that is necessary for and to His people, both for eternal life and for a blessed life in this world before He returns. As verse 10 states, believers are "complete" in Jesus. Therefore, the Colossians must not listen to the words of false authorities who seek to tempt them to abandon a faithful walk with God, by means of the lies described in verse 16 and following. God's Gospel alone promises real hope and has real value because God alone has the real power and wisdom to provide all that their hearts and souls need.

Colossians 2:13, "And you, being dead in your sins and the uncircumcision of your flesh, hath he quickened together with him, having forgiven you all trespasses"

Verse 13 turns our attention from the pictures of verses 11 and 12 back to the issue the pictures portray, namely that after God has separated His people from the penalty and power of sin, He gives them a new life. That is, it is possible for Jesus to give His people new life because He first forgave them all their trespasses.

We might think of the word "dead" as a continuation of the idea in the previous verse expressed as "buried with him." But that would be incorrect. In verse 12, the death in view is the death that pays for sin. It is the death Christians experience by sharing Jesus' "baptism." The death in verse 13 is very different. Verse 13 refers to the spiritually dead souls of unbelievers. That death is the condition in which "he," Jesus, finds His people before He applies His atonement to their lives and forgives them. They are dead in their "sins" and in "the uncircumcision" of their flesh. That does not refer to physical circumcision, as if to say, "and you, being Gentiles." Instead it refers to the time when they were not circumcised by God in their hearts (Rom. 2:29), when they were unsaved and dominated by their sins and the desires of their flesh.

The words "having forgiven" are not cheap words. God does not say, "I'll be big-hearted and just forget your past foolishness." The forgiveness is based upon a legal condition, a prerequisite that allows forgiveness. That condition is atonement, a very expensive proposition for God. As we read in Hebrews 9:22, "and without shedding of blood is no remission," in which the word "remission" is the same as the word "forgiven." In order to send our sins away, all of them, past present and future, permanently, He had to do it in a proper way. The demands of the law had to be satisfied. Otherwise, the law could still claim its right to condemn all who are found to have trespassed it. The point of verse 13 is that all the details of Christians' liability before the law has been taken care of. The complete forgiveness of Jesus is a testimony to the completeness of His work of atonement.

We now look at the words, "hath he quickened together with him." Notice that these words come before the words "having forgiven," but in our analysis of this verse, we look at them now. That is, our study does not follow the sequence of the words as they occur in the verse. The reason we consider the words in this order is that the words "hath he quickened" follow the forgiveness of God in His economy of the salvation. That is, forgiveness precedes quickening because forgiveness is the basis for quickening. The atonement provides the legal basis for giving dead people life. And it is not just any life. It is life "with him." That does not mean Christians were raised physically with Jesus about 2000 years ago. Rather, it means when Jesus was raised physically, it guaranteed that the work of the atonement was complete and anticipated all the individuals in the future who would experience the resurrection, both in their souls when they became saved and in their bodies at the end of time.

Being quickened, or made alive, is not a poetic expression. It is very real resurrection, life from death. What is that new life? On one hand, the new life is not an autonomous existence, for Christians do not live independent lives from God or each other. The Bible states that Christians have Jesus' own eternal, holy life in them (Gal. 2:20). That is, they live by means of His power, motivated by His desires and objectives. On the other hand, the new life does not remove their individuality. People who are saved do not melt into God somehow and lose their unique God-created personality. Christians are completely distinct from God and yet they are completely dependent and identified with Him, much like two married people have their own identity while they are in union with each other.

Colossians 2:14, "Blotting out the handwriting of ordinances that was against us, which was contrary to us, and took it out of the way, nailing it to his cross"

This verse explains more about Jesus' work upon which forgiveness of sinners is based and ultimately upon which Christians' new life is based.

The words "blotting out the handwriting of ordinances" can be pictured by someone using a rag to wipe off words on a slate or using an erasure to rub out words on a piece of paper ("blotting out" = "shall wipe away," Rev. 7:17). But the words blotted out are special words. They are words of a king, as the word "ordinances" is used (as in a decree from or of Caesar in Luke 2:1 and Acts 17:7), words written by a king's own hand. In this case, the words are God's handwriting, His Law (Ex. 32:16). That does not mean that God's Law was wiped out and no longer exists. The Law said that the wages of sin is death and that law still applies. But the Law no longer comes down upon saved sinners to condemned them for their sin. The Law is no longer their adversary. As far as saved sinners are concerned, because of Jesus' death, the condemnation of the Law was taken far "out of the way," as if it did not exist.

The words "nailing it to his cross" are a straightforward reference to Jesus sacrificial death, as advertised on the cross. It was a special death, a cursed death (Gal. 3:13), because that was the demand of the "handwriting of ordinances" for sin. The complete demands of the Law were met for all Christians, past present and future. The Colossians' new life is secure, never in doubt and in need of no augmentation or adjustment, despite the claims of false teachers who try to "spoil" them.

Incidentally, because of a persistent false teaching about Judgment Day, it is appropriate to emphasize an idea that comes out of this verse. The false teaching is that Christians' thoughts and conduct will be reviewed on Judgment day, for the equitable distribution of rewards. However, Judgment Day is a time when the "handwriting of ordinances" will be used as the standard of evaluation. But they do not apply to Christians, so no review is possible. Anyone who is subject to the jurisdiction of those ordinances will receive only one verdict, guilty, and one sentence, a cursed death, the same as Jesus had to endure.

Colossians 2:15, "And having spoiled principalities and powers, he made a shew of them openly, triumphing over them in it."

The word translated "having spoiled" conveys the idea of stripping as in removing clothing. The word is used in Colossians 3:9 as "have put off."

The words "principalities and powers" are neutral terms that can refer to secular authorities to which Christians must submit (Titus 3:1) or demonic influences with which they wrestle (Eph. 6:12). Clearly, they are Jesus' opponents whom He "spoiled," and therefore must refer to Satan and his host. This verse states that, in addition to removing the condemnation of the Law, Jesus removed the claims of Satan upon His people.

How did Jesus do that? The verse states Jesus "made a shew of them openly." The idea is that Jesus completely exposed Satan in the sense that Satan's wicked, rebellious objectives and his evil, devious methods were on display for all to see. We should add that the word "openly" means "confidently" or "boldly," as the word is used in Acts 4:31 ("boldness") and Acts 28:31 ("confidence"). The idea is that God is in complete control as a successful Savior and Conqueror over Satan, and He knows it. The cross is the final victorious statement of a sovereign God who has supreme authority over all creation to judge all His enemies and to save all His people.

The verse also states that Jesus triumphed "over them in it." The word "it" refers to "the cross," or rather, His atoning death which the cross advertised. The word "triumphing" is used only here and in II Corinthians 2:14 as "which causeth us to triumph," to refer to Jesus' victory over Satan (II Cor. 2:11). From that point of view, Jesus completely exposed Satan in the sense that Satan was vulnerable to Jesus' wrath.

We should mention that the confrontation and conflict between Jesus and Satan was necessary because Satan had the right by virtue of conquest to rule over Adam who foolishly heeded his tempting call. Satan now rules over all unsaved men. But God came to reclaim His elect for Himself. Man in Adam submitted his will to Satan in Eden. God came, in Jesus, to release men from their enslavement to Satan and make them His subjects (Heb. 2:14, John 12:31, Luke 10:18, Rev. 12:8, 12, 20:2). Like the claims of the victor in battle, Jesus "spoiled" the camp of the enemy by taking His people home. God's people are under His new authority (Isa. 26:13,14).

In addition, the principalities and powers had dominion over His people before they were saved in the sense that His people were under the power of their own sinful flesh, and Satan could control them through his appeal to their flesh as well as their fear of God. When Jesus removed the penalty and power of sin in the lives of His people, Jesus broke Satan's control and released them (Matt. 12:29, Col. 1:13, Heb. 2:14, Rev. 20:2).

Colossians 2:16, "Let no man therefore judge you in meat, or in drink, or in respect of an holyday, or of the new moon, or of the sabbath [days]:"

If it is true that Jesus has done those things described in chapter 2, verses 9 through 15, the Colossians must "let no man therefore judge" them. Chapter 2, verses 16 through 23, explain the motives and methods rival, false authorities use to "judge." The verses also explain the weakness of their message.

God gives power and wisdom to all His children who ask and even to those who do not ask or ask amiss. But they are not marionettes. Christians are commanded to "**let** no man therefore judge you." Sometimes they foolishly ignore the warning to their sorrow. Many times they heed it to their benefit. The blessing is that Christians are kept from the worst damage that their own foolishness and the false shepherds can inflict. And when they do stray, they are eventually restored by grace to a more faithful walk.

The words "let judge" are translated from a word that often is used as "judge," with the verdict of condemnation in view. For example, it is used as "might be damned" in II Thessalonians 2:12 to describe the judgment of God against sin in Romans 2:12, and 16. Colossians 2:16 highlights a common method false teachers use to control other people. They blame and condemn people for not following the religious rules they promote, claiming that such disobedience jeopardizes their relationship with God.

The words "meat and drink" refer to the laws in the Old Testament, such as those laws found in Leviticus 11 concerning the "meat" of clean animal that the Jews could eat and the "meat" of unclean animals that they could not, as well as laws about the "drink" that comes in contact with unclean animals (Lev. 11:34). There were other laws too. The words "holy days," "new moons" and "sabbath days," including the 7th day Sabbath, refer to the laws concerning proper worship of God (Lev. 23:3, I Chron 23:31, Psalm 81:3,4). These are the physical rituals that were part of the Old Testament. These laws were pictures of the Gospel to be fulfilled in Jesus Christ. The real danger is to trust, for righteousness, in keeping these laws instead of trusting in the Savior to whom they pointed and anticipated (Gal. 2:16, 3:2,10,11, note Gal. 4:9,10). It is true that a weekly Sabbath day continues, but now as a 1st day Sabbath that points to, among other things, Jesus' resurrection on Sunday that completed His work of atonement (Matt. 28:1-6).

In a passage that explains the character and methods of false teachers, this verse gives the third warning. The warning is that often those who bring a false gospel, because they do not have authority over men or have the power to cause men to comply to their demands, must be forceful. We must beware of anyone who operates by means of accusations and intimidations. It is all a scare tactic, calculated to have an influence and control over other people. But only weak people, people who do not trust in the completeness of salvation found in Jesus, are impressed by the threatening bluffs of those bullies and are susceptible to their deception. It is not that false teachers personally threaten other people, although that is sometimes the case, rather the threat can be expressed as, "if you don't obey what I say, then you are in big trouble with God."

Human authorities, which rival God's authority, condemn all those who do not follow their ways. External rules, such as those listed in verses 16-23, are vital to rival authorities. They use rules to try to control their followers. But external rules have no power in taking care of the demands of the flesh in an honorable way (verse 23). That is evident in the sinful life of themselves and their followers.

In contrast to that is the gentle persuasion of the faithful teachers of the Gospel (II Tim. 2:24-26). They are motivated out of concern for the souls of others (II Cor. 5:10) rather than their own advancement or reputation. They are sustained by a confidence that it is God's Gospel. He invented and He will see to its distribution and effect. All they must do is trust and obey Him.

Colossians 2:17, "Which are a shadow of things to come; but the body [is] of Christ."

A shadow is not the real object. A shadow is only a vague silhouette of the object that casts it. In this verse, the object in view which casts the shadow is Christ Himself. He is the fulness of the shadow.

The "holyday(s)," "new moon" and the "sabbath(s)" refer to the laws in the Old Testament that are the shadows of Christ. They give a vague picture of Christ, but they are not Christ Himself. Christ is the complete "object," in a manner of speaking, to which the law points (Romans 10:4).

Jesus says, "I have taken care of the demands of the law and the ceremonies point to me." The rivals say, "you can take care of the demands of the law yourself and the ceremonies show you how to do it." The crazy thing about all of this conflict is that the law and the ceremonies were established by God Himself. The challenge to God' authority is in the name of God! How insane!

Colossians 2:18, "Let no man beguile you of your reward in a voluntary humility and worshipping of angels, intruding into those

things which he hath not seen, vainly puffed up by his fleshly mind."

The word "beguile" is not a translation of the same word found in Colossians 2:4. In fact, all five words "let ... beguile ... of your reward" are a translation of one word in Greek, composed of a prefix *kata*, meaning "down," and a root, whose form here is *brabeutoo* and is translated "rule" in Colossians 3:15, as an umpire would in a sports contest or a judge in a court room. The idea of the warning in Colossians 2:18 is "don't let any man judge you or have authority over you, deciding if you are right with God by measuring your performance against his own standards."

The word "voluntary" is the common word used as "willing." It is found in Colossians 1:27 and 2:1 as "would" to mean "want to" or "according to the will of." So the words "in voluntary humility" point out that the humility of false teachers is self-motivated. It is not a fruit of the Holy Spirit. In the context of verse 16, the idea is that a man sets himself up as a judge, motivated by his pride of self-righteousness and uses the law as his criteria for judging others while at the same time he wears the outward cloak of false self-willed humility.

The phrase "worshiping of angels" refers to the worship of the messengers who bring the message, worship of man rather than God. It is a problem that troubled the Corinthian church then (I Cor. 1:11,12) and plagues churches or ministries today. The phrase does not refer to some kind of bizarre cult of worship of spiritual beings, even though that kind of perversion has been part of the history of man. Rather it is a worship of men who give the appearance of being a wise teacher but who are blind leaders of the blind.

In a passage that explains the character and methods of false teachers, this verse gives the fourth warning. The warning is that we must beware of any ministry or message in which a single man is prominent. Even if Jesus is praised and all the right doctrine is taught, one man must never be the focus of or dominate a faithful Gospel ministry, for it leads people to honor that "angel," or messenger, rather than to honor the One who sent that messenger.

The words "intruding into" come from a word that is used only here but is composed of the prefix meaning "in" and the root derived from the word "feet." Also, contrary to what is sometimes taught, the word "not" belongs in the passage because it is part of the original Greek text (Textus Receptus). The idea is that the false teachers have entered into the subject of the law, something of which they have no knowledge or experience. Their threats are an ignorant bluff, which if challenged by the truth, would dissipate like a mist in the morning sun. In fact, their threats are a self-deception. They think they see but they are blind, as we read in John 9:41. What they see is an imaginary idea of the law, a shadow of the law that causes them to be "vainly puffed up" by their "fleshly mind." Their teaching of the law is vain because it inflates their view of themselves and because it is empty of wisdom.

According to Matthew 16:17, flesh and blood do not reveal God's truth, so what false teachers say is not of God but out of their own head. Also, since what they say is a product of their own imagination and work, they are proud of it. Pride is the root of their desire to have the acclaim of followers and the desire for power over men. False teachers are self-deluded. They do not have real authority. Yet what they say it is cleverly designed to successfully catch foolish men.

Colossians 2:19, "And not holding the Head, from which all the body by joints and bands having nourishment ministered, and knit together, increaseth with the increase of God."

The word "holding" is a participle. That is, it is verb that acts like an adjective that describes the subject. We could say the false teachers were "not-head-holding" kind of people. It was their nature to not hold the head, which refers to Christ. The word "holding" also is a cousin to the word translated "strength" or "dominion." Altogether we can think of the words "and not holding the head" to mean the false teachers who came to the Colossians did not have God's power to hold on to Christ. They are not a true branch, which abides on the vine by the power of God. Their weakness was evidence that they were not true messengers, for God nourishes and increases the life that He gives to all of His people.

We could express Paul's message as, "the men who try to beguile you are false teachers who have no power from God. They have no power over Christians because their power is human and weak. Nor do they understand half of what they talk about. So, don't pay any attention to their huffing and puffing. What they say is not based on fact or the spiritual experience of salvation. They come in their own authority, and not Christ's."

Colossians 2:20,21, "Wherefore if ye be dead with Christ from the rudiments of the world, why, as though living in the world, are ye subject to ordinances, Touch not; taste not; handle not."

The words "wherefore if ye be dead" remind us that believers died with Christ. Like a dead man who no longer is subject to the laws of the land in which he lived, Christians no longer are subject to the demands of the law of God, from the perspective that they do not have to obey the law in order to be right with God.

The "rudiments of the world" are the physical elements of the world (II Peter 3:10,12), which people can "touch," "taste" and "handle." Here the focus is upon the laws of God that use physical objects as pictures of the greater spiritual realities, for example, laws about meat and drink that pictured the Gospel. We can apply the same idea to today's laws about water baptism and the communion supper.

The words "are ... subject to ordinances" are a translation of one word that is in the middle voice, a grammatical construction that refers to a reflexive action. That is, Paul learned that the readers, as they were "living in the (physical) world," were putting themselves under the bondage to the laws concerning physical rites and ceremonies. That is surprising, inasmuch as we read that they had a reputation for living by faith (Col. 1:4).

We can understand the comment, "why ..... are ye subject to ordinances," which questions their behavior, when we think of it in combination with the conditional statement "if ye be dead with Christ." The idea is that Paul's words are addressed to people who are "dead with Christ from the rudiments of the world" and they are just being temporarily foolish. That is, Paul does not say to them what He said to the Galatian congregation, "I am afraid of you, lest I have bestowed upon you labour in vain" (Gal. 4:11) because, although some of the Colossians were showing a weakness, the congregation was still quite faithful. The true believers in the Colossian congregation were not actually subject to ordinances as if they trusted in them for their own righteousness, as unsaved people do. Instead, they had experienced a momentary lapse or a dangerous leaning which required the authoritative words of Paul to correct before too much damage was done. The false teachers were beginning to have an influence in their lives and that had to be stopped.

Colossians 2:22, "Which all are to perish with the using; after the commandments and doctrines of men?"

The "commandments and doctrines of men" refer to the "ordinances" of God, instead of some laws that men have made up.

However, they are the ordinances of God that men misapply. The false teachers were bringing the ordinances of God but their explanation, interpretation and application were "the commandments and doctrines of men." These men taught that God's Laws must be obeyed in all their physical dimensions in order to be right with God.

To properly understand this verse we should remember that at one time God expected unswerving outward compliance to His "ordinances." The commands to "touch not," "taste not" and "handle not" had to be strictly obeyed. But those "ordinances" were a "shadow of things to come." When Jesus finally did "come," He "blotted out the handwriting of ordinances." For, by "nailing it to the cross," He took the condemnation for His people's disobedience "out of the way" and He completely fulfilled the terms of the ordinances so that His people no longer have the obligation to adhere to the ordinances' physical obligations to be right with God. The physical objects that were instructional props pointing to greater spiritual realities could be abandoned. The ordinances are not essential for salvation. They are dispensable shadows of salvation.

Verse 22 adds the observation that the physical objects of which the "ordinances" speak are "all subject to perish with the using." The word "perish" is not the same as we read in John 3:16, referring to the judgment of God. It is a word that is translated in Romans 8:21 as "corruption," referring to the effects of God's curse upon this world as an answer to man's sin. Therefore the physical objects mentioned in God's laws are perishable because they are part of a cursed world. They will be destroyed along with the physical world at the end of time. That means the objects in the "ordinances," the objects upon which the false teachers focussed, had no power in themselves and indeed would someday vanish.

The question that ends with verse 22 began with verse 20. If we put the whole question together we can rephrase it in this simple way, "Why are you submitting yourself to those physical ordinances that are subject to the curse of God and to the coming destruction of the world? How dumb, how sorrowful, if you claim to be saved, to submit yourselves to something that has less power over sinful flesh than you have in Christ and to something you will outlast."

Unsaved people live in a world that is perishing. Yet, unsaved people have a natural propensity to seek something in the physical world to protect them from the corruption and death they fear (Heb. 2:15). False teachers take advantage of that tendency by claiming that obedience to the physical rules that God originally ordained is necessary to be right with Him. However, any plan of salvation that includes observance of physical rules sustains the bitter fear of God, not the fear that leads to wisdom, but the dread of God that drives people to hide or cover themselves by means of their own efforts.

People who insist upon or focus upon anything physical in a Christian walk demonstrate a serious spiritual problem in their lives. We should beware of anyone who makes a big deal about anything physical in the Christian life.

Colossians 2:23, "Which things have indeed a shew of wisdom in will worship, and humility, and neglecting of the body; not in any honour to the satisfying of the flesh."

The "things" which have a "shew of wisdom" are the physical rites, ceremonies and rules found in God's ordinances, but from the point of view that people pervert them into obligations for righteousness. The word "shew" really means "word," as it is used in Colossians 1:5. That is, the good things of God are distorted into "the commandments and doctrines of men," and have a apparent word of wisdom.

People use God's ordinances together with their own "enticing words" (Col. 2:6) and "philosophy and vain deceit" to present an apparently wise path to God. And yet, all their words are only "will worship" meaning worship designed and motivated by their own will rather than God's. People are good at affecting an appearance of piety, especially in the words they use, but without a heart that trusts and seeks to obey the Lord. For example, the words of people promote a false "humility" that looks gentle and submissive but really is prideful submission to their own rules and a faithless denial of God's finished salvation work in Jesus. Also, their words are focussed upon "neglecting the body." This does refer to people's self-denial of sinful physical desires in an attempt to be faithful to God in response to His grace but to people's self-denial of some physical desires in order to please God by their own actions or impress and gain the confidence of men.

The words "not in any honour to the satisfying of the flesh" tell us any plan that insists upon obedience to physical rules soon reveals its lack of wisdom and power. There are many desires of the flesh that are legitimate, created by God Himself. But there is only one way to honorably fill those desires. For example, God creates human sexual desire, but false teachers have no power to prevent its perversion in their own lives or their hearers'. The idea is that false teachers emphasize the importance of obeying physical rules and promise peace and liberty but their own dishonorable lives in the flesh reveals their weakness and slavery to their licentious desires (II Peter 2:19).

In a passage that explains the character and methods of false teachers, this verse gives the fifth warning. The warning is that, as Jesus taught in Matthew 7:15-20, false and deceitful prophets are identified by their evil fruit, and the evil fruit of people who follow them.

Verse 23 brings another idea to mind. People see the world perishing and are afraid. False teachers make use of unsaved people's natural trust in the elements of this physical world to allay their fear of death (Heb. 2:15) by claiming that physical rules are essential for being right with God. However, any message that is worldly and physical sustains that bitter fear, not the fear of God that is the beginning of wisdom but the dread of God that drives people to hide or cover themselves by their own efforts. A barometer of the truth of a message, a one litmus test, is to ask, "does the message promote that unholy kind of fear or does it encourage a fear that leads to submission to the Gospel of sovereign grace?"

Additional notes related to Chapter 5

Colossians 2:4-22

Additional notes for Colossians 2:6, **"As ye have therefore received Christ Jesus the Lord, so walk ye in him."**

This verse helps us understand true Christian growth and maturity. There is a commonly held but wrong perception of Christian maturity that is dismissed and corrected by this verse. The wrong attitude can be expressed in the following way: "Oh yes, the basic doctrines of salvation are great, but we cannot always stay with the milk. The mature Christian should go on to the meat or the deeper things of the Lord."

When people make distinctions between different doctrines and decide some are more important that others, they have a very wrong view of Christian maturity. For example, some people isolate the doctrine of the return of the Lord and called it one of the deep things, the meat of the Bible in contrast to what they say is the milk of the basic doctrines of salvation, as if the ideas of trust and repentance are reserved for baby Christians. Often, their view of the return of the Lord is quite complex and involved. It is deep only in an artificial or man-made way, in a wrong way.

It is true that the doctrine of the return of the Lord is deep, as all doctrines are. But it is deep because it comes from the deep, unfathomable mind of God. However, it is not as complex as many describe it. As it turns out, the doctrine of the return of the Lord can be expressed in the following simple way, "Jesus came the first time to save all His people out of all nations and will come the second time, at the end of the world, to judge all unbelievers and gather all His people to be with Him forever in the new heaven and earth." It is no more complex or mature than the doctrine of redemption, which states, "Believe on the Lord Jesus, and you will be saved." The distinction made between doctrines, that some are for new Christians and others are for older, more mature Christians, is wrong and leads to serious errors in understanding the Bible.

As it turns out, all doctrines are tied together. When we properly understand one doctrine, we will have the foundation for properly understanding another. Conversely, incorrect understanding of one leads to error in understanding another. That is the value of the principle found in verse 6. It isn't that a Christian learns more and more deep doctrines as he matures, but that he learns more and more deep things about the same basic doctrines. A mature Christian understands the same doctrines he understood early in his faith, but he understands them better and with far more conviction. He sees how the basic doctrines are found throughout all of the Bible and how they tie together.

Additional notes for Colossians 2:9, **"For in him dwelleth all the fulness of the Godhead bodily."**

When the Bible states that in Christ dwells the Godhead "bodily," it does not mean that God and man are mixed up somehow as in a soup. It does not mean that God and man are separate, as two different people in one shell. It does not mean the Son of God reduced His divine nature or attributes when Jesus was conceived and born of Mary. Rather, in Christ, God and man are distinct but united, connected in a mysterious way that is not possible for us to really understand.

Nevertheless, the Son did become flesh and dwell among people. It is an historical fact of which we can't help having some thoughts. In order to avoid vague and careless ideas about the incarnation, we offer the following weak but accurate and serviceable analogy. Hopefully it will point us in the right direction. Consider a room added to a house. The new room is distinct from the house that was already there. But the whole structure is all part of one house. The pre-existing structure is not affected by the addition, and yet the whole house in no longer the same, for the new room is part of the house. Similarly, in the incarnation, the Son added or attached to Himself a human nature. The Son is now God-man even though the human part did not change the divine part.

In many ways the incarnation is beyond our limited human mind to fully grasp. And yet, there are some things about it we can and should point out. First, the incarnation is a display of the Son's authority, for it is His voluntary, personal will that keeps His divine and human parts together (Phil. 2:7). Second, the incarnation is an unbreakable attachment or union because it is a fulfillment of God's promise (Heb. 10:5-7). Third, rather than a display of weakness, Jesus' confinement in a body shows that God has the wisdom, ability, power, and right to be a Savior (Heb. 2:14-18).

The reason God attached to Himself humanity was to do what is human, that is, die for sin as a human. The Son of God did not become man-like. He became fully man. Jesus did not just look like a man. He really became a specific human like all other humans. He is part of the human race that can trace His lineage from Adam. He was unlike Adam in that he did not share in the condemnation before the law or the curse of God due to His own sins, but He was fully human and therefore a fit candidate to be the Savior of men (Matt. 1:23, Gal. 4:4, I John 1:1-3).

We also should add that we must not say too much about the fact that Jesus died in His body. We cannot say that God died, although the Bible does say that Christ died (I Cor. 15:3). For one thing God cannot die because He is eternal. But more pertinent is the fact that God's death would not be a satisfactory atonement. The law is uncompromisingly fair. Man sinned and man, and only man, must pay for sin. That is the way in which we must think of the death of the man, Jesus. It is true that the Son is God Himself and we must focus upon the total person and not try to dissect Him like some laboratory specimen. But, when we think of the wounds that He bore for His people, it is like we hurt the hand and so we hurt the person whose hand it is. In other words, Jesus Christ is the perfect man and so He is the worthy sacrifice to bear the sins of many (Phil. 2:8, Heb. 2:10-18).

Additional notes for Colossians 1:16, **"the sabbath (days)"**

According to this verse, the Old Testament Saturday Sabbath is included in the list of the "ordinances" or ceremonial laws. Therefore, it is not to be observed today. If we observe it in an attempt to be obedient to God, then we put ourselves under the law and are cursed (Gal. 3:10).

Additional notes for Colossians 1:17, **"which are a shadow of things to come; but the body is of Christ."**

One fascinating aspect about this universe is that God uses physical things as tools to lead people to spiritual truth. But the physical world into which God has placed us, the physical things that surround us and adorn our lives can be either a blessing and a curse. The physical world and all that is in it can illustrate the truth (Matt. 6:26-29). But it also can hide the truth, even be a barrier to finding the truth (Isa. 44:9-17). Physical things can be a guide to show us life or a trap to seal us in death. One dramatic example of this is a shadow.

All material things cast a shadow in the presence of light because they are part of the physical creation. In the presence of light all objects cast a shadow. A shadow reveals something of an object that casts it. For one thing, it reveals that the object is material, part of the created universe. For another thing, a shadow shows something of the object's outward form. A shadow is somewhat faithful to the shape of an object. For example, a shadow of a tree is not the same as the shadow of a bicycle. It is not the same a shadow of you.

But, a shadow is a thin dark shape that tells only a few things about the object. The object and not the shadow has three dimensional size and weight. In addition to that, a shadow is a very weak thing. It depends upon the light and the object. The object and the light do not depend upon it. It is not just that a shadow disappears on a cloudy day, while the object remains. But it is that the shadow is not the object itself.

In Hebrews 10:1 we read, "For the law having a shadow of good things to come, and not the very image of the things, can never with those sacrifices which they offered year by year continually make the comers thereunto perfect." According to this, the shadow we find in the Bible refers to the law. The law is a shadow, a silhouette of "good things." According to Romans 10:15, the good things are the Gospel. Hebrews 10:1, like Colossians 1:17, says the good things are "to come." This does not mean they are not yet here and only in our future. It means, the good things come after they have been promised in the Old Testament. The law is a shadow that takes the faithful shape of the true Gospel. That is, it isn't the shadow of a false gospel. However, the law is not the Gospel itself. It is only a shadow. We must also keep in mind that a shadow, like its physical counterpart, is a weak picture of the real thing.

Since the law is a shadow of the Gospel, let us be sure we understand what the law is. The law expresses the will of God. In the law we see the thoughts and intentions of God's mind and heart. The law contains the promise for both good and for bad. The law does not contain the actual good and bad things. Instead, it contains the threat of death and judgment - that is bad. It says "obey and live. Disobey and die." And the law contains the promise of eternal life - that is good. It says, "seek the grace and mercy of God in Jesus alone and live."

If we try to be "good boys and girls" and seek to please God by our own efforts to obey the law, we have a wrong view of the law. If we try to be "better" then we have been and try to make up the difference in our past behavior, we have a wrong view of the law. The law is only a shadow. The law provides no comfort for our sad and lonely souls.

It only points out our frightful sinful situation, that we are sinners and God is angry with sinners. The law is a shadow that provides no protection from the blast of God's wrath. It only reminds us of our sin. The law provides no warmth of forgiving love for our hearts and souls. It is our accuser. The law does point us to the real comforter and His spiritual blessings. But the law is only a shadow, a promise of all those good things. Also, it is a threat for all who see the shadow of the Gospel and who do not seek the blessing of the Gospel that casts the shadow, but who hope in the shadow itself.

Therefore, the law is the shadow of the true Gospel. It is a dark but faithful picture of the Gospel. Also it is weak, like the shadow of a sword that cannot kill or the shadow of the cross that cannot save. Only God Himself can kill and make alive. We do not fear the law, we fear the God whose shadow it is. We do not seek salvation from the law, we seek salvation from heavenly things, whose shadow it is.

The lesson of Colossians is: Beware of the shadows if you think that is all you need for your protection and comfort. The Colossians were warned not to put their trust in the shadowy Old Testament ceremonies. Today, we would say physical things like water baptism, communion or the Lord's Supper, physical circumcision, and any other physical phenomena must not be our spiritual comfort and hope.

Colossians 2:17 states, "but the body is of Christ." The body which casts the shadow is Christ. Now, God is a Spirit and so does not cast a shadow. But when He was on earth Jesus Christ cast a shadow on a sunny day. The message here is that, in Jesus, the Son entered into His creation. He attached to Himself a human part, to do what only a human could do, namely die for the sins that humans committed. The Son of God was born of a woman and His name was called Jesus because He was the Savior of His people. The fact that Jesus cast a shadow demonstrates that He became part of the created, human race. That is a revelation of the amazing condescending, self-sacrificing saving love and grace of God. Immanuel is God with us, who willingly became a man, part of the created world, a man who cast a shadow like we do, especially who on a sunny day cast a shadow on Mount Calvary.

Before we leave this, we should understand that from the Bible's point of view, a shadow is not darkness. A shadow is a dim picture of the whole Gospel of God. But darkness refers to the judgment of God (Matt. 8:12, II Peter 2:4). In Psalm 107:10 we read, "Such as sit in darkness and in the shadow of death, being bound in affliction and iron." Notice both "darkness" and "the shadow of death." But a shadow is not the same as darkness. A shadow is cast only as long as the light still shines. Darkness means that there is no light. Darkness, the outer darkness of eternal condemnation and rejection by God is a hopeless situation. It is true that Jesus finds His people in darkness. But that means they are headed for eternal wrath, and pain and sorrow. But they have not been actually cast into the punishment of darkness because Judgment Day has not yet come. They have been rescued out of darkness (I Peter 2:9). In addition, there is the present darkness of foolish, sinful unbelief which engulfs the minds and hearts of unsaved sinners. So in Romans 13:12 we read, "let us cast off the works of darkness" (Prov. 4:19).

The law is the shadow of the whole Gospel, not just the threat of darkness, but also the promise of light. Happily, we read in Psalm 17:18, "shadow of thy wings" in Psalm 36:7, "shadow of thy wings" and in Psalm 91:1, "shadow of the Almighty." Jesus is the body that cast the shadow of comfort and hope. Today there is still hope. Today is a time for the shadows of the whole Gospel, both of the warning of judgment and the promise of forgiveness in Jesus. Today is not the darkness of God's wrath. That real threat, of eternal death, is only a shadow now. We have time today to look to the Gospel that casts a shadow of salvation and find Jesus.

Additional notes for Colossians 2:23, **"a shew of wisdom."**

In the main part of this study, we mentioned that the word "shew" is the word for logic or word. So, we can say that this phrase in verse 22 relates to the wisdom of men expressed through the words they say or write.

The contrast between God's wisdom and man's wisdom is dramatically illustrated by how unsaved people answer the question, "Why is there evil in the world?" If man does not have true knowledge, then he has a wrong view of the universe in which he lives and is unable to answer this question. He must, instead, resort to human "philosophy and vain deceit." Without Christ, man cannot reconcile the existence of evil in the same universe with God. If the Creator is perfect and powerful, man cannot explain why God allows evil to exist. Man asks, "Why doesn't God intervene (that is, why doesn't God intervene in the way I want Him to)?" And so men imagine their own answers

One answer of men is that the physical universe is evil or that God is evil. This is the basis for the worship of the occult. The idea is that the world is under the control of one or many god's who must be tricked or appeased lest they bring disaster. Or the idea is that evil gods compete with good gods and people are caught in the middle of the conflict, suffering innocently as a by-product.

Another answer is that after God made everything, the universe was left to itself and God either will not or cannot intervene. The material world continues independent of God with a life of its own. Or God is part of the material world with limited influence or an influence dependent upon the actions of men. Or God is a non-personal and non-rational force that must be tolerated and to which people must be resigned.

Another idea is that there is no God, that the material world is all that there is. Things are just what they are, morally neutral without an dimension of good or evil. The idea of God and evil are human inventions. There are no absolute truths and no supreme authority. Whatever happens and what any one does is morally neutral. So anyone can do what they want without thinking that it is bad. We also can describe this idea as an attempt to put God into a box in order to make Him safe and manageable . Unsaved people want a god who is small and weak enough to be controlled. They do not want any competition for authority over their lives. Any philosophy or religion they propose is designed to satisfy their own material and intellectual desires, to justify their own their cherished lifestyles, and to preserve their own egos. They are in love with the notion that what happens in their lives in totally up to themselves.

All these ideas are bankrupt. All these philosophies are only "a shew of wisdom," and nothing more.

The Bible has another view. It says the material universe is under a curse. Something is wrong. The universe was originally created good by a personal God. The Bible teaches sin is the root of all problems and is an intrusion into a world created "very good" (Gen. 1:31). The problem isn't in the material universe. The problem is sin, human rebellion against God's authority and God's required curse in answer to that sin.

If we deny the fact of God's personal authority over the universe, then we are left with the scenario that the evil in the universe is normal, part of the basic design or structure of the universe. We are left with an existence in which God is absent, the world is a machine without any purpose, cruelty is OK and there are no answers to our questions. Essentially, madness prevails. But since that is not true, since God has designed the fabric and function of the universe according to His will, people must live a schizophrenic life in which they deny absolutes like truth and love but live like those absolutes are real in order to function and fulfill their own needs. But only the Bible is honest and offers real hope..

Maybe we can understand the difference between men's view and the Bible's answer to the problem of evil by means of the following comparison. What do you do with a broken watch that you need to use? You try to fix it. However, unbelievers do not think the universe is broken. For them, the corruption of the universe is the way things are supposed to be. The question of a curse makes no sense to them. Therefore there is no hope for anything to be different. But God says the universe is broken and that He will repair it in Jesus, in the sense that he will create a new life in each of His people as well as create a new heaven and new earth.

The fact is matter isn't evil. It isn't even indifferent. It is inert, lifeless. The problem is man himself. Man gets the blame for the evil in the universe, even though God gets the credit for the curse. Man is blamed for his deliberate, hateful, insulting, spiritual rebellion. Sin and evil are all man's fault alone and came into God's perfect universe through man (Rom. 5:12). The big truth is that God does care, and He is able to plan and do what is necessary to overcome evil. He has done what is necessary to rescue men from evil.

Man does not want to face the real root problem or the solution required. For one thing, man loves this material world. Man despairs at its demise and cannot bear to think that it will be all put away. Secondly, man loves his sinful ways. Man cannot bear to think he is the cause of the problem and must change his ways as well as be held accountable for his thoughts and actions. So, when the Bible brings its message, man seeks a hiding place: in work, in entertainment and sports, in family, in education and academic, in drugs, in religion, in anything that will drown out the Bible's message and help him forget the truth about himself.

Chapter 6

Colossians 3:1-25

Colossians 2 warns Christians about spiritual dangers that assault a Christian from without, especially dangers of false teachers. Chapter 3 counsels Christians about spiritual dangers from within, dangers from the sinful desires of their own bodies. We could think of Chapter 3 as a program for successfully dealing with those inward threats.

Colossians 3:1, "If ye then be risen with Christ, seek those things which are above, where Christ sitteth on the right hand of God."

The word "if" begins a conditional statement. That means the counsel of the chapter does not apply to everybody. It is reserved for someone who meets the requirements that are given in the verse. The instruction of Colossians 3 is **only** for someone who is "risen with Christ." The idea can be expressed as, "These words of help in dealing with sin are intended for the properly qualified person."

The word "ye" is plural. It is an inclusive word. The instruction of the chapter is for **everyone** who is "risen with Christ," without exception. There are no people who are "risen with Christ" to whom this counsel does not apply. That means people who are "risen with Christ" will not find another way to deal successfully with sin. No one has their own private or secret plan for dealing with sin. The point of the word "ye" is that the counsel of this chapter applies to every qualified person's life situation and sin problem. In other words, if someone is "risen with Christ," they will follow this counsel and eventually will successfully deal with those sins God brings to their attention.

The word "then" implies a connection between the contents of Colossians 3 and the contents of Colossians 1 and 2. That is, chapter 3 reminds us of and continues some previous ideas. One idea is expressed by the words, "Who hath delivered us from the power of darkness and hath translated us into the kingdom of his dear Son" (Col. 1:13), implying that those people who are "risen with Christ" are under a new authority, Christ's and no longer Satan's. Another idea is expressed as, "and you, being dead in your sins and the uncircumcision of your flesh, hath he quickened together with him, having forgiven you all trespasses" (Col. 2:13). This implies that those people who are "risen with Christ," in addition to a judicial pardon, have received a life they never had before. That new life is Christ's own eternal life (Col. 1:27, Gal. 2:20). Therefore, those who are "risen with Christ" are expected to be different than they were before, both inside and outside (II Cor. 5:17). The intent of the word "then" from this point of view can be expressed as, "if, then, your situation is so different than it was before, both because you are in a new place (in the kingdom of God) and because you are a new person (with a new life), let me give you the following counsel."

The word "then" also introduces a conclusion. Colossians 1 and 2 described the necessity and value of doing things God's way, in contrast to some other way. We can summarize the discussion of the previous two chapters in the following way. The basis for the victory God's people have over their own personal sin is Jesus Christ, who is God Almighty (Col. 1:15, 2:9). Jesus is sufficient for all His people's needs (Col. 2:10). He alone has the authority, wisdom and power to keep His people faithful as they face the challenges of personal sins. Jesus separates His people from the penalty (Col. 1:14) and power of sin (Col. 2:11,12). He removes them from the dominion of Satan (Col. 1:13, 2:15). He gives them a new life and continues to sustain them as they deal with sins each day. These blessings display the value of being under the Lord Jesus Christ's supreme authority. He used all of His authority to design and fulfill an effective solution for the real sin problem of His people.

Colossians also describes the contrasting human attempt to deal with sin, based upon philosophy, empty promises, vain traditions, and a physical focus (Col. 2:8). The programs men invent and peddle to others for overcoming their wicked habits may sound good, but they do not help people deal with sin in an honorable way (Col. 2:23), that is, in a way that honors God's just demands. Their plans might temporarily make some people look and feel godly, but their plans have no sustaining power to help people rule over the desires of their flesh now, or to face the consequences of their sin at the end of time.

Having looked back at the previous two chapters, we "then" see that the futile plans men make to deal with sin are quite different from the effective power of the Gospel. The difference is revealed in the lives of God's people who successfully deal with sin in their lives. From that point of view, the idea of the word "then" can be expressed as, "with all that we previously have said, we can conclude that if you are risen with Christ, rather than relying upon human wisdom and strength, you must proceed in the following way in order to successfully deal with your sins."

The phrase "be risen with Christ" refers to someone who has been raised from the dead. That is, before they were saved, Christians were dead in sin (Eph. 2:1, Col. 2:13). Furthermore, they died the death of the wrath of God in punishment for sin. They did not endure that wrath personally, but in the sense that Jesus represented them when He paid for their sins. Nevertheless, before they were saved, Christians were just as dead as Christ was, who paid the penalty of death for their sins (Isaiah 53:5, Rom. 6:3-4, Col. 1:14,22). After they are saved, Christians have life (John 5:24, Col. 2:13). So, before people are saved they are not kind of dead, or mostly dead. Instead, before people are saved they are just as spiritually dead as people in a cemetery are physically dead. However, after they are saved they are alive. Since believers have the same body they had before they were saved, they must have been raised in their spiritual part, in their souls. Although not visible to the human eye, the resurrection of their souls is just as real as a physical resurrection. Therefore, the phrase "be risen with Christ" is not a poetic or figurative term. It refers to a real from-death-to-life experience, even though it is a spiritual experience.

The words, "with Christ," link the reality of believers' resurrection to Jesus' own resurrection (Eph. 2:6, Col. 2:13). Believers were as dead as Christ was, who paid the penalty of death for their sins. Believers were raised from that death as Christ was, who now reigns over all (Eph. 1:19-21, Phil. 2:9,10).

Altogether, the phrase, "be risen with Christ," means to be saved by the grace of God, which includes not only what God does **for** His people judicially in paying for sins, but also what God does **to** His people in bestowing upon them a new life. So the intent of the phrase, "if ye then be risen with Christ," can be expressed as, "If you are saved, I have some advice to help you deal with your sins."

With all of this in mind, we can say that a more complete title for Colossians 3 would be God's program for dealing with sin **in a Christian's life**. That is, the counsel of this chapter is meant exclusively for Christians. **Only** Christians want the advice and **all** Christians have the power to apply it to their lives. We do not imply that Colossians 3 has no message for unbelievers. God uses all of His Word to deal with them, too. After all, God uses His Word to call to salvation all those whom He intends to save (Rom. 10:17, I Peter 2:23). As long as someone is physically alive, there is hope. So, God can use the opening "if" statement of Colossians 3 to graciously call people into His Kingdom. Furthermore, God uses His Word to prepare for judgment all those who refuse to submit to His will (John 3:19, 12:48).

Nevertheless, when we think of Colossians 3 as a guide to help people gain victory over sin, then we must understand that it is intended for believers.

The word "seek" is a word of action. We find it translated in Acts 21:31 as "went about." This word is in a grammatical form that indicates a command. It is a command given with the expectation that a person who is "risen with Christ" will obey. From this we have one of two fundamental principles which form the foundation of God's plan for gaining victory over sin. The first principle is that a true, born again believer **can** obey and turn from his sin.

Colossians 3:1 teaches that a believer can walk obediently because he has been raised to a new life in Christ and has the greater power of the resurrected life within him (II Cor. 5:15, Phil. 2:12,13, Col. 2:12,13, Gal. 2:20, I John 4:4). He does not have to sin (Rom. 8:12-13).

One conclusion we can make is that when a believer sins he realizes he can blame only himself (James 1:14). A believer does not react to the discovery of his own sin with alibis, rationalizations, or excuses. Instead, he cries out in sorrow (Psalm 32:5, 51:3). His wickedness defiles and fights against his new nature (Gal. 5:17). Also, his sin is a grief to him because his wickedness is a personal insult to God, who has shown him so much love in the Gospel (Luke 22:62). Furthermore, he is saddened by the fact that his sin dishonors God whom he claims to follow and represent in this world.

Another conclusion we can make is that a believer recognizes that while he may be born with a particular strong sin tendency, peculiar to his own personality, he does not have to indulge it. Instead, he recognizes God knows his weakness better than he (Psalm 103:14), and that he must not neglect the divine wisdom and power available to him (Phil. 4:13,19, Jude 24).

A final conclusion we can make is that a person who continues unsuccessfully to struggle with his sin must take the constant defeat seriously, especially in light of the power that is available to someone who is "raised from the dead." A person whose life is dominated by a particular sin must not casually think, "I made a profession of faith" or "I am a member of the church, therefore I am saved, even though I happen to be living like the world." Rather, a person must seriously think, "No matter what I said or did outwardly in the past, if I continue to live like the world, am I really saved?" No evidence of seeking means no evidence of salvation, for a true believer can seek the things above.

The word "seek" is a word of action with a purpose or objective, described as "those things which are above." So, dealing successfully with sin requires a heavenly goal. It is not true that to be heavenly minded is to be of no earthly good, as if someone who is always thinking of Heaven is incapable of being any use for the practical affairs of daily living on earth. In fact, the only way to be of any earthly good is to be heavenly minded. There is nothing more practical than salvation and God's momentary aid in a person's daily struggle with sin.

The words, "seek ... above" remind us of prayer. That vital ingredient in gaining victory over against sin and temptation will be discussed later when we look at the phrase, "and be ye thankful," found in verse 15. For now we can say that there must be a heavenly focus in the business of daily life, especially in the struggle with sin.

The words, "where Christ sitteth on the right hand of God," do not mean Jesus sits in repose, detached from the affairs of His people. Rather, the "right hand" of God is the place of supreme authority (Eph. 1:20,21). Jesus sits and reigns with supreme authority as the Creator (Col. 1:16) and as the Redeemer of His church (Col. 1:18). Since Jesus sits on the right hand of God, He rules with sufficient authority to cause His people to deal successfully with their sin. They no longer owe obedience to sin (Rom. 8:12), for it is no longer their master (Rom. 6:17,18). Jesus is. Sin has no overwhelming control over them. Jesus has. Therefore, the command to "seek" is accompanied by the authority and power of God to help fulfill that command. That is why the first principle is true. With that in mind, the issue of dealing with sin comes down to the question of, "Who is your Lord and Master?" That is, "Are you saved and so is Jesus your Lord? Or are you unsaved and under the authority of your own sinful desires and Satan's influence?" (Rom. 6:16)

In addition to that, according to Ephesians 2:6, people who have been "risen with Christ" sit where Jesus does. They rule with authority, too, "as kings" (Rev. 1:6). It is not that they are rivals to Jesus' authority or that they have jurisdiction in a part of the universe that is equal to or exceeds Jesus' authority in some way. Instead, their authority is expressed in different ways, two of which are as follows. When Christians bring the Bible's message of the Gospel, not only is what they say backed by the authority of God Himself, but also God works through their testimony to save some people and prepare others for judgment (II Cor. 2:15-16, 5:20). Also, Christians rule over their own sinful flesh (Rom. 6:12-14). God's resurrection power within them enables the desires of their soul to reign over the desires of their flesh so that they can live obediently (Rom. 5:17,21).

We must remember that the reason believers are successful in their struggle with sin is that they do not fight the battle themselves. God fights for and in them. Their victory is based upon Jesus' personal victory over sin and death in His sacrifice before the law, together with His abiding work in their hearts. That victory is seen at the present time in Christians' ability to walk after the Spirit (Rom. 8:1-5, Gal. 5:25), and will be revealed at the end of time in the renewal of the universe, which includes believers' bodies, too. Again, the principle is that believers **can** do the will of God.

Colossians 3:2, "Set your affection on things above, not on things on the earth."

The word "affection" in the King James Bible is really the word "mind." However, the word "affection" is quite appropriate because a man thinks about things for which he has an affection. An unsaved man loves this world. For him Heaven is so remote, if he thinks that it exists at all. Besides, the exciting physical universe is a good place to hide or cover up the guilt that he feels. So an unsaved person has given his heart to the world and sets his mind upon its charms. A believer is also part of this world, at least in his body. But, unlike an unbeliever, he is not of this world (John 15:19). He is really a citizen of a different world (Phil. 3:20, Col. 1:13). He really wants to do the will of his heavenly Master. His heart has been captured by Jesus and his mind is full of His words, which he dearly wants to obey. A believer's focus is upon his Lord who is sitting enthroned in Heaven, not in leisure but in control.

Therefore, Colossians 3:2 introduces the second fundamental principle that forms the foundation of God's plan for gaining victory over sin. The second principle is that a true, born again believer **wants to** obey and does not really want to sin. It is true that sin is attractive to a believer's flesh, which has not yet been changed (Rom. 7:18-24). So, in a superficial way, he does want to sin. A believer is aware that it is easy to develop an affection and appetite for sin. Sin is fun and delicious, for a while, even when a person realizes the bitter fruit of misery that it produces (Rom. 6:21). Yet, when a believer does sin, his reaction is quite unlike that of an unbeliever who tries to justify himself. A believer cannot continue in his sin. It violates his new nature. Deep in his heart and soul he does not want to sin. So, after he sins, he reacts in brokenness and sorrow (Psalm 51:4, II Cor. 7:10). A believer is honest about his situation and has a heart that earnestly seeks to turn from his sin and please God.

A person's desire, or "want to," is the seat of sin. Sin is a matter of the will (Col. 3:24). Maybe for a short time one person can force another person to do outwardly what the Bible commands. However, no one can make another person want to do God's will, no one can except God Himself. Only God can change a person's "want to," or rather exchange it. Only God can replace a sinner's old heart and its affections with a new heart and its affections (Ezek. 36:25,26). That is why salvation is the only hope for dealing with sin. The Gospel alone is the power for salvation and the power to help people set their affection on things above. That heavenly desire is a big witness to the fact that they are "risen with Christ." That desire is a big witness to the fact that God indeed has worked and continues to work in their lives with resurrection power.

Although the word "affection" is really the word "mind," we are not counseled to meditate our way out of sin and temptation. God's plan is not "mind over matter," at least not man's mind. Nor can we say that accurate thinking based upon correct knowledge is enough to assure victory over sin. A good education simply makes educated sinners. Rather, the idea is that God works through the minds of His people by His power so that they do His will (Rom. 12:2, I Cor. 2:16, Phil 4:6-9). That is why, as we shall see, the counsel of Colossians 3:16 is so important.

The focus of Colossians 3:2 is upon the mind because that is the factory of sin. That is where sin begins and where the battle must be won. Let us trace the way of sin in our minds. When a sinful thought comes into our minds, the tendency of our flesh is to focus and dwell upon it. For example, sometimes we fondle our sin thinking that a little taste is all we need at the moment. We turn it over in our minds and it grows bigger and bigger, soon dominating almost every waking moment of our day. We feel sorry for ourselves when we have an affection for something and cannot have what we yearn. We are afraid of losing it. We feel deprived of something special and want it in contradiction to God's will. The next step is capitulation, no matter what God says. In another example, sometimes we foolishly think we are in control and try to "figure out" our sin. We try to "better understand" it by analyzing it in order to get rid of it. At that point we are ripe for surrendering to it. The message of Colossians is that we must not think about it at all. We must think about things above. We are not so in control of the situation or of ourselves. We must flee such thoughts the moment they come to our minds and, as this verse says, turn the focus of our attention upon God.

As they fill their minds with and meditate upon the things above, Christians will reveal the work of God within them. In addition to that, they will gain the peace at heart which is a testimony to themselves and to others that they are "risen with Christ" (II Cor. 10:5, Phil. 4:7-9, Col. 3:15).

Before we continue with a brief examination of the following verses, it would be good to summarize the main ideas of verses 1 and 2. Colossians 3:1 and 2 are like two thesis statements. They state two principles which are developed in the rest of the chapter. The first principle can be stated in this way: People who have been "raised with Christ" do not have to sin. They can obey their Lord. Colossians 3:2 states the second principle: People who have been "raised with Christ" do not want to sin. They have a holy affection for the things above which is greater than their sinful affection for the things of this world. These two principles give the basis for a believer's victory over his own personal sin.

Colossians 3:3, "For ye are dead, and your life is hid with Christ in God."

This verse gives the reason why the principles stated in verses 1 and 2 are true. Christians are able to gain victory over their sins because they are "dead." At this point, we must make sure that we understand what is in view when the Bible uses the word "dead." The word can refer to at least three different but closely related ideas.

One death is physical death (Eccl. 12:7). That is a death which is experienced by all men, both unsaved and saved, except for those people who are physically alive when Jesus returns to conclude history on earth. That is not the kind of death in view here because the Colossian readers were still physically alive, as are all who read these words today.

Another death is spiritual death of the soul (Col. 2:13). That death also is shared by all men, but is the death from which God's people are resurrected when they become saved, and is the death in which all unsaved people remain eternally. That, also, is not the kind of death meant in verse 3 because the word "dead" is applied to believers' present situation. Believers were dead in their souls before they were saved, but they are no longer dead in that way.

Still one more death is the death in Hell. It is referred to in the

Bible as the "second death" (Rev. 2:11, 20:6, 21:8) because it is an event that follows the 'first death,' namely physical death (Heb. 9:27). It is the payment required for sins, which is eternally enduring the wrath of God. In other words, it is the death that accompanies condemnation. The death associated with God's wrath is also shared by all men. However, that is the death that saved people experience differently from those who are never saved. Those who are saved experience it in Jesus, since He died for them, while all who are not saved will experience that death on the their own. This is the death upon which Colossians 3:3 focuses.

The death in view is the death that believers experience as part of the salvation work of Jesus. That is, when Jesus died He took their sins with Him. In effect, they died, too (Col. 2:12). But more than a judicial compensation, more than fulfilling the command that the "the soul that sinneth, it shall die" (Ezek. 18:4, Rom. 6:23), Jesus' death also was a release. That is the implication of the prefix "away from" which is attached to the front of the word translated "dead" in Colossians 3:3. Those who are "risen with Christ" no longer obey their former master because they have been set free from that master and belong to a new Master (Col. 1:13).

Now that we have a clearer view of the word "dead," let us try to understand the message of Colossians 3:3. We shall begin by thinking of people as beings who are created in two parts, body and soul. Because of the sin of Adam, all people inherit a dead soul and a body full of sin. Since they have no life in their souls, unsaved people are dominated by the sin in their bodies. The lusts of their bodies draw unsaved people into sin, unimpeded by any resistance to sin which would come from their souls, which are dead. The Gospel changes that situation.

One result of the Gospel is that believers are "dead" with Christ. The simplest way to think about this is that death separates people from their bodies. People who become believers do not die physically, but the separation of believers from their bodies is just as real. This is important because it means believers are separated from the sin that is in their bodies in the sense that sin no longer has dominion over them. That is why Romans 6:2 states that they are dead "to sin," rather than dead to their bodies.

Another result of the Gospel is that believers are "risen with Christ." (Col. 3:1). The simplest way to think about this is that believers' souls are no longer dead but alive. They have experienced a spiritual resurrection in their souls. People who become believers have a new life, not just a restored life in the image of Adam, but an eternal life. It is eternal life, not only in the sense that it is life without end, but also in the sense that it is the life of the eternal God. It is the life of Jesus Himself who is within them (John 14:6, Gal. 2:20, Col. 1:27). Therefore, eternal life is a statement of quality as much as it is of duration. This is important because it means believers, who continue to live in their sinful bodies until they die physically or until the Lord returns, now have the power of Jesus' life in their souls that enables them to resist the pull of the sinful desires in their bodies. They both can and want to do God's will.

Therefore, the reason the principles stated in Colossians 3:1-2 are true is that Christians have died to sin, or rather to the power of sin, and have the greater power of the resurrected life within them (Col. 2:12,20). Again, they both **can** and **want to** do God's will.

Colossians 3:3 adds that believers are "hid with Christ in God." The word "hid" is used to highlight the fact that the blessings of a new resurrected life are not recognized or understood by unbelievers (II Cor. 4:3). The whole idea of dealing with sin makes no sense to people who are not saved. Anyone who willingly denies himself the pleasures of sin in order to serve God is strange in the eyes of unbelievers (I Peter 4:3,4), and is either pitied or mocked by them.

Colossians 3:4, "When Christ, who is our life, shall appear, then shall ye also appear with him in glory."

This verse states the objective of the two principles given in verses 1 and 2. The objective is that when Jesus Christ "shall appear, ... then shall ye (Christians) also appear with him in glory." How is that important in Christians' struggles against their sins?

For one thing, verse 4 promises that Jesus shall indeed "appear." That means believers will not struggle with their sins forever. Jesus will return to remove this sin-cursed world and replace it with a new incorruptible one (II Peter 3:13), which includes Christians' glorified spiritual bodies (I Cor. 15:42-44). So their struggles with sins will eventually end in complete victory. Christians will be given victory in the sense that they will be free from the present demands of their sinful flesh, which annoys and grieves them. They also will be given victory in the sense that they will be free to honor and praise God perfectly, as He deserves, and as they yearn to do, without the impediments and blemishes of sinful motives and actions. But for now, they must keep their focus on things above, as they deal with sin here on earth.

The present victories which Christians experience in this corrupt material world show that their hope in the future appearance of Jesus is not misplaced or some "hope-so," "pie-in-the-sky-by-and-by" mental invention. Their present victories over their sins are witnesses to the reality of God's promises and power, for anyone who has eyes to see. Jesus' future appearance is as real as His power to give them present victories over their sins. Christians must not faint or grow weary in their struggles with their sins. The struggles are abiding, wearing and a source of sorrow for now, but the promised end is in sight and makes the struggles worthwhile (II Cor. 4:14-18).

In addition to that, when Jesus appears, Christians will "appear with him in glory." It is not that by gaining victory over sin, Christians earn the right to appear with Jesus in glory. Rather it is that, thinking back to verse 3, the victory reveals that their "life is hid with Christ in God," or to verse 1, they have been "risen with Christ." When Jesus appears, Christians will not be separated from Him as guilty criminals. Instead, they will be with Him as dear children, sharing the blessings of His grace. They are people who have been made ready by God's grace to meet Jesus inasmuch as they are in God as a shelter, hidden from the judgment that will come when Christ appears (Psalm 27:5, 32:7, 90:1, Rom 8:1).

Colossians 3:5, "Mortify therefore your members which are upon the earth; fornication, uncleanness, inordinate affection, evil concupiscence, and covetousness, which is idolatry:"

Verses 5 through 9 develop the first principle. The verses show how the power of the resurrected life within believers overcomes the power of sin in their members so that they can obey. They do not have to sin (Rom. 8:12).

The word translated "mortify" in verse 5 means to put to death. The word "members" refers to the residence of sin, a person's body of flesh (Rom. 6:12,13, 7:23). The counsel is that Christians who seek to gain victory over sin must kill their members (Gal. 5:24). There is no easy way out. We cannot escape this procedure. God expects His people to mortify their members.

This verse does not promote physical mutilation (c.f. I Kings 18:28). Besides, that would not help anyone refrain from sin. Only complete physical death would. Nor is this verse a call to suicide, which is self-murder. Interestingly, in the other two places where this form of the Greek word is used, namely the one translated "mortify," it does not actually refer to physical death. Instead, the idea can be expressed as "a body that is alive but unable to function, as if it were dead" (Rom. 4:19, Heb. 11:12). To deny a sinful desire of the flesh is the same as killing it, because it is the same as if the desire were no longer there. A member of a Christian's body may scream its desire, but by God's grace a Christian will not listen. It is as if his member were dead.

The word "mortify" is a sever, decisive and uncompromising word. It implies that dealing with sin God's way means to be ruthless. Christians must cut off **any** opportunity to think of sin and avoid any situation that would feed their appetites for sin. That means they must limit what they see, hear and do. They must always be ready to separate themselves from any person or deny themselves anything that might encourage them to sin. They must take firm and deliberate steps to mortify the members of their sinful flesh. Do they hear dirty stories or gossip? They must walk away. Does the TV, radio program or book use bad language or present scenes and situations to which Christians should not expose themselves? They must turn it off or throw it away. Does their eye wander to a place or a person that it shouldn't? They must look aside, or avoid the person or place. As long as they live in their bodies on the earth, that is their full-time job.

As we mentioned in our examination of verse 2, sin is attractive to a believer's flesh, which has not yet been changed. A believer is aware that it is easy to develop an affection for sin. Yet a believer does not want to continue in his sin. He hates it like God hates it. He wants to deal with it how God will deal with it on Judgment Day. He is alarmed that sin has captured him for the moment, and he takes steps to "mortify" or kill it. By killing it, we mean that a true believer will take the necessary steps to turn away from anything that attracts him to sin. He will act to remove sin's influence in his life, so it is as if the sin does not exist for him, as if he has killed it.

We also must remember that sin is not an alien force that has invaded Christians' minds and bodies from outer space. They are not victims of an evil foreign agent who has taken them captive. In fact, they initiate sin. It starts with them, in their members. They are willing participants in sin because in their flesh they enjoy sin. It is a delicious habit to which their flesh is addicted. So, they are not surprised by sin unawares. In fact, the tendency of their members is to look for opportunities to sin. In their flesh, they too easily study to do their own will in opposition to doing what God says in His Word. So the call to "mortify" is urgent and insistent.

The word that best describes the intent of verse 5 is "repentance." At this point it is important to set aside some common misunderstandings about repentance. Repentance is not a word that means Christians regret or feel sorry about the horrible consequences of their sins, which they and others must bear, although that certainly is a proper Christian attitude, for when he does sin, a true believer reacts in brokenness and sorrow. Neither is repentance a word that means Christians seek to do something to compensate for their foolish disobedience. Repentance is not an act of restitution or compensation. Instead, repentance means to make a U-turn in the road of life and go the opposite direction, with purposeful strides away from self-desires and toward God's will.

In addition to that, the deliberate action which is the mark of repentance is not a virtue that makes Christians particularly endearing. They do not gain honor for turning away from something that they had no business doing in the first place. Recognizing the foolishness of doing something sinful and belatedly turning from it is an expected and obligatory action. Repentance may be a refreshing change from a former life of wickedness, but it does not change the facts. Repentance does not erase the record of the numerous and odious sins Christians commit, nor does it absolve Christians of those sins. Repentance may begin the healing process, but doing the right thing does not make someone a hero. Repentance is simply a necessary step in God's economy for dealing with sin. Repentance begins with Christians' eye-opening honesty about their own wickedness and continues with their deliberate steps away from it. A believer is candid about his situation and has a heart that earnestly seeks to turn from his sin and to please God.

Finally, we must understand that repentance is not an action motivated and sustained by the person who turns from his sin. Repentance is a gift of God (Acts 5:31, 11:!8, II Tim. 2:25). Unless God grants the desire and power to repent, no one would. An unsaved sinner may turn from a particular sinful behavior because of his own decision. But that apparent repentance is short-lived. All too soon, unsaved people return to serve their natural sinful desires (Prov. 26:11, II Peter 2:22). Also, it is not real repentance because it is motivated by self-centered interest, with an eye to personal advantage.

It is hard to repent. Why? First of all, Christians' sinful desires that come from their bodies are as strong as ever. Without the changed heart and divine power that accompany salvation, repentance is impossible. It is easy to excuse an indulgence in sin. For example, sometimes people do not want to turn from a sin because they are afraid that they will miss some special earthly joy. Or sometimes other people encourage them to sin and they do not want to lose the esteem and companionship of their "friends." But if they refuse to turn from their sin, they must wrestle with the fear and doubt that they may not be saved.

Despite the value of the wisdom that comes from verse 5, we must emphasize that repentance alone is not enough. A Christian may cease to do that which is wrong, but that restraint is not sufficient to gain victory over his sin. The complete picture is to replace the business of sin with the business of obedience. To the negative call to "mortify," verses 10 and 12 add the positive call to "put on," or in the words of Romans 6:13, "yield yourselves unto God." Christians are counseled to be busy, to use their time in holy pursuits (I Tim. 6:11). They must make an effort to fill their minds with anything that redirects their focus away from whatever tantalizes them to sin. They must seek to be occupied with service to God.

Verse 5 also uses the word "your." As we mentioned earlier, in any attempt to gain victory over sin, the spotlight must not be upon the sins of others, as obnoxious and numerous as they are. Nor should we dwell upon and crusade against the social injustices or the general moral depravity of mankind. That is just a ruse to take the attention and blame off of our own sin. Besides, the sins of society or of mankind as a whole are nothing more than the collective sins of each person in that society, including "your" sin. As it turns out, Christians have no time to look upon any other person's sins, because they should be too busy dealing with their own sins (I Tim. 4:16). The emphasis must always be upon "your" individual personal sin. That keeps the effort to gain victory over sin simpler and more in focus.

All the sins listed in verse 5 are the same in the sense that they are all equally wicked, no matter what the unique characteristics of each sin are. To demonstrate that fact, we point out that the word "idolatry," at the end of the verse, does not refer only to "covetousness," the word next to it. Rather, "idolatry" refers to all the sins in verse 5. Any sin is idolatry because it puts that desire above the will of God. Capitulating to any sinful desire is to worship and serve that desire rather than God. Therefore, the need to "mortify" is not related to the peculiar character of a sin or to how bad the sin is. Mortifying is always an important and urgent item on our agenda for gaining victory over sin because there are no unimportant or little sins (James 2:10).

Related to the idea of sin as idolatry is the danger of incomplete or selective repentance. In other words, a person could turn from many sins and yet face one that seems impossible to abandon because he cherishes it too much. Whether he eventually repents of it or not reveals the true devotion of his heart, whether to God or to the idol of his sin.

It is true that dealing with sin is a life-long occupation. On a Christian's last day on earth, there will be many sins in his life of which he should have repented but did not, either because he never became aware of them or because he died before he could deal with them as he should. And it is true that a Christian takes time to repent of some sins, resisting for a while any change in a sinful behavior which his flesh cherishes. However, when God brings a particular sin to a Christian's attention and calls him to repent of it, under normal circumstances he eventually will repent of it. The reason is that God is the source of true repentance (Acts 5:31,11:18, II Tim. 2:25). He creates in His people the desire to call upon Him for all things (Isaiah 57:19), including the desire and power to repent from sin. And He then answers their request (Psalm 37:3,4).

Colossians 3:6, "For which things' sake the wrath of God cometh on the children of disobedience:"

The words in verse 6 provide motivation for repentance. They remind us of the threat of an existence under condemnation and, by contrast, the relief of a future life without it (John 5:24, Rom. 8:1). In other words, as an encouragement to repent, verse 6 reminds us of "the wrath of God" upon sinners.

A great deal is at stake as people struggle with sin. Christ, the supreme authority, will appear. What will those people do who despise His authority and who show it by their abandonment to their carnal desires? If people's sins cause them to wonder about their spiritual situation, great! They must deal with it now before it is too late. In contrast to that, if their sins are not accompanied with a fear of wrath, horrors! For people who are headed for a Christ-less eternity in Hell have no fear of God (Psalm 36:1, Rom 3:18).

True believers, who are not personally threatened by condemnation, who are secure in God's love, still find motivation to repent in the reminder of "the wrath of God." They understand the enormity of their sin, of the insult it is to God. They understand that God reacts personally in wrath against sin because it is meant personally, for sin is deliberate rebellion against God. They agree that wrath is a just response to sin because they understand God's wrath is a true measure of how bad sin is. Also, believers are distressed that their sinful behavior is such a disregard of Him who has shown so much love to them and whom they claim to love. It is not that they feel sorry for Him or that He needs protection and cannot take care of Himself, but that they love Him and are ashamed for the personal offense against Him that their sin is. They are grateful that they have been given a heart to hate sin, an attitude that accompanies their salvation. Their awareness of the nature of sin is wisdom that motivates them to put legs on their desire to repent (Job 28:28).

The words "the wrath of God" also provides a practical tip in dealing with sin. It reminds us of God's attitude toward sin, an attitude which Christians must share. Sometimes we are afraid that if we give up our sin we will miss something special, some kind of irreplaceable joy. It is so easy to feel sorry for ourselves, and say, "Poor me. I deserve a little indulgence." However, verse 6 puts things in proper perspective. We must look at our sin the way God looks at it, namely, with hatred, as the word "wrath" implies. We must despise and loathe it for what it really is. If we do not have that holy hatred for sin, then our battle against sin must begin there. We must ask God in prayer for the eyes to see how disgusting and repulsive our sin is to Him and ask for the hatred that He has toward it. It is easy, too easy, to be angry at the sin of others. But only God can show us the nature of our own sin and create in us an emotion that matches His.

In support of the need and value of hatred for sin, we read in Ephesians 4:26, "be ye angry, and sin not: let not the sun go down upon your wrath." This verse is not an accommodation to people's natural propensity to lose their temper. The verse is not saying, "I know that you are going to get angry. But at least don't get so angry that you lose control and sin. Make sure that you resolve your anger before the day is through." After all, anger is sin, as we read in Ephesians 4:31. That is, all anger is sin except one kind, the kind which Ephesians 4:26 points out. What kind of anger is that? According to Ephesians 4:26, it is the anger that leads us to "sin not." We recognize that as the anger against our own sin, the same anger mentioned in Colossians 3:6.

Incidentally, hatred toward our sin does not mean that we focus upon it and brood over it. That tactic leads to more sin and is really a form of pride. No, we must have a cool deliberate hatred that translates into a swift and decisive action. Then we can move on to "seek those things which are above," in order to do God's will in our lives.

Our hatred for sin is related to shame. Believers represent the Holy

God in this world and are saddened when their sin dishonors Him. Our hatred for sin also is related to fear. Believers tremble at God's Word (Isaiah 66:2), knowing with great relief the disaster they escaped and knowing the terror of that awaits all the unsaved.

Colossians 3:7, "In the which ye also walked some time, when ye lived in them."

Verses 7 through 9 provide some additional motivation for repentance. They remind Christians of their horrid past life of enslavement to sin (Rom. 6:21). And, by contrast, verse 10 through the end of the chapter highlight the obedience that marks Christians' present lives (Rom. 6:17). Altogether, verses 7 through 25 remind us of the difference that can be expected between those who do not live under God's authority (Titus 3:2) and those who do (Titus 3:8).

The words "in the which" refer back to the sinful tendencies of their "members," described in verse 5. The word "walked" means to walk in circle. The idea is that, before they were saved, the Christians in Colossi walked under an unbreakable habit of sin. So, verse 5 describes their past lives, and verse 6 describes their past spiritual liability. Was such a life worth it? (Rom. 6:21).

If we are Christians, we still may wince at the memory of our past wickedness. We may be embarrassed when we think of our past foolishness. We may regret the loss in our own personal lives and the harm in the lives of other people that are consequences of our sins. We may wonder, "why do I recall these sad experiences? Are these memories an indication of my lack of faith in God's forgiveness?"

We should be thankful for those memories. Paul brought them to the attention of the Colossians purposefully. And God allows them to come to our minds for many reasons. Although God has forgotten our sins in the sense that He does not hold us accountable for them, and although in eternity our sins will be remembered no more, our memories of our sins perform a valuable service. Memories of our past help us in the present. For one thing, the memories keep us humble, reminding us of our mean heritage and evil tendencies, which we were helpless to change. Secondly, the memories refresh our gratitude for God's atonement, forgiveness and new life in Christ. Thirdly, the memories renew our sympathy and patience with other people who are struggling with similar sins. Fourthly, the memories provide us with the understanding we need to effectively explain the Gospel to others.

Colossians 3:8,9, "But now ye also put off all these; anger, wrath, malice, blasphemy, filthy communication out of your mouth. Lie not one to another, seeing that ye have put off the old man with his deeds."

The idea of these verses can be expressed as, "Your former pattern of behavior, from which you are called to repent, although awful, was understandable inasmuch as you were an unbeliever, but now you must put all those things away." The words "put off" in verse 8 and "have put off" in verse 9 are not translations of the same Greek word, but they hold similar ideas. The first emphasizes separation or disconnection from sinful behavior that is part of the process of mortification and the second emphasizes removing and setting aside something, like clothing. The point is that Paul can expect the Colossians to take deliberate steps to separate themselves from all those patterns of behavior that mark a unbeliever's life. The word "mortify" is not a suggestion or a possibility. It is a command that actually is obeyed in the life of anyone who is "raised with Christ." That is the message in other parts of the Bible (Gal. 5:24,25) and is the example of other believers (Titus 3;3,8).

The sins listed in verse 8 are all are basically the same, describing what comes out of a person's mouth. And as we read in Luke 6:45, a person's mouth speaks from his heart. The idea is that a person's words represent his "communication" or whole life style. People can use fair words to hide their evil heart for a while, but the deception will not last for long. A person's words will eventually, sooner than later, expose his heart. "Anger" and "wrath" have a character that is especially revealing because they are fueled by egotism, which promotes and protects self above anyone else, including God.

Verse 9 seems to isolate and therefore highlight the sin of lying. Although all sins are the same before God, lying is one of the marks of Satan (John 8:44), the rival authority, from whose dominion Christians have been released. With that in mind, we see that repentance is not only expected but also imperative, inasmuch as to continue in sin is to act on behalf of Satan.

Verses 7 through 9 are both humbling and encouraging to people who are saved. They are humbling in that they remind Christians of their shameful heritage. They have a previous record that should check their tendency to boast in their present victories over sins and motivate them to be sympathetic and patient with other people who also struggle with sin. But the verses also are encouraging in that they speak of things gone by that no longer dominate them. They are never totally free of any of these things until they leave this earth, but their sinful desire is no longer their master, a fact that is food for praise to an amazingly gracious God.

Colossians 3:10,11, "And have put on the new man, which is renewed in knowledge after the image of him that created him. Where there is neither Greek nor Jew, circumcision nor uncircumcision, Barbarian, Scythian, bond nor free: but Christ is all, and in all."

Verses 10 through 17 develop the second principle. The verses show how the power of the resurrected life within Christians shapes their affection so that they do not want to sin (Rom. 6:17-19, 8:5).

First, let us think about the words "the new man," in verse 10. Actually, the word "man" does not exist in this verse, but it is not such a foreign idea, being included in a similar discussion in Ephesians (Eph. 4:24). If we allow the word "man" as a valid insertion, then one way to think about this is to recognize that the "new man" is Jesus Himself. It is Jesus within His people (Col. 1:27). That is, Christians "put on" Jesus Christ (Rom. 13:14) and display a life that is "the image" of Jesus (Rom. 8:29), so what He wants is what they want. That is why they do not want to sin but want to do God's will.

If we deny the insertion of the word "man," then the focus of verse 10 is upon a Christian as a new creation (II Cor. 5:17), created in Christ Jesus (Eph. 2:10). As someone "new," a Christian has a new "want to." Being new does not mean being a different person. God uses the word "new" in the Bible to mean fulfilled, especially in connection with the Gospel. The Old Testament is the Gospel promised. The New Testament is the Gospel fulfilled. Both testaments describe the same Gospel. It is just that the New Testament explains something new about it, namely, that it is completed in Jesus. Similarly, a Christian is new in the sense that Jesus dwells within him so that he can fulfill the purpose for which he was originally created. A Christian has the same personality and unique identity created by God, but now he is free to serve God with his new, implanted life, out of love (Gal. 5:1,13).

We can combine both views of the words "new man" when we also think about the words "after the image of him that created him." That is, Christians are saved to be an image of Jesus, to spiritually look like or resemble Him who created them (Rom. 8:29). This is revealed by a totally new pattern of behavior motivated out of a new heart (Ezek. 36:26, Rom. 6:17) that does not want to sin but wants to obey, in great contrast to the "children of disobedience."

According to verse 11, the heart desire to obey God is common to all of His people, regardless of their cultural or ethnic background and experience. If a Christian belongs to Christ, superficial physical differences do not matter (Acts 17:26). Unlike unsaved men who try to separate people by race or culture, the Bible unites them. Verse 11 states, "Christ is all (that is important) and in all (His people, no matter what their past or present physical situation)." He is their common unifying identity. Therefore, all true believers are "raised in Christ," no matter what their human heritage, and all want to obey their Lord. What each one now wants as a "new man," or as an "image of him that created (them)" is described in verses 12 through 14.

Colossians 3:12, "Put on therefore, as the elect of God, holy and beloved, bowels of mercies, kindness, humbleness of mind, meekness, longsuffering."

We can read this as "elect of God (and therefore) holy and beloved (of God)." That is, God's people are elected for a reason, one of which is to be "holy," as He is (I Peter 1:15,16). Christians are saved to display God's glory and honor (Isaiah 43:21, I Peter 2:9), which their willing obedience does.

The word "bowels" highlights the fact that all the things a person does are motivated from his deepest part, from his heart. As evil things came from their hearts (Col. 3:8) so now do the good things listed in this verse. Of course, a few acts do not tell the whole tale, and the true motivation of a particular act is often obscure. But over time, what a person does is a window that reveals what he is, or rather what God has made him to be.

The list of virtues in this verse are the adornments we see in a person life after he has put on the "image of him that created." That is, the virtues of kindness (Eph.2:7, Titus 3:4), humbleness of mind (Phil. 2:5,8), meekness (Mat. 11:29) and longsuffering (I Tim. 1:16, II Peter 3:9,15) all are attributes of Jesus Christ which decorate a Christian's life after he has put on the "new man." These are spontaneous qualities that flow from Jesus' life within him, for a Christian has a heart that delights to act in the way this verse describes. In contrast to the character of "anger" and "wrath" mentioned in verse 8, the character of "kindness," "humbleness of mind," "meekness" and "longsuffering" are based upon a self-sacrificial promotion and protection of others. More than just refraining from the evils of verses 8 and 9, the testimony is that Christians "bringeth forth fruit" (Col. 1:3-6), as listed in Colossians 3:12.

Let us think a little more about the fact that in the business of gaining victory over sin, God insists that we put on "kindness, humbleness of mind, meekness, (and) longsuffering." In Ephesians 2:7, kindness refers to God's gracious forgiveness of the sins of sinners. In Philippians 2:3,5-8, humbleness of mind refers to a desire to reduce ourselves for the spiritual benefit of others. In Titus 3:2,3, meekness refers to not speaking evil of other people's sins, in full recognition of our own sinfulness, in accord with the saying, "the pot should not call the kettle black." In II Peter 3:15, longsuffering is directly connected to God's desire to save sinners.

Having briefly looked at the virtues listed in verse 12, we see a common attribute that leads to an important principle. The principle is based upon the fact that Christians are not islands but connected to each other through the bonds of mutual, spiritual concern. The principle is that is a person's attitude toward his own sin is linked to his attitude toward the sins of other people. More specifically, we can state the principle in this way. Christian's success in his attempt to gain victory over his own sin is dependent upon his gracious forgiveness of the sins of other people. This leads us to the message of the next verse.

Colossians 3:13, "Forbearing one another, and forgiving one another, if any man have a quarrel against any: even as Christ forgave you, so also do ye."

The word "forgiving" is based upon the word for grace or God's mercy to sinners. The key to understanding the logic of this verse is found in the words "even as." The idea is that Christians' attitude of forgiveness matches Jesus Christ's. This is true from two points of view. First of all, what Christians do comes out from their own saved hearts. With that in mind, we can say only hearts that first have been shown mercy from God can show mercy to others. Someone who is not saved himself has no desire to forgive nor does he understand what forgiveness means in the first place. Secondly, what Christians do comes out from "Christ in you" (Col. 1:27). That is, hearts that show mercy to others are expressing the mercy of the God who dwells within them.

We can explain the relationship between a Christian's attempt to gain victory over his own sins and the message of forgiveness mentioned in this verse in the following way. First of all, many of our sins are connected to other people, such as theft, anger, lust, and covetousness. So, if we have not resolved our differences between ourselves and other people, then we have not resolved our sins. Secondly, some of our sins that seem to be only related directly to God, such as lack of trust and some doctrinal errors, are also connected to others in the sense that we are supposed to love other people enough to bring them the true Gospel. So, if we demonstrate a lack of trust and are not correct in what we say about what the Bible teaches, then we are not "forbearing," "holding up" or bringing people to God so that they may find true forgiveness.

Incidentally, the word "if" does not imply, "maybe there is someone who has a quarrel against any of you. In the occasional time that you have a quarrel, then forgive." Instead, the idea is that "since there are quarrels among you, you must always be ready to forgive." Forgiveness is always needed because quarrels are always present. In other words, since it takes two to have a quarrel, it is imperative that we examine our motives and methods to see if we are willing to recognize that we are vessels of clay who are many times in error. We must be sure that we are willing to defer on issues that are not spiritually significant, willing to endure loss for the spiritual benefit of others and willing to abandon our own pride for the sake of a peace between us and our opponent that promotes his peace with God.

Colossians 3:14, "And above all these things put on charity, which is the bond of perfectness."

God is "perfectness." So, when we put on love, we put on Jesus (Rom. 13:14). He is the bond to God and the bond between men.

The idea of the verse is that the grand objective of successfully gaining victory over sin is not just for the personal benefit of the person who has gained that victory, but also for what value his victory has for other people. Christians seek victory over their sins out of the love they have for God, but also, as this verse mentioned, out of love for other people. That is one reason God gives His people the desire and power to gain victory over their sin. It must be the goal of God's people too.

In what way is the success of a Christian in dealing with his own personal sin a benefit to other people? It is a benefit in the sense other people do not have to put up with a Christian's sometimes annoying self-centered behavior. It is a benefit in the sense that other people are not harmed by a Christian's sometimes foolish and evilly motivated actions and words. It is a benefit in the sense that a Christian is more able to contribute something worthwhile to other people's lives, such as a witness to the Gospel in both his words and his example. That is, gaining victory over our own personal sin has evangelistic consequences.

Colossians 3:15, "And let the peace of God rule in your hearts, to the which also ye are called in one body; and be ye thankful."

The command "let the peace of God rule in your hearts" can be obeyed only by the people for whom Jesus is the supreme authority. Since Jesus, the Peace of God (Eph. 2:14), is the authority of all believers, they will not seek another. Jesus is the "peace" who rules over a Christian's heart and its affections by virtue of His redemption. In a way we could entitle Colossians 3, or the whole book of Colossians for that matter, as <u>The Peace-ruled Heart</u>.

According to Luke 6:45 and 12:34, the kind of heart a person has is revealed by who rules over it. And that rulership is displayed through the life that he leads. That is, we can tell our own hearts (I Cor. 11:28, II Cor. 13:5). We cannot necessarily tell another person's heart (James 4:12). After all, would we include David, who committed fornication with Bathsheba and was responsible for her husband's death, among the heroes of faith (Heb. 11:32)? If we did not have God's personal statement that he was a "man after God's own heart" (I Sam. 13:14, Acts 13:22) or if we did not read that his heart was smitten when the prophet Nathan accused him (II Sam. 12:13, Psalm 51:1-4), our verdict would probably be that David was unsaved.

The words in Colossians 3:15, "and be ye thankful," that is, "thankful to God," remind us of the importance of prayer in the business of dealing with sin (Psalm 32:5,6). The moment a believer begins to think about sin he should pray, especially prayers of thanksgiving. The prayer of thankfulness means that a believer recognizes he is dependent upon God's care and has found God's supply in every needful occasion (Phil. 4:6-7,19). A believer recognizes that, in his struggle to turn from sin, he must walk one step at a time. Sometimes, as he seeks to stop thinking of the attraction of a particular sin, he must earnestly pray for God's help to take him through the next hour, or even the next minute. Then, as he finds that God has given him the victory for that span of time, he continues to pray for strength during the next hour or minute. Each succeeding victory gives him confidence to continue through the present struggle and gratitude for God's past faithfulness. His success in dealing with sin vindicates his trust in his Lord to lead him moment by moment safely through each future challenge.

The prayer of thankfulness also means that a believer recognizes all that the Lord has done for his salvation to prepare him for the hazardous Christian walk. Cheer replaces self-pity, as he focuses upon the blessings of God. In prayer his mind is not sin-occupied but love filled, that is, full of the words and love of his Savior. He also discovers that he must be looking, not for an excuse to fulfill his own desires, but for an opportunity to complete God's will for his life (Matt. 6:10, Col. 3:23).

The prayer of thankfulness maintains the genuine peace and joy that sin cannot provide and that the world can neither understand nor take away. Above all, a believer is relieved and thankful that God is the supreme authority in the universe and that He is the Lord of his life. Knowing what a mess he has made in the past and could make in the future, he is happy that now Jesus is in charge.

The words "in one body," brings a Christian's attention back to the fact that he is not living an isolated life. Everything he does has an effect upon others because he is part of "one body." This is an reminder of what was taught in verse 15 about the love connection Christians have with others, especially to those in the "body."

Colossians 3:16, "Let the word of Christ dwell in you richly in all wisdom; teaching and admonishing one another in psalms and hymns and spiritual songs, singing with grace in your hearts to the Lord."

This verse states two excellent strategies for dealing with sin. One strategy is found in the words, "let the word of Christ dwell in you richly." Again, where does sin begin? It begins in our minds. We always think about sin before we commit it. It doesn't ambush us "out of the blue." The counsel is that as soon as the thought of sin pops into our mind, we must ask for God's forgiveness and His mercy to help us focus on His Word instead. But we must know God's Word in order to think about it and in order to for God's thoughts to replace our own sinful ones. Like a pot full of sand that has no room for anything else, a mind full of God's Word crowds out evil thoughts. The idea is we must meditate upon God's Word when sinful thoughts assault our minds (Psalm 37:31, 119:11, Prov. 7:1-3).

Bible study and memorization are what a Christian does as part of his preparation in advance, before going out into the world and struggling with a particular sin (Psalm 119:11). It is not wise or possible to strap on a sword and armor when in the middle of a battle. Therefore, by means of prior Bible study and memorization, a Christian acquires abiding attitudes which can check his impulsive reaction to follow the appeal of his flesh, a reaction that may be hard to control in the press of a temptation. In fact, the activity of a Christian's preparation is itself an effort that displays he is serious enough about his sin to be diligent as he strives to gain victory over it. Also, through the Bible a Christian gains the insight and skill to make correct decisions in a complex and messy struggle with sin.

Another strategy is found in the words, "teaching and admonishing one another in psalms and hymns and spiritual songs, singing with grace in your hearts to the Lord." Christian songs are wonderful devices to train our minds to think about holy things, especially in the passionate, stressful and confusing times of temptation. The idea is that as soon as sinful thoughts enter our minds, we should replace them by "singing with grace in your hearts to the Lord" (Psalm 51:14).

However, according to verse 16, the music must both teach and admonish. And in I Corinthians 14:15, we learn that we must sing with "understanding," that is, with an understanding of the Bible. In other words, to be most helpful, the lyrics must be faithful to the Bible and be more substantive than simple repetitive choruses. The songs not only must be uplifting, as music often is, but also must include the darker reality of the consequences of sin, namely warnings about the judgment to come (Psalm 101:1). The empty and self-centered lyrics of secular music are repetitive and ubiquitous. But we should sing songs that teach themes found in the Bible, such as those that warn us about the need to forsake our sin and walk faithfully with God as well as those that declare the mighty works of God (Exod. 15:1,21, I Chron 16:9,23, Isaiah 44:23, 49:13, Rev. 5:9). Music is not only a wonderful device to train our minds to think about the things of the Lord, but also a wonderful way to witness about His gospel of judgement and salvation.

The fact that Christians are expected to sing "with grace" in their hearts means many things. The most important is that they sing only because God has worked in their hearts in the Gospel so that can and want to sing. Their songs of salvation are a testimony to the deep trust they have in God's salvation and the personal assurance salvation is for them too. There is a total commitment of some one who is saved to He who is their Lord.

As a final comment we must notice that music is not primarily for our own enjoyment, although we do enjoy it and God does bless us with the ability to perform and appreciate music. Instead the verse says we sing, "to the Lord." That is, our music is our offering to God. We should think of the music we perform and listen to as something holy that we give to Him rather than something that we use only of our own amusement and indulgence. We sing songs that He would want to hear, rather than songs that are popular with the world and that satisfy our own carnal tastes. That is why our songs should be shaped by the Bible, for His own words are sweetest to His ears. The words "to the Lord" also mean that what we sing is a prayer. If we have "risen with Christ," the desire of our hearts should be, "Oh, may we not join the world that sings its wild and foolish melodies. May we join the host of heaven that sings praises of and to the Lord, the Creator and Savior of the universe!" (Rev. 5:9-10)

Colossians 3:17, "And whatsoever ye do in word or deed, do all in the name of the Lord Jesus, giving thanks to God and the Father by him."

The word "whatsoever" means that Christians are never "off duty" in their fight against their sin. There is nothing Christians do that is so unimportant that it need not be measured against God's Word. There are no times in Christians' lives that they can call their own and do as their flesh pleases. Guarding against their sin is a never ending obligation. Turning from sin's appeal and walking according to God's will is a full-time business.

The point of the words "in the name of the Lord Jesus" is that no matter what Christians' do will reflect upon their Lord Jesus. His reputation is at stake among men (Matt. 5:16, John 15:8, Phil. 1:11, I Peter 2:12). The reason is that Christians' behavior reflects upon their Lord's wisdom and ability to guide and control them. So, based upon the fact that Christians love their Lord Jesus and are jealous of His honor, they do not want to sin.

Notice that the verse says "do all ... giving thanks to God." Life is hard for someone who not only tries to do all that life requires but also tries to avoid its spiritual pitfalls on his own strength. He might worry about some unsaved loved one and feel he must work hard at making them a Christian. He might be concerned about a future event, a present decision or a struggle and exhaust himself working out a solution. But Christ is in control. Rather than give in to frustration or worry, a Christian gives "thanks to God" because he trusts that Christ is competent, informed and wants the best for him. Armed with that truth, he can give thanks, even before the tale is finally told, that God will give him the victory.

Colossians 3:18, "Wives, submit yourselves unto your own husbands, as it is fit in the Lord."

Verses 18 through 22 illustrate the two principles. Everyday events of life will show that Christians are under Jesus' authority, that they are willing and able to do "all in the name of the Lord Jesus" in different life situations. Christians' own flesh, as well as their many human relationships either provide occasions to sin or opportunities to demonstrate resurrection power. We can see that power in Christians' relationships to their marriage partners, to their children, and to those in the hierarchy of human authority above and below them.

First, let us think about the counsel of wives. Husbands can be foolish and abusive. They often do not deserve the submission of their wives. That fact could encourage the tendency of wives, as all people, to heed their fleshly desire to feel sorry for themselves and lead them to take more control of their own lives. Yet the counsel of the Bible is that a wife "submit" to her husband. A Christian wife's submission to her husband reflects her submission to the Lord, and is a witness that she really is "in the Lord."

It is not easy for a wife to "submit." For one thing, as sinners, they lack a naturally submissive spirit. Also, many suffer under incompetent, hurtful husbands. However, knowing all of that, God has a chain of command among men and women (I Cor. 11:3). And based upon the power of the resurrected life, a wife can submit. A true Christian wife's focus is upon spiritual things (I Cor 7:14-17, I Peter 3:1-4), upon what things "fit the Lord" rather than what fits herself.

Colossians 3:19, "Husbands, love your wives, and be not bitter against them."

Next, let us think about husbands. Wives are sinners, too. It is as easy to find a reason to be "bitter against them." That fact could encourage the tendency of husbands, as all people, to heed their fleshly desire to selfishness and impatience, and lead them to abrogate their responsibility to sacrificially care for their wives, as well as seek the sympathetic companionship of other women. Yet the Bible commands husbands to "love" their wives, not just in word but in deed. A

Christian husband's love for his wife reflects the love that has been given to him in the Gospel.

Based upon the power of the resurrected life, a husband's focus can be upon spiritual things and he can love her, as Christ loved the church (Eph. 5:25), not because she pleases him in some physical way, but because he is committed to doing whatever is the very best for her soul. He knows that his wife is God's gift to him, just as Christ was given His people, the elect (John 6:37,38, 17:6,9,12), and is dedicated to her alone. It is his obligation, to which he is obediently attentive, not for personal gain or with an emotionally detached conviction of duty, but out "love." His love is the love of Christ expressed through his attitude and behavior toward his wife. He sees his wife as a unique person created by God, with a precious eternal soul. He understands that like he, she is a sinner, so he loves without any great expectations of love in return. His love is purposeful, maturely ignoring her foibles and sometimes foolish or hurtful words and actions for the greater goal of her spiritual benefit.

Colossians 3:20, "Children, obey your parents in all things: for this is well pleasing unto the Lord."

Now, let us turn to the counsel for children. Parents can be hypocritical and unfair. They may be right in some things, but not in "all things." That fact could encourage the tendency of children, as all people, to heed their fleshly desire to rebel and lead them to both question and challenge authority. Yet the counsel of the Bible is that children "obey." Christian children's obedience is not just to their parents, but also is a reflection of the fact that they are under the control of Jesus Himself and should seek to please their Lord.

Children are placed in a certain family by God's authority (Psalm 127, 128). Sometimes rebellious children will complain that they were not asked to be in the family in which they find themselves. But God does not have to consult them to know what is best. He is in control. He knows what He is doing and always does what is best (Acts 15:18). Rebellion to parents can be traced to rebellion against God.

Notice that the verse says, "all things." This brings to mind the tendency of children to look for special cases when it is OK to disobey parents in order to justify the pursuit of their own desires. The excuses children give for not obeying their parents multiply when they compare the prohibitions in their own lives with the privileges children in other families are given. It is true that a parent may demand that a child do something that is a sin. In that case, a child respectfully can refuse in the sense that he seeks to do God's will as revealed in the Bible. But in general, including cases when it is not clear if the parents wishes are right, children must not try to take control of their own lives. Unless they are clearly told to violate God's law, children must obey. The reason is that doing something that may be wrong but with the attitude of submission to parents in an attempt to be submissive to God is acceptable to God. By that obedience they are demonstrating a real trust in God's design for their lives and His care for them in all situations. It is a demonstration of faith that pleases God (Heb. 11:6,8).

Colossians 3:21, "Fathers, provoke not your children to anger, lest they be discouraged."

From this verse, we gain the following wisdom for parents. Children can be immature, exasperating and unthankful. They often operate in a thoughtless and self-centered manner. That fact could encourage the tendency of parents, as all people, to react in kind, and lead them to set a poor example, which would encourage their children to sin even more. Yet the counsel of the Bible is that a parent "provoke not ... to anger."

This verse is many times misunderstood to mean "fathers do not make your children angry. Do not let your discipline get out of hand. Do not punish your children so harshly that you break their spirit as well as their will." However, that is not a correct way to think about this verse.

The word "anger" is not in the original Greek text and should be left out. The words "to anger" are in italics in our English Bible to highlight the fact that they were inserted by the translators, probably because the translators held the common misunderstanding of the word translated "provoke." The Greek word translated "provoke not," is used only here and in II Corinthians 9:2 as "hath provoked." In I Corinthians 9:2 it implies "to create a zeal by example." Therefore, we can more accurately understand Colossians 3:21 to say, "Fathers, do not, by your personal example or in your interaction with them, encourage your children in their natural desire to sin." That will lead to their lack of interest in the Lord and lack of desire for living obediently to Him. Christian parents who are careful about their own walk with God before their children, show that they have been "raised with Christ."

Perhaps we could ask, would a father, or a mother for that matter, want to discourage a godly walk in their children? Some unbelieving parents do indeed deliberately seek to turn their children away from the Lord. However, more often, children are discouraged in an indirect way. For example, parents, especially fathers, insist on pleasing themselves at the expense of or the neglect of their children's spiritual benefit. Parents can neglect the spiritual instruction of their children. Parents can destroy a worshipful attitude in their children by insisting on their own amusements or desires on Sunday. Parents can spiritually demoralize their children and encourage a rebellious attitude by fulfilling their own physical interests at the expense of time and resources that could be spent on their children. Parents can be thoughtless and careless about their witness at home.

God gave children to their parents as a gift. Children are in a home by the authority of God. Parents have an awesome charge and God expects them to raise their children in the fear and admonition of the Lord (Eph. 6:4). Therefore, parents' reaction to God's call has a big and lasting effect on their children and succeeding generations. Incidentally, the words "provoke to wrath" in Ephesians 6:4 are a proper translation. The word "wrath" is part of the verse. It is helpful to compare it with Colossians 3:21. They are related but not identical. The message of Ephesians 6:4 is " don't act in a way that will encourage your children to be angry, that is, against God. The message of Colossians 3:21 is "don't act in a way that will encourage your children to indulge in sin."

Interestingly, what a person really is on the inside often is revealed most clearly in his relationships to children, especially to his own children. If a person is selfish, cruel and self-interested, it will come out many times as he relates to children. Why? Because children make many demands upon grown-ups without having the ability or sometimes the willingness to give much in return. A person who is not under the authority of the Lord Jesus will be frustrated and angry with the immaturity of children, always seeking to fulfill his own desires no matter what it costs the children. A person who is kind, forgiving, and sacrificial often displays his heart when children interfere with and conflict with the attainment of his own desires. A person, including a father, who is under the authority of the Lord Jesus will be understanding and patient with the imprudence and absurdity of children, always seeking to fulfill his children's real needs no matter what it costs himself (Psalm 103:13,14).

As it turns out, children know deep in their hearts the right way to act. They recognize the virtues that come from God in the behavior of their parents and recognize when their parents fail to live up to their responsibilities. Children, especially when they are very young, respond to the authority God has delegated to their parents, even though they are sinners and are eager to fulfill their own will. Children usually want to please their parents, even if only in an outward way, and readily follow the spiritual leadership of their parents. It is the job of parents to encourage their children to walk obediently to God and to discourage a life of sin.

Colossians 3:22, "Servants, obey in all things your masters according to the flesh; not with eyeservice, as menpleasers; but in singleness of heart, fearing God:"

Finally, we are given the example of servants. In the times in which Paul and the Colossians lived, servants were usually slaves, owned for life by their masters, who had complete dominion over them. However, the wisdom of this verse applies to anyone who is obligated to submit to the authority of another human being, even to the less restricting situation of a hired hand who is free to quit and seek employment elsewhere.

Masters can be unreasonable and tyrannical. They often can forget that their servants also are people, created in God's image, and order them about in an insensitive and even abusive manner. That fact could encourage the tendency of servants, as all people, to lazy indifference of duty or service that is motivated only by self-preservation. Yet the counsel of the Bible is that a servant "obey ..... in singleness of heart." Christian servants' obedience to their masters is not superficial but from the heart, and shows that they "fear God," who is their real Master. "Singleness" means "liberal" (II Cor. 8:2) or "bountiful" (II Cor. 9:11). They don't do the minimum, but work in a way that is best for their master because they care for him, from the heart

According to the Bible, being in physical bondage cannot stop a Christian from obeying his Lord (I Cor. 7:21-24). For one thing, service is a matter of the heart. A Christian can be faithful in his heart no matter what physical constraints to which he may be subject. For another thing, as always, God is in control. The physical limitations of God's people are not a barrier for Him. Nothing can stop Him from doing a His will, even though, from a servants perspective, his own situation is greatly confining (Phil. 1:12-14).

We might look at servants who have "masters according to the flesh" and think that is all there is to their lives, that they have no hope of doing anything worthwhile for the Savior. But that is not the whole story. According to the Bible, God puts servants into their physical situation. God is really over all men, so a servants' attitudes and reactions to their fleshly masters are the same as their attitudes and reactions to God. They must trust that God has a work for them to do that is designed specifically for their situation (Gen. 39:1-4, 45:5-8).

Christian servants obey their masters, "fearing God" because they know what is at stake (II Cor. 5:11). That is, there is a fear of judgment, if not for themselves then for the poor souls they meet each day, including the masers they serve. Christians also serve "fearing God" because they have a respect for the people whom they serve as image bearers of God (Rom. 13:7). More than that, as we saw in verse 17, they have a high regard for the name of Him whose name they bear and who is their real Master.

Colossians 3:23, "And whatsoever ye do, do it heartily, as to the Lord, and not unto men."

Verses 23 describes the proper motivation that must be behind the application of the two principles.

Verse 17 and 23 begin the same way. And their messages are related, for doing anything "in the name of the Lord," particularly to remove sin, should be done "heartily, as to the Lord." That is the only true and acceptable motivation for seeking victory over sin and serving the Lord faithfully. Christians serve out of the love they have for their wonderful God and Savior (Col. 3:14,23), whose sacrifice is completely sufficient for all that they need. Romans 13:10 teaches, "love is the fulfilling of the law" (I Tim. 1:5). Love for God is the only real basis for gaining victory over sin. In fact, seeking to gain victory for any other reason is sin.

Christians do things "unto men," of course. Christians do not live in isolation. Christians live among people. Christians work with and for people. But whatever they do, they must do it "as ... not unto men," as if a human being was not their boss or people were not the recipients of the benefit of their efforts. When Christians do anything here below on earth, they must think that it is to honor and benefit God in some way, out of a heart that loves Him. Whatever pleases Him should be their ultimate objective. That, incidentally, will turn out to be the most beneficial for the people whom they serve directly.

Colossians 3:24,25, "Knowing that of the Lord ye shall receive the

reward of the inheritance: for ye serve the Lord Christ. But he that doeth wrong shall receive for the wrong which he hath done: and there is no respect of persons."

Verses 24 and 25 continue to discuss Christians' motivation. Christians can be expected to "serve the Lord Christ" because of what He has done to free them from the power of sin and because He has given them the desire and power to do his will. However, Christians' inward motivation that drives their outward performance is often misunderstood. These two verses help us set aside two serious and commonly taught errors concerning why Christians seek to gain victory over their sin and faithfully serve their Lord.

First, let us consider the error that is a result of a misunderstanding of verse 24. It is often taught that believers receive rewards in heaven based upon a measure of their faithful obedience during their lives on earth. The idea is that missionaries and other workers in the Gospel who have sacrificially and faithfully served for years will receive more in Heaven than other Christians who lived negligent and indulgent lives or Christians who died hours after Jesus saved them.

The Bible teaches something very different. First of all, the Bible teaches that Christians are promised no extra inducements, honors, or rewards for anything they do on earth other than the gift of eternal life that is common to all believers. Verse 24 will help explain that fact. Secondly, the Bible teaches that Christians do not seek or expect any personal gain in compensation for their obedience to their Lord.

Let us look at verse 24 a little more closely. It states that "the reward" Christians will receive in Heaven is "the inheritance." We discussed the idea of inheritance when we examined Colossians 1:12, but we can briefly recall some points to help us in our evaluation of this verse. An inheritance is a unilateral promise that someone makes to another person. A person who makes the promise pledges his commitment to give another person something valuable, but the gift is not dispensed until after the person who made the promise has died. It is important to notice that, as an "inheritance," the "reward" is something bestowed upon Christians independently of anything that they have done in the past or do on earth after they are saved. The contents of the gift and the identity of the beneficiaries of the promise have been determined by God before creation (II Tim. 1:9). The reward promised is a blessing of sovereign grace.

If we study the Bible a little more, we will discover that the "reward" that is received by Christians as an inheritance is not something that God distributes to His people, but rather is God Himself, as we read in Genesis 15:1 (Psalm 90:1, Isaiah 28:5). That is, Christians do not just receive Jesus' blessing of salvation, they receive Jesus Himself (Col. 1:27, 2:6). Everything that Christians need and are promised is found "in him."

From this we can make some conclusions that help us set aside the wrong notion that a Christian can expect a reward in Heaven that is more than another Christian receives, based upon a his faithful life on earth. One conclusion is that, as we just stated, Christians receive Jesus as a reward. What more can anyone desire or hope for than Jesus Himself? Another conclusion is that, as we read in Romans 8:17 and 32, Christians are joint-heirs with Jesus, receiving "all things" that He is heir to (Heb. 1:2). What more can anyone receive than ALL things? A third conclusion is that, all the blessings Christians receive come from God as an unmerited gift unconnected to their own behavior (John 3:27, Col. 1:27, 2:6). The Bible states in Matthew 20:15 that all believers receive the same because the reward, like an inheritance, is based upon the decision of the giver and not upon the behavior of the receiver. It is true that deep in their hearts all Christians want to be more faithful, but some are more obedient than others. And yet, what differences will there be in the positions in heaven between the thief on the cross and the apostle Paul or John? The Bible says in Luke 18:28-30 that it is not related to what they do on earth. Is that fair? No, it is not fair. It is more than fair! The reward is all of GRACE to people who deserve wrath, including the most faithful missionary.

To that we can add the fact that faithfulness does not merit any special blessing or reward because faithfulness is a Christian's expected obligation (Luke 17:10,18). As Colossians 3:24 puts it, "for you serve the Lord Jesus." That implies Christians are His servants and they simply do what their Lord commands, humbly and gratefully. He is their Lord, whom they love because He first loved them. What else can they do? To see a more complete presentation of what the Bible says about the idea of rewards, please turn to the additional notes for Colossians 3:24 at the end of this chapter.

Now, let us consider the error that is a result of a misunderstanding of verse 25. It is often taught that Christians who neglected prayer, avoided Bible study, failed to deal with sin in their lives and did not witness to people as they should can expect some loss or embarrassing exposure on Judgment Day. The idea is that at the end of the world Christians are graded upon a review of their lives and then may lose some blessing based upon their performance. But that is a terribly wrong and spiritually dangerous idea.

The Bible's does not teach that at all. From the Bible we learn that there are no reviews on Judgment Day for anything Christians neglected to do or did not do properly on earth. The purpose of standing before the Judgment throne is always to pronounce innocence or guilt (Rom. 2:5-11, Rev. 20:12,13). Since all men are sinners, they will be condemned and experience God's wrath. The relief for Christians is that Jesus has already withstood that judgment for all of His people (Gal. 3:13, I Pet. 2:24). In fact, the Bible teaches that Christians will not only escape judgment, but also they will participate in the judgment of the unsaved (I Cor. 6:2-4).

If we look at verse 25 a little more carefully, we will see that the word "he," found twice, refers to unbelievers, for whom dealing with sin now is unimportant and unsuccessful. This observation is supported by the phrase, "and there is no respect of persons (with God)." According to Romans 2:11, the fact that God is "no respect of persons" is the reason why His judgment will descend upon all unbelievers, no matter what their national or ethnic background. The point is that, if there is no evidence of resurrection power in a person who claims to be a Christian, then it is not that he will be shown His errors on Judgment Day prior to being admitted to Heaven. Rather, it is that he will be revealed to be unsaved, to never have been a Christian at all.

Therefore, Judgment Day is not an time of evaluation, a grading period with the result that saved people will not lose their salvation but nevertheless will be embarrassed and sorrowful after a disclosure of their sins of omission and commission. As we indicated, judgment is always for evaluation of guilt or innocence, never a accounting for distribution of rewards. According to Roman 8:1 and John 5:24, judgment is passed for believers independent of their actions on earth. Since Jesus endured their judgment (Rom 8:3, I Peter 2:24), they are not motivated to serve out of fear of Judgment at the end of time. Fear is the beginning of the gospel experience, but fear brings sinners to Jesus and in Jesus they both find mercy and experience an operation of God upon their hearts, that consequently beat with a love for the Judge and Savior of the world (I John 4:17,18). To see a more complete presentation of what the Bible says about the idea of judgment, please turn to the additional notes for Colossians 3:25 at the end of this chapter.

The point of verse 24 is that Christians serve the Lord out of love because of all the unmerited blessings the have received and are promised. Christians do not obey out of gain because they have everything already (1:12). The point of verse 25 is that Christians serve the Lord out of love because He has removed the threat of the Lord's condemnation. Christians do not obey out of fear, for they are at peace with God (1:20). As we read in Colossians 3:23, the only one true and acceptable motivation for serving the Lord is out of a right heart, that is, out of a love which believers have for their wonderful God and Savior. Jesus' sacrifice is completely sufficient for all that a sinner needs. Therefore, all that a sinner does after he is saved is done in adoring gratitude for that sacrifice.

This idea is more understandable when we compare it to the normal relationship between a child and its mother. Is a child threatened or bribed to love its mother? No, a child can't stop loving its mother, it wants to, sometimes even amid abuse from its mother. Similarly, Christians love God with all their hearts. So the question is, when we seek to turn from our sin and serve the Lord, is it because we love Him, as His child?

All the things that God commands Christians to do are not things that they **must** do to be right before Him, instead, they are things that they **want to** do please Him whom they love.

Additional notes related to Chapter 6

Colossians 3:1-25

Additional notes for Colossians 3:1, **"If ye then be risen with Christ, seek those things which are above, where Christ sitteth on the right hand of God."**

Since Colossians 3 is addressed to people who are "risen with Christ," that is, to people who are saved, the implication is that Christians sin. Do Christians sin? Oh yes, many times. That is what God teaches in Romans 7:18-25. But they have the power within them to turn from a particular sin that is attracting and tempting them. Also, as months and years go by, Christians more and more conform their behavior to the will of their Lord. When Christians sin, they realize that they can blame only themselves (James 1:14). However, they also realize they can call upon God for help who is ready to give him them the wisdom and strength to gain victory over their sin.

The realization that they sin arrests Christians' tendency to pride. The message is, "Don't think that you are perfect, super holy and without sin. That is a conceit and a deceit that fools no one but yourself" (I John 1:8). Also, the realization they sin provides solace. The message is, "When you sin don't be overly discouraged or fearful." It is important to understand that the presence of sin in a Christians' lives is not an indication of a loss of salvation. It is a reminder of the fact that after a they are saved, they are a walking civil war (Rom. 7:17-24). This is an encouraging fact because the conflict reveal they are true Christians. If they were still spiritually dead, they would conform to the desires of their flesh without an intense or prolonged conflict. But since they are alive, they have both the desire and ability to fight against their flesh. Finally, the realization they sin provides the encouragement of companionship, for the word "ye" is a plural pronoun that embraces many people. The message is, "Don't think that you are the only one who is struggling with sin. You aren't weird or especially wicked." That is, not only does a Christian still sin, but all his brethren do too. It is not that a Christian is happy that other Christians agonize over their sins. Rather, the struggles he observes in other people's lives reinforce the thought that God has not abandoned him and that he must not be weary in well doing, but press on.

Christians should never be so surprised at the wicked things they say and do. After all, what else is new? What do they expect, especially when they remember that they are still encumbered by a body infected with sin? The issue is not whether Christians sins but "what do they do after?" Colossians 3 explains what should come after, if a person is truly raised with Christ.

Additional notes for Colossians 3:23, **"do it heartily, as to the Lord."**

God changes a person's heart on order to change his life. So whenever sin comes into a person's own life, either because he listens to the rival authority of his own desires or the words of another person, he must always ask, "What is the matter with my heart that I don't love and serve God? Who is ruling in my heart?"

As we mentioned before, the fact that sin bothers a believer is a good sign. It is a sign that sin is alien to his new nature; and with God's power and wisdom, he will once again be set on the right way to walk. For that a believer is thankful.

The prayer of thankfulness reminds a believer that he is dependent upon God's care, that he must walk step by step, that he must not be full of self-pity, but focus upon the blessings of God, that his mind must not be sin-occupied, but full of the words and love of his Savior, and that he must be looking, not for an excuse to fulfill his own desires, but to seek the opportunity to complete God's will for his life. There is a real peace and joy in obediently submitting to the authority of God. It is a joy and peace that sin cannot provide and which the world neither understands nor can take away. Above all, a believer is relieved and thankful that God is the supreme authority in the universe and that He is the Lord of his life.

Additional notes for Colossians 3:24, **"the reward"**

The Bible teaches that Christians do not receive special rewards for faithfulness which are to be bestowed at the end of time. Some verses which seem to contradict this statement are listed below, together with a brief explanation of their meaning.

1. I Peter 5:4 seems to imply that believers get crowns of glory. However, from Isaiah 28:5, we learn that our crown is God Himself.

2. II Corinthians 4:17 seems to hold the promise of special glory for those who suffer. However, from I Thessalonians 2:14, we see that

our glory is Jesus Christ Himself. The Bible also teaches that all believers suffer. It is their common lot (II Tim. 3:12). No special reward can be expected for those who endure it.

3. Luke 14:14 seems to imply that a recompense is due to believers. However, that verse also states that the recompense is the resurrection of the just, which is the reward of all believers, rather than the recompense of an especially faithful few.

4. Luke 19:12-27 seems to imply a position in heaven according to works on earth. However, there is no significance to the fact that one man received five and another ten. After all, why didn't the man with five pounds also get some of the money from the man with one pound (verse 24)? Therefore, the issue is not the five or ten.

5. John 4:36 seems to imply a wage for effort. However, the wage is eternal life given to all believers.

Here are some verses that support and clarify the statement that Christians do not receive special rewards.

1. Colossians 3:24 teaches that a believer's reward is an inheritance. There is a work in salvation for which a reward follows, but the work is all God's. The reward is secured by God and given in grace, willed, as a free inheritance to all of God's own. God's reward is their inheritance.

2. Romans 8:17,32 and Hebrews 1:2 teach two important facts. One is that all believers get the same inheritance. Another is that Christ is heir of all things and believers are joint heirs with Christ. Based upon these, we can conclude that there is nothing more that God can give one person than another. Essentially, there is nothing left which God can give as a reward.

3. Matthew 20:15 teaches that what God's people receive is God's prerogative. As the giver, God is sovereign, and what a believer obtains is not related to anything which he does.

4. Luke 17:10 teaches that all of a believer's work is nothing special. It is just their duty (Rom. 12:3).

5. Romans 4:1,4 teaches that grace and earned rewards are mutually exclusive. What God has in store for His people is not what they can earn by their own efforts. Their works before their salvation merit death (Rom. 6:23). Their works after salvation are done for love alone (Rom. 6:17).

6. Luke 18:28-30 tells us that the disciples wondered about rewards too. Jesus answered, "On this earth you will get blessings when you live obediently to God, but in Heaven the reward is always the same, eternal life."

7. Corinthians 9:17,18 teaches that a believer's expectation is only to bring the Gospel freely.

8. Genesis 15:1, Psalm 90:1, Isaiah 28:5 teach that the real reward is God Himself.

At the root of it all, our view of rewards reflects our view of God and of ourselves. We must recognize that God is all powerful, perfect, who does everything for us without any contributory works by us. We must also recognize that we are weak, sinful creatures who are blessed to have anything, even a scrap from God (Matt. 14:27,28). Therefore, we must live a life of humble gratitude and love to God our Savior without even a thought of rewards. More than that, any idea of rewards and works brings us back to salvation in which our efforts count for something and the cross is not totally sufficient. This is not the salvation of the Bible.

Additional notes for Colossians 3:25, "....shall receive for the wrong."

The Bible teaches that Christians do not stand for judgment of any kind at the end of time. The following verses support and clarify this statement.

1. Romans 2:6-11, Romans 14:10, II Corinthians 5:10 teach that all men, without exception, must be judged. However, the purpose of the "Bema" or judgment seat mentioned is not to evaluate the performance of a Christian with a view to reprimand or reward. The purpose of judgement is always to adjudicate. The question is, "Is a person innocent or guilty?" Every man's verdict is the same, guilty (Rom. 3:19).

Now, the Bible teaches that Christians faced judgment in Christ on the cross. All of their sins were judged (Rom. 8:3; Gal. 3:13; I Peter 2:24). Unbelievers, on the other hand, will face judgment on their own (Rev. 20:12).

2. Romans 3:22 teaches that believers receive God's own righteousness and so cannot be judged.

3. II Corinthians 5:8 teaches that believers go to heaven immediately after they die. No additional clean up is necessary. There is no evaluation of a believer's life at that time or later.

4. John 5:24 and Romans 8:1 are flat declarations that, for believers, there is no judgment. This is based on Christ's finished work of paying for their sins.

5. Hebrews 8:12, 10:17 teaches that God's attitude toward the believers is that He does not remember their sin anymore. He recognizes nothing for which he can judge the believers.

6. I Corinthians 6:2,3 teaches that at Judgment Day believers will actually be with the Judge participating in the judging process.

At the root of it all, our view of judgment reflects our view of God and of ourselves. We must recognize that God is all powerful and perfect, who does everything for us, without any clean up by us. We must recognize that we cannot lose our salvation, which standing for judgment would imply (John 10:28, Eph. 1:13). Therefore, we must live a life of gratitude and love to God our Savior without a thought of fear of judgment. More than that, any idea of judgment or accountability of Christians brings us back to a salvation in which God's work is not complete and somehow we must live a careful life after we are saved, or else we are liable for judgment. However, the salvation of the Bible is a one time act of God in which Christ paid for all of our sins, past, present, and future.

****

For the sake of completeness and to avoid some misunderstanding it is important to present a some companion ideas to discussion concerning the struggle Christians have with their sins.

a. Salvation is the foundation for gaining victory over sin

Based upon the phrase "be risen with Christ," we can state that salvation is the foundation for gaining victory over sin. We can understand this observation in two ways.

First of all, salvation is the foundation for gaining victory over sin in the sense that people first must be saved in order to deal successfully with it (Rom. 8:1-4). For people who are not Christians, successfully dealing with sin begins with seeking the mercy and grace of God for salvation. For Christians, the first step in dealing with sin is to "make sure that you are saved!"

As we face the so-called "practical" issue of dealing with sin, we must keep in mind that there is no separation between the doctrines of salvation and advice for Christian life. Truth in one leads to truth in the another. Error in one leads to error in the other. A person who does not correctly understand the doctrines of grace will eventually show it by how he lives his life. Conversely, any sin of attitude or behavior to which a person clings will eventually affect his understanding of salvation. That is why the best basis for a faithful walk with God is a correct understanding of salvation. Similarly, only a person with a humble willingness to submit to God's commands for his life is open to the truths of salvation as presented in the Bible.

Maybe we can better understand the idea that salvation is the basis for gaining victory over sin by asking the following questions. Is God's counsel, "Let me tell you how to do a better job than Adam and Eve"? Does God point us in the right direction and send us off to just try harder? Is our task to copy Jesus' life more carefully? Is the key to solving our sin problem leading a good life and going to church? Does a sincere effort count? The answer to all of these questions is, "No." Anyone who seeks to take the necessary steps to gain victory over the sins in his life, must understand that Colossians 3, or any part of the Bible for that matter, is not a do-it-yourself kit. As we said, dealing with our sins is really a salvation issue.

People who are not saved have no interest in denying their sinful desires and have no ability to turn from their sin, even if they wanted to. However, people who are saved have the desire and power to turn from their sin. Jesus Christ has given them a new life. They are animated by new motivations, objectives and abilities. Therefore, gaining victory over sin is first of all not a moral issue of performance, but an issue of salvation. Dealing with sin begins with redemption, which is a rescue from the wrath of God, and is accompanied by the resurrecting power of the Gospel. The expected moral and spiritual virtues that attend salvation are the resulting fruits, not the initial objective of the Gospel.

The answer to the question, "What can I do about my sins?" is "You can do nothing about it yourself." One reason is that we have accumulated a record of disobedience, for which we are accountable, that we are not able to erase by our own efforts. An inventory of our sins is not a list of wrong or neglected actions which we simply need to properly complete, in order to fulfill our obligation. In other words, solving our sin problem is not just a matter of eventually finishing what we were supposed to do. Nor is solving our sin problem a matter of adding acts of obedience to our record that hopefully will balance out or compensate for our acts of disobedience. The answer to the question "What can I do about my sins?" never is "Do better next time" or "Try to redo the job and fix what you did wrong in order to make up the difference for your mistake" or "Be good so your deeds will out weigh or cancel your bad behavior." No one can start life again with a clean slate. No one can go back, erase, and correct his acts of wilful disobedience. Every sin is a permanent, indelible mark in the book that God will open on Judgment Day in order to confirm the frightful destiny of every unsaved sinner (Rev. 20:12).

Another reason the answer is "You can do nothing about it yourself" is that we can do nothing in our own wisdom and strength. When God first meets us, we are dead. Turning from our sin and obeying God are impossible tasks (Matt. 19:26, Mark 10:27, Luke 18:27). We cannot raise ourselves from the dead. But what is impossible with man is possible with God. Only God can remove the judicial barrier between a sinner and His grace, and only God can raise up that which is dead.

We must keep in mind that our sin problem is really God's problem to solve. He first removes the penalty and power of sin through the sacrifice of Jesus. He then continues to deal with sin in the lives of His people after they are saved. It is all of God. Therefore, victory over sin begins by heeding the warning, "be sure that you are saved!"

In addition to that, salvation is the foundation for gaining victory over sin in the sense that after people are saved they must apply the same principles to their sin problem that brought them salvation in the first place. As we read in Colossians 2:6, Christians walk in Christ the same way they receive Him. Let us examine the process or means though which God saves people in order to understand how to gain victory over our sins.

We begin with the fact that God causes people whom He saves to recognize and focus upon their own personal sins (Psalm 32:5, 38:18, Prov. 28:13, I John 1:8,9). That is, in any situation that might lead Christians into sin or in which they have sinned, they must focus upon their own sin problem and not on the sins of another person, as real and as aggravating as the other person's sins may be. In any situation, especially when their sin involves a conflict with another person, they must contritely recognize their own culpability. They must face the shame associated with their own sin as well as be aware of the consequences they deserve, whether they are spared those consequences or not. That personal focus will make their sin problem clearer in their minds and make their struggle with sin less complicated.

Next, we turn to the fact that God causes people whom He saves to trust Him (Phil. 1:29). In any situation that might lead Christians to sin or in which they have sinned, they must believe the promise of His grace, trusting that He will forgive according to His Word. Also, they must trust His control over all things in their daily lives. For example, when their carefully prepared plans fall apart, when they are arrested from attaining something they want, or when they wonder about an unfair situation, they must not impatiently and aggressively strive to achieve what they want through their own wisdom and strength. Neither must they compare their situation with that of another person and become jealous, frustrated, bitter or vengeful. Rather, they must trust that God is always in control and can change any situation as He sees fit. They must conclude that things are the way they are because God has allowed them to be so. Then they must abandon themselves to God's management over the affairs of each day, expecting that God's ways are best and that He will direct things for their good and His glory. They must trust that no situation is more than God can handle. No situation can prevent Him from doing His good and perfect will.

Associated with the need to trust in God is the principle that people cannot serve two masters (Matt. 6:24). In addition to trusting God, people who seek to deal with sin must simultaneously relinquish control of the things that they treasure (Phil 3:13). They must give all those things to God. They must abandon all of own their plans, jealousies, resentments, hurts, fears, desires, or anything else that would divide their loyalty and keep them anchored to this world. On one hand, people who trust God must understand that God means what He says when He threatens to destroy all idols, together with the people who cling to them (I Cor. 6:13). On the other hand, people who trust God must delight more in the Lord than in any earthly pleasures or treasures.

The things of this world, which includes the desires of their flesh, work against their efforts to gain victory over their sin and their efforts to serve God whom they claim to love (Gal. 5:17). Therefore, anyone who trusts God in a half-hearted, double-minded way will never receive victory over his sin (James 1:6-8).

Finally, we face the fact that God causes people whom He saves to take deliberate steps of contrite repentance (Psalm 37:23, 143:8). In any situation that might lead Christians into sin or in which they have sinned, they must never think that a little indulgence does not matter or that they can take care of their sin sometime later. Sin problems only get worse. Sloth in this area often leads to great sorrow later. In fact, some people's procrastination may be an indication that they have no interest in God's will because He really is not their Lord and Savior, even though they might think He is. On the other hand, a true believer can take and wants to take prompt steps to change his attitude and pattern of behavior.

We can conclude our observation that salvation is the basis for dealing with sin by looking at I Corinthians 10:17. According to I Corinthians 10:17, God makes a "way to escape" for people who face sins and temptations. The word translated "way to escape" is used only twice in the Bible, once in I Corinthians and once in Hebrews 13:7 as "end." In Hebrews, it refers to the faithful lifestyle of rulers, whose way the other members should follow. The word translated "way to escape" is a combination of the prefix "away from" and the root, "feet." The root is used only in Acts 3:7, to refer to a man's restored feet as a picture of salvation. Our conclusion from all of this is that I Corinthians 10:17 teaches we have a "way to escape" only if God has given us "feet" to walk "away from" the sins and temptations. Those are feet that accompany salvation. The point is that a Christian's ability to deal successfully with sins and temptations begins with and continues all his life by God's work of grace (II Peter 3:18).

b. A finished work of God

Being "raised with Christ" does not mean people are raised part way or raised by installments. Salvation is an all-or-nothing proposition. In terms of John 15, a person either abides in the vine and produces fruit or he does not produce fruit because he is not in the vine. The fact is that the Holy Spirit fully equips a Christian to deal with sin (Rom. 8:13,14).

Since God's work of salvation is something that He does without any participation by those who are saved, it is a perfect and complete work that needs no amendments. Therefore, a Christian's objective for gaining victory over sin is not to prepare himself for entrance into Heaven. Colossians 3 is not a plan to help him be good enough to be accepted by God or to allow him to fix something in his life before he meets God. The notion that gaining victory over sin is a clean-up in preparation for entering Heaven implies that Jesus' atonement was insufficient, and that something is missing which is supplied by our own works or the work of someone else on our behalf. However, Jesus alone made full access to the Father for all of His children, inasmuch as he disposed of the barrier to Heaven that their sins erected. That access is available, both now in prayer (Eph. 2:18, Heb. 4:16) and after death when Christians go to be with God (Phil. 1:21-23). That is both a relief and a caution. It is a relief for Christians who understand that their right to enter Heaven is independent of their uncertain efforts in dealing with sin, and a caution for people who think that it is not.

c. Christians still sin

Colossians 3 is addressed to people who are "risen with Christ." The idea is that the counsel of the chapter is meant for Christians because they need it. The implication is that Christians sin. Do people who have the heart and the power to do God's will still sin? Yes. That is what God teaches in Romans 7:18-25. Keeping that fact in mind helps Christians deal with their sin.

First of all, the recognition that Christians do sin arrests any tendency to pride. The message is, "Don't think that you are perfect, super holy and without sin. That is a conceit and a deceit that fools no one but yourself" (I John 1:8). Christians must never attempt to protect their pride and self-respect because that action would be a barrier to gaining victory over sin. Christians must be humbly honest about themselves and their need of God's help. Their souls are righteous, the proof of which is that the moment they die they go to Heaven in the presence of a Holy God (II Cor. 5:8). However, while on earth, they are in a sinful body that continues to delight in its own sinful desires (Rom. 7:17-20).

Secondly, the recognition that Christians do sin provides solace in their struggle. The message is, "When you sin don't be overly discouraged or fearful." It is important to understand that the presence of sin in a person's life is not an indication of a loss of salvation. It is a reminder of the fact that after a person is saved, he is a walking civil war (Rom. 7:23). This is both an encouraging and a sobering fact.

A person is encouraged by the fact that he struggles because the battle shows he has life within him. We can compare this to a fish in the water. A dead fish is swept along with the prevailing tides and currents. But a fish that is alive often swims and struggles against them. Similarly, a Christian's struggles against sin is good news because those struggles reveal he is a true Christian, that he is spiritually alive. If he were still spiritually dead, he would conform to the desires of his flesh without an intense or prolonged conflict. But since he is alive, he has both the desire and ability to fight against his flesh.

A Christian must keep in mind that a person who is saved can never lose his eternal salvation (John 10:27-29, Rom. 6:23, Eph. 1:13). He can trust God's promise to keep him (Phil. 1:6, II Tim. 1:12). Although sin is found in his life, repentance and faith will follow, because he really is saved. That realization should drive him to seek the wisdom and power of God he needs to turn from his sin. And as time goes by, he will gain victory over this sin and that sin, never completing the job but always showing evidence of striving to be more faithful (Phil 3:13,14).

Thirdly, the recognition that Christians do sin provides the encouragement of companionship, for the word "ye" is a plural pronoun that embraces many people. The message is, "Don't think that you are the only one who is struggling with sin. You aren't weird or especially wicked." That is, not only does a Christian still sin, but all his brethren do too. It is not that a Christian is happy that other Christians agonize over their sins. Rather, the struggles he observes in other people's lives reinforce the thought that God has not abandoned him and that he must not be weary in well doing, but press on.

Finally, a person is sobered by the fact that he continues to struggle with a particular sin because a besetting sin could be an indication that the sin is par for the course in his life, that the sin is dominant and in control, that he is really not saved and has never been saved, despite his outward claim. That realization should drive him to seek the salvation of the Bible. When a person sins, it is always appropriate for him to reassess his spiritual condition and ask "Am I truly saved?" (II Cor. 13:5) If he really is saved, then he will be assured of his salvation by the Word of God (Rom. 8:16, 10:17). But he should never be so surprised at the wicked things he says and does. After all, what else is new? What does he expect, especially when he remembers that He is still encumbered by a body infected with sin? The issue is not whether a Christian sins, but "what does he do after?" Colossians 3 explains what should come after, if a person is truly raised with Christ.

Incidentally, the words, "Whosoever is born of God doth not commit sin; for his seed remaineth in him: and he cannot sin, because he is born of God," found in I John 3:9 do not contradict our claim that Christians still sin. In fact, the book of 1 John itself states, "If we say that we have no sin, we deceive ourselves, and the truth is not in us" (I John 1:8). I John 3:9 refers to the "inward man" which delights in the law of God (Rom. 7:22). A person who is saved is perfect in his soul. We say that based upon statement that, after a Christian dies, he goes directly to God's Holy heaven without any intervening purification (II Cor. 5:8).

d. Christians are victorious

In Colossians 1:3-6 we read, "we thank God ... since we heard of your faith ... and bringeth forth fruit, as it doth also in you." The fact is that Christians do eventually gain victory over a sin with which they are struggling (Col. 1:10, 2:5). That is what we read in Romans 8:1-5.

The realistic message of Romans 7, that Christians struggle in this world with the sins that so easily beset them, is followed by the message of Romans 8, that Christians do gain victory over sins. That victory is the hallmark of a true Christian's life. Even if, as Romans 7 points out, Christians temporarily lose some battles with a particular sin, they always win the war, because that sin cannot determine their eternal destiny, nor can it continue to determine their behavior. The point is that when a Christian submits to God's plan, there is a real expectation of success.

However, victory over sin is not a testimony to Christians' personal diligence and valor. God does not design a wise plan to overcome sin, disclose it to Christians, then equip them to gain the victory independently by their own earnest efforts. Rather, the victory is God's (Rom. 8:37, I Cor.15:57, II Cor. 2:14). It is God's victory in the sense that He has done all that is necessary in Jesus' atonement to vanquish His peoples' sin. And it is God's victory in the sense that He is the one who animates His people to deal with their sin (Gal. 2:20, Phil. 2:13).

Also, victory over sin does not mean that the propensity to fall into the same sin has been totally eliminated or that Christians will never sin in a particular way again. Instead, the victory is in the sense that, as time goes by, Christians grow and are more and more successful in recognizing and avoiding a particular sin that God brings to their attention. That is, Christians learn to depend more and more upon the wisdom and power of God in different situations (Prov. 3:5,6), recognizing that though they are weak, He remains faithful (II Tim. 2:13).

From that point of view, we could say that Colossians 3 presents two strong evidences that a person is a true believer. That is, if his greatest desire is to serve God and not himself, and if he reveals the power to gain victories over sins, then he reveals that he is indeed saved, and is under the authority of God.

e. Vigilance is required

Hebrews 12:2 warns that we must be aware of "the sin which doth so easily beset us." Sin is handy. It is as nearby as our flesh. The potential for becoming entangled in sin exists in every life situation. Therefore, the struggle against sin is a 24-hour-a-day job. Also, it continues until the day Christians die. The message is Christians must recognize that the struggle against their sin requires that they constantly be watchful. It can be expressed as, "Don't think you can let down your guard."

For example, Christians must understand that even though, by God's grace and abiding power, they have resisted the attractions of a particular sin for a time, that sin and its appeal never completely disappears. They must ever watch lest they once more heed and answer its appeal to their flesh. In another example, while God in His wisdom removes some issues of sin early in Christians' lives, He allows many others to remain so that they must deal with them, one at a time, over the remainder of their lives on this earth. That is, when God gives them victory over a particular sin, another sin that they had not previously noticed soon demands their attention. So they must begin to work on it. And yet each victory gives them wisdom to effectively struggle with the next sin, as well as confidence in God, who used His power to help them deal successfully with their past sins.

Christians must be diligent in Bible study and prayer in order to be prepared to deal with the temptations to sin they face every moment. Only through those two means will Christians have the wisdom and power to remain constantly vigilant, which is part of their struggle with sin as long as they live on this earth.

f. Why do Christians sin?

The Bible teaches, which our own experience supports, that Christians sin because they still live in their sin-corrupted bodies (Rom. 7:17-19). However, at this point we could ask, "Why would God allow Christians to sin, especially when we think about the great problem it is for them? Couldn't God prevent them from sinning? Doesn't I John 4:4 state that God is stronger than sin and Satan?" Yes, God could prevent Christians from committing many of the sins they do. The fact is that He does restrain sin in their lives, much more than in unbelievers' lives. In fact, it is only because of God's power that anyone turns from sin and obeys Him at all. Nevertheless, God does not prevent every sin. He allows some sins to continue in the lives of His people until the day they die. Is there any possible reason for that?

We do not know all that God knows or intends to do through the affairs of men, including the lives of His people. But some things are easy to understand. One reason God allows sin to persist in Christians' lives is that it teaches them something about God. They learn that when he does prevent any sin it is because He is so gracious and kind to people so undeserving (Psalm 107:9-13).

A second reason God allows sin to persist in Christians' lives is that it teaches them something about themselves. Christians' sins humble them as their sins force them to have a realistic self-image. Their sins remind them of their personal sin-tendencies and highlights their dependence upon God's abiding care (Rom. 7:24,25).

A third reason God allows sin to persist in Christians' lives is that it teaches them something about the Gospel. As Christians eventually gain victory over particular sins, they see that the promises and power of God's Gospel are real (Titus 3:3-6).

A fourth reason God allows sin to persist in Christians' lives is that it teaches them something about other people. On one hand, they observe other people struggling with a common foe, and are reminded that all people are earthen vessels, weak and in need of patience and mercy (II Tim. 2:22-25). It causes Christians to be sensitive and sympathetic with other people. They learn that other people should be targets of Gospel comfort, rather than criticism. On the other hand, as Christians slowly over time grow in spiritual strength, they become wise to the wiles of the world and the spiritual attacks of their enemies. So it causes Christians to have a realistic image of other people, and to trust God rather than men (Psalm 108:12).

g. Struggle with sin and assurance of salvation

When a verse such as Colossians 3:4 reminds people of the appearance of Christ, there are two possible reactions in their hearts. One is joy (Jude 24) and another is fear (Rev. 6:16). The reactions are based upon whether a person is saved or not.

It is a wonder that Jesus came to earth the first time to save His people from their sins. That work provided a certain and eternally secure salvation, that no one can erode or reverse. To that we can add another wonder, namely, believers can be absolutely sure they are saved. In other words, not only can believers know that God's salvation is true, but also they can know it is true for them. That personal conviction is called assurance.

God's people are not left to question if their Christian experience is a mental or emotional illusion. The message of the Bible is that "we know" (I John 4:13, 5:13). The assurance God's people have is based upon facts. They have evidence that they have been transformed by God's grace. According to Colossians 3:1 and 2, the evidence is that they can and want to obey their Lord. How is this evidence seen? The book of I John lists some of the ways. God's people have dealt with their sins in Christ (I John 1:9, 2:12) and continue to live faithful, obedient lives (I John 2:3,5,29). They are able to recognize and endure spiritual attacks (I John 4:4, 5:18). They genuinely love their brothers (I John 3:14,18,19). And they have the Spirit within them, Who bears witness with their spirits that they indeed are the children of God (Rom. 8:16).

Every person struggles with his own personal sin problems. Those struggles can cause him to question his spiritual situation. If discouragement and doubt dominate a person, if fear persistently lingers in his heart, then it is appropriate for him to ask, "Why do I fear? Is it because I am not saved?"

A true believer can draw upon those things he has close at hand in order to keep his thinking straight about his own spiritual situation. A list of those resources includes the true propositional statements of the Bible, prayer, and his past record of obedience amid temptations, as imperfect as that record is. With the evidence in place that he is saved, he can welcome the promise that "Christ ... shall appear." A person who is assured that God loves him as His child has inner peace, boldness before God and courage before men.

Chapter 7

Colossians 4:1-6

Colossians 3 describes how Jesus uses His authority to shape a believer's inward life. Colossians 4 describes how Jesus uses His authority to shape a believer's outward life, his calling or life of service.

Colossians 4:1 "Masters, give unto [your] servants that which is just and equal; knowing that ye also have a Master in heaven."

We might be inclined to consider this verse to be a continuation of the of list of examples begun in Colossians 3:18, inasmuch as the break at Chapter 4 is artificial because Colossians originally was a letter rather than a book. However, there is even better reason to think of this verse as a shift in thought, especially since it comes after Colossians 3:23-25, which interrupts the list of examples and turns our attention to the proper motive that ought to drive Christians' behavior. It will be our view that Colossians 4:1 turns our attention to a subject which is related to but different from the subject of Colossians 3. The main idea of Chapter 4 is that, having discussed a believer's proper inward character that is displayed in his properly motivated relationships with other people, Paul then turns his attention to a believer's outward service on behalf of his sovereign Lord.

Before we look at the details of verse 1, we can set aside its apparently narrow focus. It applies to more than the situation of human masters and servants. We can broaden the message to include all believers when we remember that this verse is part of the Bible and it is intended for all people of God (II Tim. 3:16,17). Additionally, when we learn what the verse commands, we will see that it does indeed fit the situation of all believers. Therefore, we can consider the example of "masters" in verse 1 to be an argument from the greater to the lesser. That is, if "masters" ought to do what is here stated, then we can expect all people with lesser authority to do likewise, no matter upon what rung of the ladder of authoritative hierarchy they happen to be.

Verse 1 begins with the command that "masters" must "give." Give what? The answer is, "give ... that which is just and equal." The idea behind the words "just and equal" is not as it is used by children at home or on the school playground to mean that believers must be fair and not cheat. Nor is the idea, as is sometimes mistakenly taught, that masters must not prejudicially give less to one person and more to another or that masters must not hold back wages but give to servants all that they have earned. A proper understanding of verse 1 begins when we recognize that the words "just and equal" are not a comment upon the amount of what is given or the manner in which it is given. The words "just and equal" are descriptions of what is given. Believers must give something that is called "just and equal."

The word "just," *dikaion*, sometimes translated "righteous," identifies God Himself (John 17:25, I John 2:1) or those things that belong to God, such as the Bible (Phil. 4:8). The word "equal," *isotees*, and a related word, *isos*, are used in various ways in the Bible. Sometimes the word "equal" identifies Jesus, who is equal with God (John 5:18, Phil. 2:6). Sometimes the word "equal" identifies God the Holy Spirit, who is the "equal" gift (Acts 10:45, 11:16,17 "like" = "equal"), given to all who are saved (Rom. 8:9). Therefore, we shall conclude that the phrase "just and equal" in Colossians 4:1 refers to God Himself. That is what believers must give. Masters, and so all believers, are obligated to bring God to the world. They do that when they faithfully speak the Gospel.

The words "knowing that ye also have a Master in Heaven" remind us that masters must give what is "just and equal" because that is the command of their Master, God in Heaven (Matt. 28:19,20). It is the job God has assigned to them and all Christians. That is how they can best serve God and man.

The words "knowing that ye also have a Master in Heaven" also remind us that masters must give what is "just and equal" because that is the example of their Master, God in Heaven (Matt. 9:35, Luke 4:15). Bringing the Gospel is the service God wants His people to do because it is what He wants to do. Christians want to walk in His steps, to do the same thing He does, and by grace He enables them to do it.

Evangelism is rooted upon the authority and example of God. Witnessing is the big assignment for believers, and it is that concept that helps us understand of all the rest of Chapter 4, including the following verses that speak of prayer.

Colossians 4:2, "Continue in prayer, and watch in the same with thanksgiving."

All believers, including masters, are told that continual prayer is a necessary companion to bringing the Gospel. People who bring the Gospel pray for opportunities to bring the Gospel. They pray that their motivation, attitude, words and behavior be faithful to God's word.

They pray for God's grace be upon those who hear the Gospel. They pray that God would continue to use their witness long after they have finished their testimony and have moved on.

Believers are commanded to "watch in the same." In Mark 14:38, the word "watch" means to notice and avoid temptation because "the flesh is weak." In Acts 20:31, the word "watch" is part of Paul's warning against men who "arise, speaking perverse things, to draw away disciples after them." With that in mind, and thinking back upon the main lessons found in Colossians 2 and 3, we can say that a believer's effort to bring the Gospel is hindered by his sinful desires and challenged by false teachers who oppose him. The idea of "watch" is that vigilance is necessary in bringing the Gospel.

Believers bring the Gospel accompanied "with thanksgiving." One reason for thanksgiving is the relief Christians have for the Gospel in their own lives. Another reason for thanksgiving is that they know that their "watch" will be effective, for God will keep them faithful in their own walk and in their proclamation of His Word (Jude 20-25). Still another reason for thanksgiving is the joy Christians have in delivering such a wonderful message to those in such desperate need of it (Psalm 126:6), for they are convinced their work in the Gospel will not be in vain but accomplish its intended purpose (Isa. 55:11, II Cor. 2:14,15).

We should note that, without ever seeing the results of the Gospel in the individual people to whom they witness, Christians nevertheless thank God beforehand. Why? Because they know He has the authority to accomplish His will through what they say and do (I Cor. 3:6, II Cor. 4:7). Worry, frustration or resignation over apparently disappointingly few conversions is replaced by trust and contentment. Boredom and compliance out of a sense of duty is replaced by willing, joyful obedience. Christians are thankful to know that somehow through their efforts God is glorified. Christians are thankful that, somehow through their efforts, God will find His lost sheep. They are thankful in all situations, even if their faithful witness causes them difficulty. They are thankful with whatever results from their witness, trusting that because God, the supreme authority, is in control, His will is done in His great way and in His great time.

Colossians 4:3, "Withal praying also for us, that God would open unto us a door of utterance, to speak the mystery of Christ, for which I am also in bonds."

The words "for us" are actually better rendered "around us." Paul was not asking for the Colossians' prayers because he and Timothy had forgotten to pray. Nor was he asking for the Colossians' prayers because their salvation was in question. Rather, the idea is that Paul wanted prayers because he and Timothy hoped "that God would open unto us a door of utterance." As always, God is in control of the opportunities for and results of a person's witness. He alone can "open a door" (Acts 14:27). Paul and Timothy knew that recruiting a large amount of people to pray for something was not going to affect God's plans that He had worked out from before the foundation of the world. But their call for prayer showed a God-given concern for the salvation of souls.

Unless God arranges and blesses circumstances so that His people can bring the Gospel, their labor will be as hard as going through a closed door. Any progress will be impossible. Unless God prepares people to hear the Gospel, His peoples' efforts will have no impact upon hearts closed in unbelief. Only God can make a difference (Matt 19:26). It is God alone who opens doors of opportunity to bring the Gospel and open hearts to receive it. Therefore, God people must pray. God alone has the authority and power to create opportunities and to create faith (John 6:37).

We might add that even the well known appeal in Revelation 3:20, that seems to expect people to respond to the Gospel call, means, "Go ahead and try to open the door. You won't be able to do it. The only handle on the door is on the outside." That is, God calls dead people to repentance and faith, then makes them alive whom He wills so they can respond to that call. Christians do not pray in order to change God's mind or influence Him to open a door He hadn't planned on opening. Rather, They offer prayers as an expression of their own desire for the salvation of others and as their confident expectation that it is God's plan to work through their prayers to do His will, even though they may not recognize God's specific work in response to their prayers. Christians' prayers also indicate that they are alert for opportunities to witness because they recognize the importance and urgency of the job.

The word "open unto us" imply that Paul and Timothy had their unique assignment. It is as if Paul said, "God may open a door for us and do something differently for you." All believers bring the message of the Bible, but the exact words believers use to explain the Bible and the opportunity they have to bring its message is not the same from one Christian to another. A Christian's ministry must not be a clone of anyone else's. A Christian must pursue the individual path God gives him that fits his abilities and circumstances. Not only is a person's work in the Gospel part of his unique call from God, but also his witness is a product of his individual, personal walk with God, rather than a program that conforms to some formulae or is an imitation of what seems to work for someone else.

We have already discussed the word "mystery" as an equivalent to the word "gospel" (Col. 1:27, I Tim 3:16), with the modifying premise that it highlights the gospel as a message understood by unbelievers only when it is revealed to them by the grace of God (Rom 16:25, I Cor 2:7, Eph 3:3,6,9).

The phrase "mystery of Christ" can be understood to mean the mystery has Christ as its chief content. The phrase also can be understood to mean the mystery is owned by Christ, in the sense that He is in control of the Gospel and reveals it to whom He wills.

With all of this in mind, Christian must pray for patience and humbleness when they bring the gospel remembering that God had to open their eyes, for no one can see the Gospel without God's grace. They must pray with compassion, since they realize there is much at stake. They must pray for courage and faithfulness, since they know they do not have the power in themselves to bring a true message amid certain antagonism and personal danger, to which the words "for which I am also in bonds" allude (I Cor 16:9). That is, faithful preaching will bring opposition, sometimes fierce opposition. So they pray that they may remain focussed upon the spiritual reality and need. And they pray that they will have the courage to remain faithful amid the threats, abuse and injury their enemies send their way, trusting that God is in control.   The words "I am also in bonds" mean that Paul was probably in prison at the time he wrote this letter (c.f. Col. 4:10,18). Out of that situation came his urgent appeal to the members of the church at Colosse, as well as Laodicea and Hierapolis, to look, as he was forced, beyond the harsh physical things that were so immediate and focus upon the all-sufficient Lord Jesus, who is above all circumstances. With this in mind, the words of verse 2, "continue in prayer" are especially meaningful, for prayer is needful to help maintain a heavenly focus amid earthly troubles. Also, when we combine the words "I am also in bonds" with the words "that God would open unto us a door of utterance," the message is that there is no physical situation, even something as confining and desperate as incarceration, that can prevent a believer from bringing the Gospel of his Lord Jesus. The reason is that Jesus has supreme authority and so nothing is a barrier to completing His work through His people (e.g.

Acts 16:25-40).

Colossians 4:4, "That I may make it manifest, as I ought to speak."

The word translated as "I may make ... manifest" occurs twice in Colossians 3:4 as "shall ... appear." It is used in I Timothy 3:16 to refer to Jesus' manifestation in the flesh as a human being. The words translated "as I ought to speak" could also be rendered "as I must speak," as in John 3:7 and 14. The idea of the verse is that it was just as mandatory that Paul display a faithful behavior as it was that he speak a biblically correct message. God is equally concerned with both, and so was Paul. God works through both (I Peter 3:1-4). They are equally important. Correct doctrine without a faithful live is hypocrisy. A faithful life without correct doctrine is not only impossible, it is illusion that encourages a gospel of works.

With this in mind, we can understand this verse to mean Paul wanted the Colossians to pray that he "may outwardly appear" to be an example of what he speaks. In other words, Paul wanted the Colossians to pray that God make his outward behavior match his message. He knew that his behavior was part of the witness that supported and illustrated his vocal message, so he wanted them to pray that he be as faithful in his life as he was with his words. The honor of the Lord whom he represented and the souls of the people to whom he spoke were both that important. It is true that the eternal destiny of people is in the sovereign hands of God and not in the fragile witness of a human. However, Paul's prayer revealed the work of God in his life. God purposefully planted that prayer in Paul's heart because it is through a combination of true words and a faithful life that God calls His sheep into His fold.

Colossians 4:5 "Walk in wisdom toward them that are without, redeeming the time."

We can think of the words, "walk in wisdom," in two ways. One way is to think that they mean "walk in Christ," who is wisdom (I Cor. 1:30). From that point of view the words mean "walk as someone saved," the only people who are "in Christ" (Rom. 8:1). Another way is to think that the words mean, "walk in the word of God." From that point of view the words mean "walk as someone who spends time in, understands and obeys the Bible."

The words, "them that are without," refer to unbelievers. They are people who are outside of the kingdom of God. The idea is that Christians always have a largely unbelieving audience to their witness, if not an audience who hears their words, then an audience who sees their lives (I Pet 2:15).

The words "redeeming the time" are important. It is always valuable to be efficient. Using the time that God gives us and not wasting it is part of being a faithful steward. However, the main point of this phrase is a little different than that. The word "redeeming" means to buy back" or "buy out of," and is used for Jesus' purchase of His people, as in Galatians 3:13 and 4:5. How are we to "buy back the time"? Once time has passed it is not possible to buy it back. It is gone forever. One possible answer comes from Ephesians 5:16. That verse explains "redeeming the time" is necessary "because the days are evil," and puts it in the context of a Christian's struggle against false prophets. With that in mind, the idea of the phrase "redeeming the time" seems to be as follows. False prophets try to use the time to spread their own message. But they are using time improperly. Time was invented by God so that the Gospel could go out into the world. Therefore, Christians are commanded to use time for speaking the truth that false prophets use for their own purposes. Christians are told "Don't let false teachers use all the time for their lies while you use no time for the speaking the truth. Use time to preach the Gospel so that they are not the only voice heard."

We also can think of the phrase "redeeming the time" in another way. All times are not the same. Paul wrote at a time after Jesus fulfilled the Gospel promise, at a time after He died and was resurrected to pay for the sins of His people. Paul also wrote after a time called "Pentecost," when God began to harvest souls in all the world through the preaching of the Gospel. That is, when Paul spoke it was the "time" for salvation for the people of the world (II Cor 6:2). Later there will be no time for that, either because many people die each day or because eventually time will come to an end on earth. But there was time right then. So "redeeming the time" means that there is a sense of urgency because there is "no tomorrow" for anyone who is unsaved, that is, there is no guarantee of a tomorrow and certainly no salvation after they die (Heb. 2:3, 3:3, 9:27,28) or after the end of time (Rev. 10:6,7).

Colossians 4:6 "Let your speech be alway with grace, seasoned with salt, that ye may know how ye ought to answer every man."

The message of verses 1 through 5 is, "Be willing and ready to bring the Gospel as God gives the opportunity. Pray for it. Be patient and content with the opportunities God gives you and the apparent results of your efforts. Be sure your behavior supports what you say." The message of verse 6 is, "Now let me tell you what you should say. Let me give you the content of your Gospel."

The words "speech be alway with grace" can refer to two different ideas. First they can refer to the content of Christians' "speech." That is, Christians must always preach the doctrine of grace, salvation by sovereign grace apart from the works of man, salvation by unmerited grace bestowed upon sinners because of God's great love. Secondly, the words can refer to the manner in which Christians bring their "speech." That is, Christians must always speak "in grace," as the words really are, or in a gracious manner. Just as God Himself brings His gospel with a meek and gentle spirit, Christians are similarly to be His ambassadors (II Tim. 2:24-26).

The words "seasoned with salt" are usually misunderstood and require a little careful explanation. Many teachers commonly but wrongly explain that the Bible uses the word "salt" to emphasize preserving, purifying, or flavoring. Some Bible teachers will say that the words "seasoned with salt" mean that our speech should include things that are a blessing to others, words that are flavorful, dynamic, and supportive of the person to whom we are speaking. If we use our common experience to decide what salt means, that would be a fair conclusion. But that conclusion is not the result of good Bible study and must be avoided. The Bible does not use the word "salt" in any of those ways.

Consistently, the word "salt" is used in the Old Testament to refer to the judgment of God (Gen. 19:26, Deut. 29:23, Judg. 9:45, Ezek. 47:11, and Zeph. 2:9). Salt also is part of the sacrifices (Lev. 2:13). However, even the sacrifices bring a message of judgment because they are figures of the sacrifice of the Lord Jesus Christ who endured the wrath of God on behalf of sinners (Heb. 10:4-14).

The New Testament uses the word "salt" in a similar way to the Old Testament. For example, Mark 9:49 quotes Leviticus 2:13 as a support to the statement "for every one shall be salted with fire," referring to the fire of sacrifice and, therefore, to the fire of God's judging wrath.

Therefore, because salt refers to the judgment and wrath of God, the counsel "let your speech be alway ... seasoned with salt," means our speech must include the judgment and wrath of God. This was certainly the content of Paul's own witness (Rom. 1:18, 5:9, II Cor.

5:11). It was consistent with Paul's faithful use of the whole Bible, with its messages of the threat of God's judgment and the promise of God's mercy (Acts 20:20,27).

Believers have a responsibility to tell the whole truth as the Bible presents it and trust that God will do His work as he has said. According to Hebrews 4:12, the Bible is a two-edged sword, and we must expect it to cut two ways, both for salvation and for condemnation (II Cor. 2:15,16).

Believers must not seek to present a gospel that is popular, that is, to talk only of the love of God which would more easily endear them to their audience. In fact the idea of the love of God does not make sense until Christians explain that God's love caused Him to send Jesus to bear the His wrath for sinners. Christians must resist the temptation to shape their witness to get the greatest response.

Also, they must not focus upon the results of their witness, and emphasize the love of God in order to woo people into the kingdom of God. Whether many or few are saved, the results of their witness are in God's hands (I Cor. 3:6). God intrusts to His people His word, which declares what He has already willed in heaven (Matt. 16:18,19). They must be faithful to that supreme authoritative Word in both what they say and what they do (I Cor. 4:2). It is the job of every believer to make sure that his "speech is always with grace, seasoned with salt," and leave the work of salvation to God.

Once God is our authority and we bring the whole counsel of God as we have just learned, then we will "know how" to "answer every man." The word "answer" does not necessarily mean "to respond to an asked question." In fact, the word "answer" could refer to someone who asks a question or it could refer to a person's response after he evaluates what he hears or sees around him (Acts 25:4,9,12,16). That is, a Christian brings the whole counsel of God as the appropriate response to every situation he encounters, whether it is a proper answer to a question or a proper response to the events that happen to and around him.

Finally, the whole counsel of God is the appropriate response to "every man." A Christian's message is the same no matter who is listening. A Christian may not say the very same words to ever person with whom he speaks, as in a memorized script, but he does bring the same message, the same Gospel. A Christian may apply the Gospel to the particular problem of the person to whom he is speaking, emphasizing one aspect of the Gospel over another, but he does not modify the warning or the comfort of the Gospel according to the culture or the desires of the people who hear him (I Cor 2:2, II Tim 2:15).

Additional notes related to Chapter 7

Colossians 4:1-6

Additional notes for Colossians 4:6, **"seasoned with salt"**

To complete our explanation that the words "seasoned with salt" refer to judgment, we also must understand two other phrases that use the word "salt." One phrase is found in Mark 9:50, that states "salt is good." How can salt be good if it is associated with the wrath of God? Is God's wrath good? In answer to these questions, it helps to look at Matthew 5:13 that states, "ye are the salt of the earth." By comparing Mark 9:50 with Matthew 5:13, we can see that salt is good because Christians are the salt of the earth. This conclusion is reinforced by the command in Mark 9:50, "have salt in yourselves." In other words, it is because Christians have salt in themselves that it is "good." To put it another way, the statement that "salt is good" is a reflection of the fact that believers have the message of salt or judgement in themselves. That means believers tell people the truth about their sin and the consequent penalty of judgment that can be expected. That message of judgement is a source of "good" to unsaved people, showing them their peril in order for them to seek God's mercy while there is still time, as we read in II Corinthians 6:2. Believers' salty witness is "good" in the highest degree when it arrests people in their headlong race toward Hell and causes those people to flee to God for mercy (Isaiah 1:18-20).

Another phrase we should try to understand, also found in Mark 9:50, is "if the salt have lost his saltness." In the physical world, salt cannot lose its "saltiness." It is either salty because it is salt or it is not salty because it is not salt. It might be disguised by other substances, but if it is salt it still has the same chemical composition and taste. There is no physical counterpart to salt losing its saltiness. Losing saltiness must mean losing salt. God uses words from the physical world, but He uses them in a way that forces us to seek a spiritual understanding of those words. The warning that salt must not lose its saltiness can be understood to mean that believers must be sure not to neglect the truth of the coming judgment whenever they witness to other people (II Thess 1:7-9). A witness that does not bring the whole counsel of God is not a faithful witness and in God's eyes is worthless and to be cast out. If people are not warned of the coming wrath of God, why would they want to flee to the Savior for protection? What are we to be saved from, if not from God's wrath? If Christians do not warn the people of the world, who will? A Christian's greatest service to people is to tell them the full story, to help them prepare to meet God.

Chapter 8

Colossians 4:7-18

These verses illustrate how God's authority shapes the lives of His people

Colossians 4:7-9, "All my state shall Tychicus declare unto you, who is a beloved brother, and a faithful minister and fellowservant in the Lord: Whom I have sent unto you for the same purpose, that he might know your estate, and comfort your hearts; With Onesimus, a faithful and beloved brother, who is one of you. They shall make known unto you all things which are done here."

We read that Tychicus and with Onesimus were two men "whom I sent" (verse 8). That seems to have been the main theme of Tychicus' life, for he also was sent to the congregation at Ephesus, as well as to Titus (II Tim 4:12, Titus 3:12). One reason they were chosen is that both Tychicus and Onesimus were "faithful" (verse 7 and 9). Another reason is that both were willing to speak ("declare, verse 7, "they shall make known,"verse 9). They were trustworthy and capable. In addition to that, Tychicus and Onesimus were good candidates to be couriers because Tychicus was from Asia (Acts 20:4), the location of Colosse and Onesimus was a Colossian ("who is one of you," verse 9). Both men knew and were known by the Colossians. Their message from Paul would more likely be received by the Colossians, and their report to Paul about the Colossians would more likely be accurate. We should add that the word "sent" implies they were recruits rather than volunteers. That does not mean they were reluctant but that they had a commission. In other words, the journey to Colosse was not their own idea. They were both sent by Paul, under the authority of God. Therefore, what they said was something to which the Colossian had to pay attention. Also, the Colossians were expected to disclose their "estate" and not hide anything.

The words "all my state shall Tychicus declare" point out that a person who is under Jesus' authority lives in a glass house (I Peter 2:12). Tychicus together "with Onesimus" was going to tell "all" about Paul. And that was OK because all that Paul did was a display of God's work. It was not that, as Paul's "beloved brother" in the Lord, Tychicus would give a biased report in favor of Paul. Rather, Tychicus, together with Onesimus, as a "brother" or fellow Christian, knew what it meant to live under Jesus' authority. He could verify that Paul's life and ministry were genuine. It is fitting that Christians confirm and support the life and work of other faithful "brothers," especially if they both are "fellowservants" in the ministry (Eph. 6:22). In fact, that two men were sent to Colosse meant, in accord with the formula in II Corinthians 13:1, they could confirm the truth of each other's report. In addition to that, the two men were expected to return to Paul with a report of the spiritual "estate" of the Colossians, as Epaphras did (Col. 1:8).

From the exchange of news between Paul and the Colossians through the two men, concerning what God was doing in their lives, we can draw an important lesson. Not only do Christians bring the Gospel of God's mighty works of salvation to the unsaved people of the world, but also they tell each other of God's work in their lives (Psalm 22:22, 107:2). On one hand, it is true that conversation among Christians often is full of the joys and concerns of family, friends, work and school. It is no surprise that Christians are interested in the minutia of the business of life on earth. That is expected and is as it should be. After all, Christians' interest in the details of each others' lives reveals a genuine mutual concern. On the other hand, Christians' also must eagerly talk about and listen to what God has done and is doing in their lives, for it is the evidence of God's work that especially gives them "comfort."

Colossians 4:10,11, "Aristarchus my fellowprisoner saluteth you, and Marcus, sister's son to Barnabas, (touching whom ye received commandments: if he come unto you, receive him;) And Jesus, which is called Justus, who are of the circumcision. These only are my fellowworkers unto the kingdom of God, which have been a comfort unto me."

These verses introduce three Christians of Jewish heritage, an observation based upon the phrase in verse 11, "who are of the circumcision." Aristarchus, Marcus, and Jesus called Justus were men who represented God's grace and illustrated His authority in the lives of the blood descendants of Abraham. The words "these only" cannot mean they were the only ones who helped Paul in the work of ministry, for Timothy and Epaphras also did. The words must mean that, in the geographical location where Paul was at that time, of those people who were of the circumcision, "these only" helped. Especially among the

Jewish leaders, Paul found enemies instead of "fellowworkers." Many considered Paul a traitor, for he now marched to a different authority.

Not much information is given about these three men, but we can make the following general comments in light of the theme of authority we have chosen to emphasize. Aristarcus was a long term companion of Paul, and courageously accompanied him at the risk of personal peril (Acts 19:29, 27:2). Aristarcus' submission to the Lordship of Jesus was not a flash-in-the-pan, emotional commitment. He continued under the service of Jesus even though, as we read in Colossians 4:10, it meant prison. And we must note that prison in those days was not comparable to a monitored, humane correctional institution of today. It was wretched confinement in a dungeon administered by the rules of that day. We see God's control in Aristarchus' live through his enduring faithfulness, not in his physical condition. Aristarcus' life is a testimony that the evidence of God's authority over a person is not necessarily related to his physical situation.

"Marcus" is the "John Mark" of whom we read in Acts 15:36-39. His life illustrated God's restored control over a lamb who became lost. Briefly, the story was that Paul was unwilling to take Marcus with him to the mission field because Marcus had deserted him and Barnabas during a previous journey. But now we read that Paul expected the Colossians to "receive him," to extend to Marcus the hospitality they should give to any minister of God (III John 5,6). In fact, Paul later stated, "Take Mark, and bring him with thee: for he is profitable to me for the ministry" (II Tim. 4:11). What a change! Marcus had wandered away as a lost sheep, but the Shepherd brought him back to the fold. Jesus' gracious, loving control over Marcus, that began before the creation of the world and continues into eternity, was unbreakable, even by Marcus' temporary foolishness. God's care for Marcus depended upon His grace and not Marcus' performance.

"Justus" was a man whose house was part of the synagogue (Acts 18:7). The Bible also says he "worshipped God." It could be that he lived next to the synagogue because he participated in the service. Perhaps Justus was a true Christian at that time and ignorantly continued some of the Jewish rituals but received Paul into his house because he was willing to be more carefully instructed in the way. Or, perhaps Justus was still of the Jewish faith but was open to hear the true Gospel. The fact is that he extended hospitality to the hated Christian, Paul. So, evidently God had taken control of his life and his house. The message is that being previously misguided, following another religion, does not disqualify someone from grace. When a man has chosen a religion and has practiced it for a while, he becomes more and more resistant to any other way. The Gospel claim of exclusive truth is especially obnoxious. The Gospel is a threat because it exposes the inadequacy of a person's imagined protection from God's wrath. The Gospel is an embarrassment because it reveals him to have been a fool all along. The Gospel is odious because it removes all the familiar comforts of religious habit and ritual. There is plenty of reason for a person in another religion to resist the Gospel. But, the Lord of all creation is so powerful He can turn any heart toward him.

Paul wrote "these ..... which have been a comfort to me." In light of Romans 10:1, Paul was comforted that some of these Jews, his kinsmen according to the flesh, were saved. They were a testimony to Paul that God has not cast off all of His people, that God has not broken His promise to save a remnant from all nations, Israel included. Normally, Jews provided Paul's greatest opposition, but by grace these men were a comfort to Paul, both because they were saved, and because, as saved men, they helped Paul and his work in the "kingdom of God.".

Colossians 4:12-14, "Epaphras, who is one of you, a servant of Christ, saluteth you, always labouring fervently for you in prayers, that ye may stand perfect and complete in all the will of God. For I bear him record, that he hath a great zeal for you, and them that are in Laodicea, and them in Hierapolis. Luke, the beloved physician, and Demas, greet you."

If the three men named in verses 10 and 11 are specifically identified as "of the circumcision," then we conclude that three men named in verses 12 through 14, by contrast, were not of the circumcision. That is, these verses introduce three men of Gentile heritage. That observation also can be inferred from the fact that Epaphras was called "one of you." That is, Epaphras was a Colossian, most of whom were Gentiles. The ethnic background of most of the Colossians can be deducted from the warning found in Colossians 2:11, which can be understood to mean, "You have a spiritual circumcision. So, don't let anyone insist that you must have a physical circumcision." That is, most of them were not physically circumcised because they were born Gentiles. Therefore, Epaphras, Luke, and Demas were men who illustrated God's authority in the lives of people who had no physical tie to Abraham. They, together with the men named in verses 10 and 11, illustrate that God's authority extends over people of all mankind (Acts 10:34,35, Rom. 3:29,30).

Based upon the little we know of these men, we shall make the following observations. "Epaphras" was a "fellowprisoner" (Philemon 23), as was the Jew, Aristarchus. So, God's assignment for His people is the same, no matter from what ethnic or cultural heritage they come. And their courageous commitment to that assignment is the same, whether Jew or Gentile.

Epaphras' commitment to the Colossians is clear from the words "labouring fervently for you." But his commitment was not primarily based upon their shared, common Colossian background, upon being "one of you." Rather, it was based upon the "great zeal" he had for the souls people, no matter who they were, whether they be from Colosse, from "Laodicea" or from "Hierapolis." God controlled Epaphras' vision to see people, not provincially, but humanly.

"Luke" was "the beloved physician." Luke was educated and trained to help people with their physical problems. Luke willingly accompanied Paul on many of his missionary journeys, to provide what help God had equipped him to supply. He was qualified to give some medical assistance as needed and to chronicle the work of the Gospel in the book of Acts (Luke 1:3, Acts 1:1, 16:10 "we," etc). But Luke learned, both from God who opened his eyes and from personal experience, that physicians do not have the ability in themselves to heal, only God does. Human physicians just bring the medicine and the therapy through which God works. More than that, Luke understood the great spiritual sickness that transcended any physical malady. So Luke was picture of someone who brings the healing of God's gospel.

Of "Demas" no comment is given. Possibly, Paul was silent because he didn't have anything to say, although Paul did tell Philemon that Demas was one of his "fellowlabourers" (Philemon 24). In II Timothy 4:10 we learn that Demas forsook Paul because he loved this present world. We cannot know from the Bible itself if Colossians with its silence, Philemon with its neutral or mildly positive comment, or II Timothy with its strongly negative comment was written first or last. The sequence would indicate if Demas' life ended in apostasy or restoration. Marcus' sad defection is found in Acts. And since the encouraging words of Colossians and II Timothy were written after Acts, Marcus' story had a happy ending. That could have been Demas' story too. Or it could be that Paul said nothing positive about Demas because he suspected something amiss in Demas' life. Even if Demas ended up as an unbeliever, we recognize God's control, for as we read in Matthew 11:25-27, the fact that Epaphras and Luke had spiritual sight and Demas possibly did not is a consequence of God's sovereign, gracious decision (Rom. 9:18). One lesson that comes out of all this is that working in the ministry is not a substitute for a personal relationship with God. According to I Timothy 4:16, "Take heed unto thyself, and unto the doctrine; continue in them: for in doing this thou shalt both save thyself, and them that hear thee." That is, there is no substitute for the cultivation and nurture of a personal walk with God (I Cor. 9:27, II Cor. 13:5).

Colossians 4:15,16, "Salute the brethren which are in Laodicea, and Nymphas, and the church which is in his house. And when this epistle is read among you, cause that it be read also in the church of the Laodiceans; and that ye likewise read the epistle from Laodicea."

Verses 10 through 14 illustrate that God's church is composed of a variety of people, like a patchwork quilt. Verses 15 through 17 illustrate that God's church is united into one body. That is, the quilt is one whole, even though it is put together of many different pieces (I Cor. 12:12). As we learned that God is in control of each individual person who hears the Gospel, whether they become saved or not, so we learn that God is in control of that the congregation which they join.

The name "Nymphas" is based upon the word for "bride"(John 3:29, Rev. 21:2,9) or "bridegroom" (John 2:9, Rev. 18:23). Inasmuch as it refers to a male, the second reference seems to be more appropriate. We are tempted to think of "Nymphas" as a picture of Jesus Christ, for all believers together are the church in His house. Nothing more is said of him personally, so we cannot learn any lessons from His life. But the image of a bridegroom is important for it reminds us of a passage like Ephesians 5:25-32, that explains Jesus' love for His church. That is a big subject that we cannot fully investigate here. However, we should keep in mind a few important ideas.

The word "church" refers both to all true believers throughout the world and time, a spiritual congregation, and to all the local congregations scattered throughout the world and time, the people who meet physically each Sunday. Of the organized church, we must make a few things clear. When a local organized congregation is in control of true, faithful believers, it is a true church. When a local congregation is under the control of unbelievers, who profess to be a may outwardly, in some aspect, appear to be true believers, it is not a true church of

Jesus, no matter what the members may call themselves. If it began as a true church, and over time unbelievers took control, then it will not continue faithful and eventfully cease to be a true church. The Bible does continue to call national Israel His in the Old Testament, His congregation, even after they went apostate. But He then says that He divorced it and it was not his bride anymore. Unbelievers were in control and God rejected it.

Today there are a variety of individual local churches scattered around the world. Some are more faithful than others. When a local church becomes under the control of unbelievers, like Old Testament Israel, it becomes apostate and is rejected of God, like Laodicea eventually was. Such a congregation is not Jesus' church, no matter what they may call themselves. However, God is merciful to in the lives of true believers, otherwise they would not be believers. God spiritually takes care individual believers and so a collection of true believers, a congregation in which true believers are in control, according to the principles and example of Ephesians 5:25-28 and Colossians 3:19. That is, according to Romans 7:18, no individual true believer and therefore no congregation of true believers are without sin, in doctrine and practice. To teach that they must be, or can be without error in doctrine or practice and to teach that God expects them to be on this side of eternity is against the Bible and a gospel of works. That is, such a notion is saying that an individual's or a congregation's standing before God is dependent upon their performance. But that is not true. Performance is important because it is proof of God's prior work of salvation (Rom. 7). But an individual or a congregation never is faithful 100% of the time on this side of eternity.

Jesus is the "Nymphas" because He chooses His bride and works to "sanctify it" (Eph. 5:26). He alone loves and sustains true believers. Even though they never, individually or collectively, are finally without sin of doctrine and practice, Jesus continually cleanses them by His Word. And, as we arrive near the end of time, the amount of true believers, the remnant, will be small. The amount will not be zero, but it will be small.

When we read the phrase, "and the church which is in his house," our focus is directed to Christians as a unit, one house of God, composed of all believers (Heb 3:6). God is concerned with the whole body of believers. God is concerned with individual believers where ever they are found in the world. But God also cares about His people's collective spiritual health and vitality, as well as their collective witness to the world. Any part of the body, anywhere in the world, that is weak will effect the rest of the body. So, the warnings in the letter to the Colossians were also needed in neighboring Laodicea. That is why God, through Paul, expected both the Colossians and Laodiceans to share their letters, especially when we consider the fact that the church at Laodicea became apostate a few years after the Colossian letter was written (Rev. 3:14-17). There is one body of God, and the same food of God's word is needed by all.

The physical riches of the church in the neighboring city of Laodicea did not lead to its apostasy until years after this letter was written. Yet Paul, knowing the tendency of all people to be attracted to and be impressed by the things of this world, may have written Colossians 1:27, 2:10 and 3:2 with that in mind. It was always his desire to guide the members of the churches to focus upon spiritual rather than earthly things.

Colossians 4:17, "And say to Archippus, Take heed to the ministry which thou hast received in the Lord, that thou fulfil it."

The name "Archippus" is based upon words that mean "chief" and "horse." We can think of the horse as the symbol of strength (Job 39:19, Psalm 147:10). Archippus also is identified by the word "fellowsoldier" (Philemon 2). Putting this all together, the picture is that Archippus represented a man of strength in the service of the Lord's army (II Tim. 2:3,4). That he was strong is not in itself bad. It is just that, as his name reminds us, people have a tendency to be impressed by human strength. It is, then, a short step to trust in that rather than God (Psalm 20:7). The words "take heed" warn Archippus that his strength must be harnessed to do God's will. It is a real temptation for someone to either feel safe or confident, supported by the human strength with which he may be gifted, but that is not the strength upon which someone who has been given a "ministry" should rely (Psalm 118:8,9,14). A person's ministry is not fulfilled upon his own strength. It is true that God uses a person's attributes to do His will, such as mental and physical talents and skills. But a Christian's ministry is successful only because God works in the hearts of the people who hear the word that he speaks or writes.

"The ministry" was what Archippus "received of the Lord" as a gift. First of all, that means his ministry was given to him by God's sovereign decision. He did not apply for the job and then was offered a place on Paul's Gospel team because he had submitted a proper resume. The message Archippus he spoke, the ability to declare it and the opportunity to share it were all gifts from God. Secondly, that means he was supposed to serve others. His ministry was not intended to benefit Archippus alone. Nor was it his to use as he wished. Archippus fulfilled his ministry when he shared what he received from God with other people. The ministry of any individual, Archippus' included, is under control of God for the benefit of the whole body (I Cor. 12:7,12).

Colossians 4:18, "The salutation by the hand of me Paul. Remember my bonds. Grace be with you. Amen."

The letter of Colossians ends with a salutation by the personal hand of Paul, a man who was an apostle, bearing the authority of God. He was a man whose hand God used to write the Bible (Gal. 6:11). Although Colossians, like all the Bible, is the work of a man's hand in real time and space, God is its Author. In fact, the Paul recognized that what he wrote was the word of God (I Thess. 2:13), as did others (II Peter 3:15,16).

The word "remember" means more than just "think about." After all, what good that do? Paul meant "remember my bonds when you go to God in prayer and when you talk about me among each other so they can pray for me too." Paul did not expect that much prayer necessarily would release him from his physical bonds, but he did expect God to work through their prayers to give him understanding of his difficult situation and give him courage to remain faithful, so that he might be a clear and effective witness. Though men, like Paul, who bring God's message may be weak and seek the supporting prayers of other people, though they may be constrained by "bonds," God's Word of grace is never bound.

The greatest message of all is that God, and God alone, gives grace to men. It is what sinners need and it is really all that they need. Paul knew that. Paul agreed to the message of grace. And grace is what he wanted for them. If the book of Colossians were only one verse long and this were it, the grace that it offered would be all that people need.

www.ingramcontent.com/pod-product-compliance
Lightning Source LLC
Chambersburg PA
CBHW071445150426
43191CB00008B/1244